HEALTHY
DEPENDENCY

HEALTHY DEPENDENCY

Leaning on Others Without Losing Yourself

ROBERT F. BORNSTEIN, PH.D.
& MARY A. LANGUIRAND, PH.D.

Newmarket Press *New York*

This book is published in the United States of America

FIRST EDITION

10 9 8 7 6 5 4 3 2 1

ISBN 1-55704-536-4

Library of Congress Cataloging-in-Publication Data

Healthy dependency : leaning on others without losing yourself— : the
four key steps to achieving balance in love, family, friendship, and work /
Robert F. Bornstein & Mary A. Languirand. — 1st ed.
     p. cm.
Includes bibliographical references.
ISBN 1-55704-536-4 (alk. paper)
1. Dependency (Psychology) 2. Interpersonal relations.
I. Languirand, Mary A. II. Title.
BF575.D34 B67 2003
158.2—dc21   2002006758

QUANTITY PURCHASES
Companies, professional groups, clubs, and other organizations
may qualify for special terms when ordering quantities of this title.
For information, write to Special Sales Department, Newmarket Press,
18 East 48th Street, New York, NY 10017; call (212) 832-3575; fax
(212) 832-3629 or e-mail mailbox@newmarketpress.com.

www.newmarketpress.com.

Manufactured in the United States of America

To Joseph Masling,
  mentor and friend

CONTENTS

How can we tell whether we're reaching out to others to learn and grow, or just to avoid life's challenges? By taking the Relationship Profile Test, you'll discover your relationship style, and learn what you need to do to recapture the healthy dependency that exists within you.

We're all born dependent, but somewhere along the way, many of us lose touch with our natural, healthy dependency needs and become overdependent or detached. What childhood events cause us to lose touch with our healthy dependency?

RELATIONSHIP GAMES
AND RELATIONSHIP TRAPS 54

How do we unconsciously "trap" other people into gratifying our unhealthy dependency needs? Can we learn to respond more effectively to overdependence and detachment in others, so we don't get "trapped" ourselves?

HEALTHY DEPENDENCY
IN LOVE 73

The intimacy of love creates unique challenges for healthy dependency. How can we recognize whether we—or our partner—have a suffocating lovestyle? An arm's-length lovestyle? And how can we replace these intimacy-destroying lovestyles with healthy dependent love?

HEALTHY DEPENDENCY
IN FRIENDSHIP 94

Every friendship is different, but in the end it doesn't matter whether your friend is overdependent or detached. Either way, you can use your healthy dependency skills to reconnect and form deeper, more satisfying friendships.

9 HEALTHY DEPENDENCY DURING DIFFICULT TIMES 193

Healthy dependency is most important during life's most difficult times. Once you know how overdependence and detachment prevent you from coping effectively, you can use your healthy dependency skills to turn loss into strength and challenge into opportunity.

10 HEALTHY DEPENDENCY AND SUCCESSFUL AGING 214

Dependency is an inevitable part of aging, but is it possible to gain confidence and strength even as you look to others for the occasional helping hand? Healthy dependency will enable you to turn late adulthood into a time of growth and positive change—for yourself and those you love.

ACKNOWLEDGMENTS

We'd like to thank the many people who contributed to this book, without whom we could not have written it. The library staff at Gettysburg College provided invaluable help in locating research and clinical information on healthy and unhealthy dependency. As always, they saw our requests as an opportunity—not a burden—and they tracked down every piece of information we asked for, no matter how obscure.

We are indebted to Carolyn Tuckey for her help in constructing easy-to-follow, user-friendly graphs and figures. Without her creative efforts, our ideas would not have been expressed as clearly, or as well.

We are grateful to Esther Margolis, President of Newmarket Press, who recognized immediately the value of our healthy dependency program. Her confidence in our ideas—and her faith in our ability to articulate these ideas effectively—made a challenging task a bit less daunting.

Many other members of the Newmarket Press team made key contributions to this project, and taught us a great deal along the way. We are indebted to Keith Hollaman, Shannon Berning, and Michelle Howry for their editorial expertise, patience, and skill. Their insightful comments helped clarify our ideas immeasurably. Together they shaped our words into sparkling text. Harry Burton, Heidi Sachner, and Julia Moberg did a superb job promoting our book, ensuring that it would reach the widest possible audience. Andrea Brown and Adriana della Porta's tremendous work on special sales and serial rights helped our ideas touch many people's lives. And we are especially grateful to Mary Jane DiMassi, whose creative, innovative design gave *Healthy Dependency* a compelling appearance that complemented and supported our message. Her efforts helped pull the entire package together.

Most important of all, we'd like to thank our agent, Joelle Delbourgo. Her unwavering support and enthusiasm helped transform our thoughts into something tangible—the book you're now holding in your hands. Without her energy, patience, skill, and encouragement, *Healthy Dependency* would never have been written.

PREFACE

No man is an island, entire of itself;
every man is a piece of the continent,
a part of the main.

—JOHN DONNE (1572-1631), *Meditation 17*

This is a book about growing stronger by reaching out to others.

It's a book about moving beyond society's not-so-subtle message that depending on people is wrong—that "mature" adults somehow manage everything on their own in a complex, challenging world.

This is a book about *healthy dependency.*

Healthy dependency? The term sounds strange. Why do we find it so hard to rely on others without feeling like a child, as if we're six years old all over again?

Therapists tell us that to be happy, we must grow up and grow strong. We must learn to be self-reliant, always independent. Maturity means fending for ourselves, so we're told—fighting our own battles without anyone's help. So this strange idea—this wrongheaded notion that dependency is bad—came from the mental health community. The very people who should be teaching us how to *re*connect instead have taught us to *dis*connect.

We were taught that, too, when we first became psychologists nearly twenty years ago. But the more we explored this issue in our research and clinical work, the more certain we became of a single, simple truth: To live life to its fullest, each of us must recapture the healthy dependency that exists within us. We must learn to balance intimacy and autonomy, ask for help without feeling helpless, and connect with other people without losing ourselves in the process.

Rebuilding healthy dependency involves changing how you think about yourself and other people. When your thought patterns change, your feelings will change as well. Your relationship goals will begin to shift—you'll find it easier to reach out for help with confidence and strength.

But it all starts with changing your mindset, and that's where we'll begin.

We've used the principles of healthy dependency in our teaching and clinical work for many years now, and we've applied these principles in our own careers, friendships, family, and marriage. We know which strategies work, and which don't, and we designed our healthy dependency program so you can move forward at your own pace, building upon existing strengths as you venture into new areas. Our healthy dependency program consists of four steps:

1) *Understand your relationship style and how it evolved.* You must begin here, because taking a good, honest look at yourself is the first step toward personal growth and healthier, more satisfying relationships.

2) *Learn how you respond to overdependence and detachment in others.* Even though you want to change, those around you might not. You need to know how other people "push your buttons," and cause you to respond in ways you don't like.

3) *Bring healthy dependency to every area of life.* Once you've mastered the basic principles, you can apply your healthy dependency skills to love, friendship, family, parenting, and work.

4) *Use healthy dependency to confront life's challenges.* You can't predict what sorts of challenges life may bring you, but whatever they are, healthy dependency will help see you through them.

A brief word of caution before we begin: As you use our healthy dependency program to learn and grow, remember that change is an unpredictable process, full of unexpected gains and frustrating backslides. Don't punish yourself if you make mistakes or progress less quickly than you'd like. Real change—deep change—is a tricky business and rarely smooth. But if you persist, you *will* get there.

And remember: No matter how quickly you go, healthy dependency is a lifelong journey, so above all, enjoy the trip.

HEALTHY DEPENDENCY:
A FRAMEWORK FOR CHANGE

Ellen and Michael were siblings, but they couldn't have been more different. Ellen was the strong one—always in charge, always in control. In high school she had been valedictorian of her class; now, twenty years later, she was president of her own Internet marketing firm, with a staff of thirty and a corner office overlooking midtown Manhattan. Ellen's business was her life, and everything else—including her marriage—ran a distant second. Many things had changed in Ellen's world during the past twenty years, but two things never changed. Everyone admired Ellen and respected her strength and insight. Yet no one felt they really knew Ellen. They just couldn't get close to her—couldn't connect.

Ellen understood how much people looked up to her, and she found great satisfaction in this. Still, sometimes late at night, when the day was done and her guard was down, Ellen felt sad, almost empty, as if somehow something was missing. She never revealed these feelings though, even to her husband. Instead, she shoved them away, controlled them, and crushed them through sheer force of will. By the time she hit work the next morning the troubling feelings were gone, and it was the same old Ellen everyone admired: strong, capable, competent, focused, always in control.

Over the years, Michael had gotten used to his sister's solitude, but he wished things were different between them. Like Ellen, Michael had a successful career, but for Michael, the main part of work was the people. He spent much of his day wondering what others thought of him, and he devoted an enormous amount of time planning things he might do to impress his supervisor, Mr. Worth. The sad thing was, no matter how much he planned or how much he did, Michael never really felt secure—the smallest slights would send him into a panic. One time when Mr. Worth walked past him without saying good morning, Michael spent two sleepless nights—two—tossing and turning, obsessing and ruminating, convinced that his boss now hated him.

Things weren't much different at home. Michael's wife Kathleen had once remarked that he was more afraid of their daughter than she was of him. Kathleen was right, too. Michael knew it. Most of the time it didn't matter: Kathleen was the "bad cop," Michael the "good cop," and things worked out okay. But two weeks ago when Kathleen was working late, Michael had given in to Kimberly's pleas, and he let her stay out past her curfew to visit a friend across town. By the time Kim got back, it was one in the morning, and Michael and Kathleen were convinced something terrible had happened—that the car had broken down...or worse. Kathleen was furious, Michael was ashamed, and both of them knew something had to change.

What in the World Is Healthy Dependency?

We can't tell you how many times we've been asked this question—by students, patients, professional colleagues, science writers, and reporters...you name it. When people first hear it, the term *healthy dependency* sounds strange. "Healthy" and "dependency"? Those words don't go together. Most of us try to *avoid* being dependent. We'd rather be self-reliant and do things on our own. Independence is good, so we're told; leaning on others for help is bad.

Or is it?

The research findings are clear: Too much dependency in our relationships creates problems, but too *little* dependency is just as bad. As we strive to make a place for ourselves, to carve out

---

HEALTHY DEPENDENCY

* * * * *

The ability to blend intimacy and autonomy,
lean on others while maintaining a strong
sense of self, and feel good (not guilty)
about asking for help when you need it.

---

our niche in a challenging world, many of us take self-reliance too far. Like Ellen, we become *too* independent, and we lose the ability to connect with other people. Or like Michael, we become overwhelmed by the demands of adulthood, and retreat into unhealthy *over*dependence. This, as we've seen, has costs as well.

There is a healthy middle ground between rigid independence and unhealthy overdependence. *Healthy dependency* is the ability to blend intimacy and autonomy, lean on others while maintaining a strong sense of self, and feel good (not guilty) about asking for help when you need it. Healthy dependency means *depending* on people without becoming *dependent* on them. It means *trusting* people enough to open up and be vulnerable, yet having the *self-confidence* you need to survive those inevitable relationship conflicts that everyone experiences at one time or another.

When you use healthy dependency to connect with those around you, you'll find inner strength you never knew you had. Friendships and love relationships will deepen, parenting and career skills will sharpen, and you'll become physically healthier—and happier, too.

How Does Healthy Dependency Differ From Unhealthy Dependency?

Several years ago, we administered a battery of personality tests and other psychological measures to a group of young adults.

We asked them to report on romances, friendships, and family relationships. We inquired about their moods, their beliefs about the future, their overall satisfaction with life, and their willingness to confide in others about life's problems. And we profiled each person's dependency style as well.

The results of our study were clear: The happiest, most satisfied, most well-adjusted people were those who showed features of *healthy dependency*—intimacy balanced with a good dose of autonomy, self-confidence blended with a generous helping of trust. Most important of all, these well-adjusted healthy dependent people had the ability to lean on others for support without feeling guilty, weak, or ashamed.

The bottom line: There's nothing wrong with feeling dependent now and then. It's a normal part of life. Problems arise when people lack one or more key healthy dependency skills, and express their normal healthy dependency needs in unhealthy, self-defeating ways. Their relationships become unbalanced and unsatisfying, their lives unfocused and unfulfilling.

By the time you finish this book, you'll be well on your way to mastering the four key healthy dependency skills, and recapturing your healthy dependency. Here's what you'll need to do:

- *Separate what you do from who you are.* Everyone needs help sometimes, but in unhealthy dependency, we confuse *asking for help* with *being helpless.* Remember: Asking for help is something you *do*, not something you *are*. When you can begin to separate the act from the person, it will become easier to ask for help when you need it—and easier to cope if help is denied. We call this *connection-based thinking*, and it is a critical healthy dependency skill.
- *Move beyond old stereotypes.* Asking for help has tremendous symbolic meaning. We associate help-seeking with insecurity, immaturity, weakness, and failure. When we reach out to others, we literally *feel* weak (and sometimes guilty and ashamed as well). Healthy dependency involves moving beyond these stereotypes, and creating new, healthier emotional patterns to take their place. As you do this, you'll de-

velop *emotional synergy*: You'll feel capable and confident when you lean on other people, so you will draw strength from their support.

- *Use dependency as a means, not an end.* In unhealthy dependency, getting help is an end in itself: Once you've gotten what you wanted, you're done—life's easy. In healthy dependency, help is a route to positive change—it's a way of becoming stronger, so next time you can do better. Think of it this way: In unhealthy dependency, we seek help to *avoid* challenges, but in healthy dependency, we seek help to *learn and grow*. This is called *growth motivation*—the third important healthy dependency skill.

- *Learn how to ask for help.* Healthy dependency means knowing how to ask for help and support, so people feel good—not trapped—when they lend you a hand. Healthy dependency also means knowing *when* to ask for help—learning to identify situations where it's okay to lean on others and situations where it's better to go it alone. This skill—called *relationship flexibility*—will enable you to bring healthy dependency to *all* your relationships.

When Healthy Dependency Is Gone, What Takes Its Place?

As we'll see in Chapter 2, many life experiences distort our perceptions of ourselves and other people, and make it difficult to acquire the four key healthy dependency skills. These experiences literally cause us to "disconnect" from others—and sometimes from aspects of ourselves as well.

When people lose touch with their healthy dependency, they usually develop one of two self-defeating relationship styles. Some people (like Michael) develop a relationship style characterized by fearfulness and insecurity—a style known as *destructive overdependence*. Other people (like Ellen) go the opposite way and develop a defensive, closed-off style known as *dysfunctional detachment*.

21

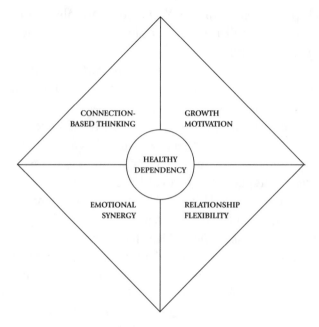

THE FOUR KEY HEALTHY DEPENDENCY SKILLS

Connection-Based Thinking, Emotional Synergy, Growth Motivation, and *Relationship Flexibility*—these are the building-blocks of healthy dependency.

As you might guess, people express destructive overdependence and dysfunctional detachment in many different ways (we'll discuss these in detail in Chapter 2). For now, let's look at the core features of these self-defeating relationship styles.

Destructive Overdependence: The Suction-Cup Relationship Style

We call destructive overdependence the *Suction-Cup Relationship Style* because overdependent people cling to others as a way of avoiding life's challenges. Overdependent people see themselves as weak and vulnerable, and believe that without a strong protector, they won't survive. Their greatest fear is that they'll be abandoned and left to fend for themselves in a frightening, hostile world.

HEALTHY DEPENDENCY
BREEDS ACADEMIC SUCCESS

* * * * *

In 1994, we made a discovery that surprised our academic and clinical colleagues: College students with good healthy dependency skills obtain significantly better grades than students who lack these skills. What is the link between healthy dependency and strong academic performance? Healthy dependent students have that elusive combination of trust and self-confidence that enables them to *depend* on their professors without becoming *dependent* on them. Because they feel good (not guilty) about asking for help, healthy dependent students are able to seek help in an appropriate way, and then use this help to build new skills they can apply on their own. The end result: An 18 percent increase in overall GPA.

Notice how all four healthy dependency skills played a role in this process:

- *Connection-based thinking* The healthy dependent students realized that asking for help was not a sign of weakness or failure.
- *Emotional synergy* Because they didn't associate help-seeking with failure, the healthy dependent students felt good—not guilty—about asking for help.
- *Growth motivation* The healthy dependent students used help the right way: To improve their performance, learn, and grow.
- *Relationship flexibility* The healthy dependent students knew when and how to ask: Not only did they get the help they needed, but their professors were impressed with their interest and their commitment to doing well.

Overdependent people are so preoccupied with maintaining ties to others—no matter what the cost—that life becomes a series of unhealthy dependencies on lovers and friends, colleagues and supervisors, physicians and therapists…it never ends. Even in the face of neglect or abuse, overdependent people find it difficult—sometimes impossible—to let go. Their self-esteem suffers, and a downward spiral ensues: The more overdependent they are, the worse they feel about themselves, and the worse they feel about themselves, the more overdependent they become.

Dysfunctional Detachment: The Teflon Relationship Style

We call dysfunctional detachment the *Teflon Relationship Style* because people who are detached let nothing stick to them, almost as if they were coated with Teflon. You can't get close to a detached person, no matter how hard you try. They keep you at arm's length—if not physically, then emotionally. And if you do somehow manage to break through the wall, even for a moment, the detached person will usually find some way to retreat—to create enough distance that they feel safe again.

Detached people see others as untrustworthy and unreliable, and believe they must go it alone. Their relationships are superficial and businesslike—they must always be in control. On the surface, detached people seem enviably strong and supremely confident, but in this case, appearances are deceiving. Studies in North America, Europe, Australia, and Asia produced strikingly similar results: Though they may *appear* strong and confident, deep down inside most detached people feel alienated, isolated, sad, and lonely.

Can We Learn to Recapture Our Healthy Dependency?

The short answer is, yes—absolutely. It doesn't matter what caused you to lose touch with your healthy dependency or which self-defeating relationship style emerged to take its place. Recapturing healthy dependency involves rebuilding the four key healthy dependency skills—*connection-based thinking, emotional synergy, growth motivation,* and *relationship flexibility*—in the context of your current relationships. This might sound like a

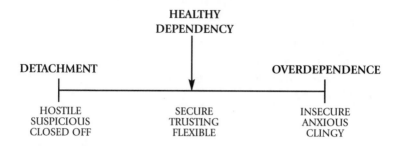

THE RELATIONSHIP SPECTRUM
As this illustration shows, healthy dependency lies at the midpoint between destructive overdependence and dysfunctional detachment.

tall order—perhaps even a bit overwhelming at first—but rest assured: These four skills are so intimately interconnected that when you begin to change in one area, change in other areas will soon follow. The hardest part is just getting started.

The Relationship Profile Test

To take that first step toward healthy dependency, you must understand your relationship style, so you can see what issues you need to focus on for growth and positive change. The *Relationship Profile Test* on the next page will help you do this. When the moment is right—when you can find some quiet time and a private place where you won't be interrupted—we encourage you to take this fifteen-minute test. Even if you're confident you already understand your relationship style, the Relationship Profile Test will still be useful: It will tell you where you stand relative to other people who've taken the test.

The only rule in taking this test is to answer as honestly as you can. No one but you needs to know your results.

RELATIONSHIP PROFILE TEST

* * * * *

Please use the following scale to rate each of the statements below. If a statement is very true of you, you'd circle a high number, like 4 or 5. If a statement is not at all true of you, you'd circle a low number, like 1 or 2.

	Not at all true of me			Very much true of me	
	1	2	3	4	5
1) Other people seem more confident than I am.	1	2	3	4	5
2) I am easily hurt by criticism.	1	2	3	4	5
3) Being responsible for things makes me nervous.	1	2	3	4	5
4) I am most comfortable when someone else takes charge.	1	2	3	4	5
5) Others don't realize how much their words can hurt me.	1	2	3	4	5
6) It is important that people like me.	1	2	3	4	5
7) I would rather give in and keep the peace than hold my ground and win an argument.	1	2	3	4	5
8) I am happiest when someone else takes the lead.	1	2	3	4	5
9) When I argue with someone, I worry that the relationship might be permanently damaged.	1	2	3	4	5
10) I sometimes agree with things I don't really believe so other people will like me.	1	2	3	4	5
11) Other people want too much from me.	1	2	3	4	5
12) When someone gets too close to me, I tend to withdraw.	1	2	3	4	5
13) I need to escape from it all every once in a while.	1	2	3	4	5
14) I wish I had more time by myself.	1	2	3	4	5

15) I prefer making decisions on my own, rather than listening to others' opinions. 1 2 3 4 5

16) I don't like to reveal too much personal information. 1 2 3 4 5

17) I'm sometimes wary of other people's motives. 1 2 3 4 5

18) I'm happiest when I'm working on my own. 1 2 3 4 5

19) Being independent and self-sufficient are very important to me. 1 2 3 4 5

20) When things aren't going right, I try to hide my feelings and be strong. 1 2 3 4 5

21) I believe that most people are basically good and well-meaning. 1 2 3 4 5

22) I am able to share my innermost thoughts and feelings with people I know well. 1 2 3 4 5

23) I am comfortable asking for help. 1 2 3 4 5

24) I don't worry about how other people see me. 1 2 3 4 5

25) Most of my relationships involve give-and-take, with both people contributing their share. 1 2 3 4 5

26) My relationships are pretty much the way I want them to be—even if I could, I wouldn't change things. 1 2 3 4 5

27) I see myself as a capable person who copes well with disappointments and setbacks. 1 2 3 4 5

28) In my relationships, I am comfortable offering support when the other person needs it and asking for support when I need it. 1 2 3 4 5

29) When I have a falling-out with someone, I am confident that the relationship will survive. 1 2 3 4 5

30) It is easy for me to trust people. 1 2 3 4 5

CONSTRUCTING YOUR RELATIONSHIP PROFILE

* * * * *

Tallying Your Scores

The Relationship Profile Test yields three scores—one for *destructive overdependence*, one for *dysfunctional detachment*, and one for *healthy dependency*. Your *overdependence* score is the sum total of your ratings for questions 1–10. Your *detachment* score is the sum total of your ratings for questions 11–20. Your *healthy dependency* score is the sum total of your ratings for questions 21–30. Once you have added up all three scores, write them in the spaces below.

Overdependence score   _____

Detachment score   _____

Healthy Dependency score   _____

Constructing Your Relationship Profile

To construct your Relationship Profile, put three dots in the appropriate places on the chart—one dot for your *overdependence* score, one for your *detachment* score, and one for your *healthy dependency* score. When you're done, draw a line connecting the three dots. This is your Relationship Profile. (Remember: The means for the three scales are not the same, so ignore your raw scores from here on out, and just focus on how you scored relative to the average on each scale.) This profile gives you a visual representation of your score—showing you which area is higher or lower relative to how others have scored.

When you've completed the Relationship Profile Test, fill out the scoring key above. This scoring key explains how to draw your *Relationship Profile* on page 29—a visual representation of your relationship style. Once you've drawn it, take a few moments to familiarize yourself with your profile. Here are some common questions and helpful tips:

How can I tell where I fall relative to other people who've already taken the Relationship Profile Test?

The dark line that runs across the middle of the chart represents the average score for each relationship style. If any of your dots

35 or above —	39 or above —	48 or above —
—	—	—
—	—	—
—	—	—
—	—	—
30 —	34 —	43 —
—	—	—
—	—	—
—	—	—
—	—	—
——— 25 ———	——— 29 ———	——— 38 ———
—	—	—
—	—	—
—	—	—
—	—	—
20 —	24 —	33 —
—	—	—
—	—	—
—	—	—
—	—	—
15 or below —	19 or below —	28 or below —
OVERDEPENDENCY	**DETACHMENT**	**HEALTHY DEPENDENCY**

are above the line, you scored above average for that style. The higher your score, the more features of that relationship style you have, so instead of thinking about your relationship style in "yes-no" terms, think in terms of *intensity*. The Relationship Profile Test not only tells you *whether* you're overdependent or detached, but also gives you a rough idea of *how* overdependent or detached you may be. (It also tells you how far along you are in developing your healthy dependency skills.)

Why do the three areas of the Relationship Profile Test have different average scores?

Because people respond differently to different types of test items, the overall means for the three Relationship Profile Test scales are not the same. For both women and men, the average overdependence score is 25, while the average detachment score is about 29 and the average healthy dependency score is 38. The best way to understand your relationship style is to forget about your raw score and focus instead on how high (or low) you scored relative to the average in each area.

My Relationship Profile isn't what I expected. What does this mean?

An unexpected pattern may simply mean you haven't thought much about your relationship style—that this is the first time you've really analyzed it. On the other hand, an unexpected pattern may mean you've been denying some aspects of your relationship style that make you uncomfortable—pushing them out of your mind so you don't have to think about them. If this is the case, take heart: You just learned something important about yourself. Insight is the first step toward growth and positive change.

* * * * *

**If you do not tell the truth about
yourself, you cannot tell it
about other people.**
—VIRGINIA WOOLF

I scored high in more than one area. Is it possible to be both overdependent and detached?

Many people obtain high scores in more than one area. This usually means they exhibit different relationship styles in different contexts. For example, some people have a detached style around their parents, but an overdependent style around their spouse. Other people are detached at home, but not at work. If you have a mixed profile, don't be concerned: Having some features of overdependence as well as detachment is a very common experience.

I'm neither overdependent nor detached. Is healthy dependency still relevant for me?

It depends on your long-term relationship goals. If you're neither overdependent nor detached, there are two ways that the healthy dependency program can be useful to you. First, it can help you strengthen your existing healthy dependency skills and apply these skills more effectively. Second, it can help you develop better ways of coping with overdependence and detachment in people around you—siblings, friends, romantic partners, children, coworkers, and others.

If someone in my life is overdependent or detached, should they complete the Relationship Profile Test, too?

It depends on whether they're willing to do it. If they are, great! You'll both learn something important. But if this person doesn't want to take the test, don't force the issue. As we'll see in Chapter 3, there are many strategies you can use to improve your personal, professional, and family relationships, even if those around you aren't ready to change.

The Story of John: Overdependence in Love, Healthy Dependency at Work

John came to one of us for therapy to deal with his insecurity around women, and as John described his problems, he certainly seemed insecure. He had great difficulty maintaining eye contact when he spoke, and he hesitated and stammered as he struggled to find the words to describe his situation. John prefaced many of his statements with self-deprecating comments like, "I'm really not much of…" and "I've never been very good at…" His lack of self-confidence came through loud and clear.

As John described it, he was so anxious around women he found it impossible to make even the tiniest relationship decision without getting his partner's approval every step of the way. Even then, John apologized repeatedly for all sorts of minor glitches—long movie lines, crowded restaurants, traffic snarls—though most of these glitches were hardly his fault. John's inse-

HOW MANY PEOPLE ARE OVERDEPENDENT OR DETACHED?

* * * * *

In 1992, we conducted our first large scale survey of destructive overdependence and dysfunctional detachment, using a diverse sample of several hundred young adults—women and men alike. We found that over 30 percent of the people we surveyed reported symptoms of overdependence in multiple areas of life. More than 25 percent of these people reported significant symptoms of detachment. Other studies have found similarly high rates of overdependence and detachment in Canada, Great Britain, Germany, Japan, Sweden, Norway, and the Netherlands.

There's no doubt about it: Overdependence and detachment are widespread problems—far more common than most people think. If you see features of destructive overdependence or dysfunctional detachment in yourself or those around you, don't despair. You're not alone.

cure, overdependent behavior destroyed each of his romantic relationships, as the women in his life eventually tired of taking all the decision-making responsibility upon themselves and playing the "mommy" role.

Would you be surprised to learn that John's behavior in the workplace was very different from his dating style? We were at first, but as we got to know John, his contrasting workplace and dating behaviors began to make sense. At work John felt confident and secure, and as a result, he had no trouble making decisions on his own—even decisions that involved important research projects and large sums of money. John had no trouble delegating decision-making responsibilities to his supervisees either. He had enough confidence in his colleagues' skills—and in his ability to cope with whatever problems might arise—that delegating responsibility came naturally to him. John trusted his coworkers enough that he frequently bounced ideas off them and sought their advice about challenging projects. John offered advice as easily as he solicited it, and was considered a model colleague and employee.

John is an excellent example of a person who has a self-defeating relationship style in one area of life, but shows healthy dependency in another area. Our task in therapy was made easier by this: We were able to help John rebuild his healthy dependency skills in the dating arena by showing him how he was using these skills to flourish at work. As John began to practice connection-based thinking and relationship flexibility in his dating relationships, his emotional synergy and growth motivation both increased. He was able to take the lead, make decisions, and stop apologizing each time something didn't go as planned. His insecure behavior began to decrease, and he began to experience the intimacy and romantic playfulness that come from inner confidence and mutual trust.

Though not all stories have a happy ending, this one does. John married several years ago, and recently his wife gave birth to their first child—a son. John's career continues to flourish, and now—after years of frustration and failed romance—his personal life is on track as well.

The Healthy Dependency Program

Like John, your relationship style might be working well in certain parts of your life, but not in others. Or, like some of our students, patients, and colleagues, you might have relationship difficulties that extend to more than one area. Either way, the healthy dependency program can be useful to you. It's flexible enough to accommodate a wide array of relationship styles and different relationship goals.

In the chapters that follow, we'll help you recapture your healthy dependency skills in stages, so that—like John—you can build upon your existing strengths as you venture into new areas. Our framework for change involves four steps:

1) *Understand your relationship style and how it evolved.* You already started this process by completing the Relationship Profile Test. In Chapter 2, we'll put your relationship style in context by tracing the roots of overdependence and detachment, and examining the most important features of these two relationship styles.

2) *Prepare for the inevitable roadblocks and setbacks.* Even though you are determined to change, those around you might not be. In Chapter 3, we show you how to recognize signs of overdependence and detachment in those around you, identify your reflexive responses to these behaviors, and alter your responses to avoid relationship "traps."

3) *Put healthy dependency to work for you in every area of life.* Chapters 4–8 provide bottom-line, practical, how-to advice that lets you apply your healthy dependency skills in love relationships (Chapter 4), friendships (Chapter 5), family relationships (Chapter 6), parent-child relationships (Chapter 7), and the workplace (Chapter 8).

4) *Use healthy dependency to confront life's challenges.* Chapters 9 and 10 illustrate how healthy dependency can be used during difficult times. In Chapter 9, we apply these skills to coping with loss and change (for example, divorce or a job transition). In Chapter 10, we show how these skills can promote successful aging—for you, and those you love.

DID YOU KNOW...?

* * * * *

People who are over-dependent or detached are at increased risk for colds *but* and flu, as well as more serious illnesses like heart disease and cancer.

Research shows that healthy dependency can lower stress, boost the immune system, and contribute to lifelong health and wellness.

Overdependence and detachment are both "career *but* killers": They prevent us from connecting with super-visors, colleagues, and potential clients.

Healthy dependency can lead to career success by strengthening leadership, followership, and mentoring skills.

Overdependence and detachment are associated with a variety of emotional *but* problems, including depres-sion, phobias, and addictive disorders.

Healthy dependency not only protects us from emo-tional difficulties, it helps us benefit more fully—and re-cover more completely—when treatment is needed.

Overdependent and detached parents raise children who are likely to *but* become overdependent and detached themselves.

Healthy dependency sharp-ens parenting skills, reducing child behavior problems, and strengthening social adjustment and school performance.

Overdependence and detachment are linked with *but* increased risk for divorce and decreased relationship satisfaction.

Healthy dependency has been shown to increase marital satisfaction and lower divorce rates.

Studies indicate that over-dependence and detachment lead to a variety of late-life difficulties, including a rocky retirement, social isolation, and increased likelihood of physical and cognitive decline.

but

Studies also show that healthy dependency promotes successful aging: By rebuilding healthy dependency skills now, your social network will become stronger, and it will be easier to ask for—and get—the help you need later in life.

THE ROOTS OF DISCONTENT: HOW WE LEARN TO DISCONNECT

The day started out well—a day like any other—but then just before lunch something troubling happened. Ellen noticed her office staff gathering in the waiting area, getting ready to head out. When she asked where they were going, they seemed taken aback. Today was An-drew's birthday—they were taking him to lunch. Hadn't anyone told her? Didn't she know?

It was an awkward situation all around, and though they apolo-gized profusely and insisted that Ellen join them, she just didn't feel right about it. A few moments later Andrew arrived, and off they went. The office was quiet.

As she sat at her desk eating lunch by herself, Ellen was confused and a little bit hurt. Had they forgotten to invite her? Left her out de-liberately? Had she offended someone? Were they trying to tell her something?

Throughout the afternoon, Ellen found her thoughts returning to the incident, so she asked her assistant to stop by at the end of the day. Ellen thought it would be helpful to get Theresa's take on things. Theresa always seemed to have her finger on the pulse of the office.

At 5:45, Theresa knocked on Ellen's door. Ellen invited her in, and when Theresa was settled, Ellen asked her about the incident. Theresa didn't say much at first—she seemed nervous, hesitant—but after a few minutes she began to speak more freely.

"The thing is," Theresa explained, "everyone really respects you. They really look up to you."

"Okay," said Ellen, "so what's the problem?"

"Well, there's no problem, really. Nothing like that. It's just that some people are a little bit, I don't know...nervous around you."

"Nervous? Around me?" Ellen was genuinely surprised. She prided herself on never losing her temper, never losing control, never raising her voice around the office—no matter how serious the problem.

"Well, yes," Theresa continued. "Not everyone of course. But some people wish....I don't know...that they could get to know you better, that maybe you'd open up a bit more."

"Open up?"

"Yes."

"How so? I don't understand."

"Oh, it's just little things, I guess. People want to know you. What you do outside work. What your husband is like. Your kids. That sort of thing."

Ellen didn't know what to say. She stared at her desk, straightened the mousepad, lined up her pens. Finally she looked up. When Ellen spoke, her voice was soft—so soft Theresa could hardly hear her.

"It's just that...I don't really...," Ellen slumped in her seat. "The thing is, Theresa, I wouldn't know where to begin."

"Where to begin?"

"You know, opening up. Talking to people. It's just not something I've ever done."

"Ever?"

"No, not really." Ellen looked at Theresa, pursed her lips, looked away again.

Ellen ran her fingers along the edge of the desk. "It's just not something we did in our family. People didn't talk. We kind of dealt with things on our own."

"Really."

"Yeah, pretty much. I talked to my brother some when we were younger, but that's about it. Not my parents though. I mean, even when my grandfather died, we never said much about it. We just dealt with it, you know? Packed up his apartment, got everything squared away, went on with our lives."

"Wow."

"Is that strange? Aren't all families like that?"

"Well, no. I mean, mine wasn't."

The two women sat quietly for a few minutes. The phone rang in the outer office, but they ignored it and it stopped. Finally Ellen smiled, bit her lip, and shook her head.

"Open up, huh? They want me to open up?"

Theresa nodded.

"I'll tell you the truth, Theresa. Even if I wanted to, I wouldn't know how."

No one is born with a self-defeating relationship style. We learn these styles through interactions with parents, siblings, teachers, friends, and others. In this chapter, we look at how people lose touch with their healthy dependency, and how destructive overdependence and dysfunctional detachment emerge to take its place.

Born Dependent: Life's First Connection

We're all born dependent—every last one of us. Like dogs and chimps and other mammals, we humans can't survive without an extended period of close parental care. We depend upon our parents for biological nourishment (like food), of course. But we also rely on our parents to provide the subtler "psychological nourishment" that every child needs—the nurturance, affection, and affirmation that help build confidence and a strong sense of self.

For better or worse, our first relationships affect us for a lifetime. And two aspects of these early relationships are particularly important in determining how we deal with dependency. Our *attachment style* affects how we *feel* about dependency—it shapes our emotional reactions and responses. Our *relationship scripts* affect how we *think* about dependency—they shape our expectations and beliefs.

39

Attachment Style

If you've ever spent time around young children, you know that each child has her own unique way of interacting with the people around her. Some children are timid and easily frightened; others are adventurous, bold, and brave. Some children are bubbly and quick to laugh; others are thoughtful, reserved, and restrained.

Early in life, we each develop our own *attachment style*—our characteristic way of relating to other people. Genetics may play a minor role, but for the most part, our attachment style is determined by how parents and other caregivers treat us during life's first few formative years.

Attachment expert Mary Main of the University of California-Berkeley found that in cultures around the world—Western and Eastern, urban and rural—children develop remarkably similar attachment styles. It doesn't matter whether they hail from San Francisco or Sri Lanka—by the time they reach preschool age, most children fall into one of three attachment style categories:

- *Secure attachment* Children with a secure attachment style are calm and confident. They see others as trustworthy and dependable, and seem certain that people will be there when needed. Securely attached children expect that things will go well, and their self-assured behavior reflects this.
- *Insecure attachment* Children with an insecure attachment style are timid and fretful. They seem anxious, on edge, as if those closest to them might disappear at any moment, abandoning them to fend for themselves in a frightening, hostile world.
- *Avoidant attachment* Children with an avoidant attachment style seem uncomfortable with closeness. They recoil—literally stiffen up—when hugged, and as they grow, they become preoccupied with keeping their distance from others. They avoid physical and emotional contact, and if you get too close, they back away.

PROFESSOR AINSWORTH'S STRANGE SITUATION

* * * * *

In the late 1960s, University of Virginia psychologist Mary Ainsworth developed the "Strange Situation Test," a behavioral measure of children's attachment. In the Strange Situation Test, a child and parent (usually the mother) are brought to a room in the psychology laboratory, and the child is placed on the floor near her mother. Then, without warning, a stranger enters. He says nothing, but simply walks across the room and sits in a chair near the opposite wall. The child's reaction to this "strange situation" tells us a lot about her attachment style. Anxiously attached children cling to the mother in fear. Avoidant children ignore the stranger completely (and oddly enough, they ignore their mother as well). Secure children are more willing to take a risk: They venture toward the stranger to see what's going on, returning periodically to the "secure base" of the mother to plan their next journey.

Do our childhood attachment styles carry through to adulthood? Studies confirm that they do. There are exceptions, of course (some timid toddlers become captains of industry). But for the most part, our early attachment style predicts how we will relate to other people later in life. More often than not, the securely attached young girl grows into a strong, confident woman. The avoidant little boy becomes a distant, detached man.

Relationship Scripts

Relationship scripts are beliefs about how other people will respond to us—how they'll treat us, whether they'll like us, what will happen when things go well, and what will result when conflict occurs. Relationship scripts are formed throughout childhood, and once formed, they help determine how we think about ourselves and other people, even years—sometimes decades—after they were first created.

Researchers have identified three core relationship scripts that help shape our later relationship style:

- *The Others-Will-Be-There-For-Me Script* The person with an *others-will-be-there-for-me* script believes that people are basically good and well-meaning and will be available to help when needed. This script stems from positive, nurturing early experiences within and outside the family, which teach the child that she is competent and capable, yet still valued and cared for.

- *The Can't-Make-It-On-My-Own Script* The person with a *can't-make-it-on-my-own* script believes that without the guidance and support of other people, he won't survive. This script stems from overprotective treatment by parents and others, which teaches the child that he is fragile and weak. The can't-make-it-on-my-own script may also result from rigid, rule-oriented treatment, which teaches the child that the way to get by in life is to become passive and do what others say.

THE FILM INSIDE YOUR HEAD

* * * * *

You can think of these scripts as scenes from a film or "internal dialogue," according to Yale University researcher Robert Abelson, a pioneer in the study of relationship scripts. When we think about a relationship, we begin by imagining what we'll say and do. This prompts us to imagine what the other person will say and do in return, and so on, until the whole interaction has played itself out. Sometimes we play these scenes over in our mind dozens—even hundreds—of times, changing small details along the way. But for most of us, the basic pattern—the core of the script—doesn't change: It comes out pretty much the same way time after time.

In this sense, relationship scripts are like "relationship blueprints": They create expectations for how things will go, and then we rehearse the scenes so often that when the interaction finally does occur, we behave in such a way as to confirm our expectations. If you've ever imagined becoming tongue-tied at the start of a date, then proceeded to stumble over your words when the night finally arrived, you've experienced the power of these oft-imagined, well-rehearsed scenes.

- *The Got-To-Go-It-Alone Script* The person with a *got-to-go-it-alone* script believes that others will not be there when needed, so the way to survive is to do everything on one's own. This script is produced when important figures in the child's life are distant and unresponsive. The child comes to believe that other people don't care—that she's somehow not worthy of other people's love.

From Healthy Dependency to Destructive Overdependence

Attachment styles and relationship scripts are important, but by themselves, they don't tell the whole story. Instead, they set in motion a process that unfolds over the years and eventually leads to a particular relationship style. Let's take a closer look at this process.

How Overdependence Develops over Time

An insecure attachment style and can't-make-it-on-my-own relationship script ultimately lead to destructive overdependence (see page 44). This takes place in four stages:

1) *The Helpless Self-Concept* An insecure attachment style and can't-make-it-on-my-own relationship script cause the child to internalize an image of himself as weak and ineffectual—what psychologists call a "helpless self-concept."
2) *Desire for Protection and Fear of Abandonment* The developing child's helpless self-concept leads to a strong *desire for protection and support,* and an equally powerful *fear of abandonment.* Insecurity and anxiety begin to dominate.
3) *Other-Centered Behavior* The child's desire for protection and fear of abandonment combine to produce what researchers call *other-centered behavior:* The child now directs all his energy outward, trying desperately to please other people and avoid conflict at all costs.

4) *Disconnection from Self* Over time, the child's other-centered behavior causes him to "disconnect" from himself—to literally lose touch with what he wants and how he feels, because he is so concerned with what *others* want and how *others* feel.

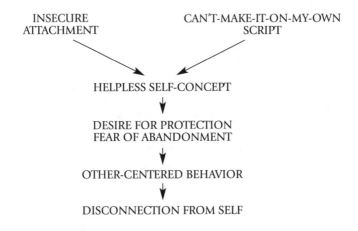

THE ROOTS OF OVERDEPENDENCE

As this figure shows, an insecure attachment style and can't-make-it-on-my-own relationship script eventually lead to a destructive pattern of overdependent ("other-centered") behavior.

Destructive Overdependence Patterns

By the time overdependent people reach early adolescence, they develop different ways of expressing unhealthy dependency needs. These patterns reflect each person's unique *coping style*—his or her way of dealing with the stresses and challenges of life.

These patterns are also a product of each person's unique relationship history: People learn to express unhealthy dependency needs in a particular way because that way of expressing dependency needs happened to be rewarded in some of their important early relationships. This is why—as we learned in Chapter 1—some people (like John) are overdependent in certain situations, but not in others. It's a consequence of their relationship history.

DISCONNECTING EXPERIENCES

* * * * *

Early experiences play a key role in shaping one's relationship style, but later experiences are important too. As we'll see, these "disconnecting experiences" promote dysfunctional detachment in some people and destructive overdependence in others. It all depends upon the circumstances surrounding the event, and the person's way of coping.

Among life's most significant disconnecting experiences are:

- being rejected by a trusted friend
- moving (or changing schools) frequently
- being singled out for public ridicule by a teacher or coach
- being taught to cover up your emotions ("Big girls don't cry....")
- being victimized by a bully (especially when adults allow the bullying to continue)
- reaching puberty much earlier—or later—than your peers
- having a weight problem, serious acne, or other physical "flaw"
- being left back in school or moved ahead a grade
- having a significant episode of childhood illness
- having an undiagnosed learning disability
- having a popular, high-achieving older sibling
- being rejected or cheated on by a boyfriend or girlfriend
- being physically, emotionally, or sexually abused by a trusted adult or older peer

Psychologists have identified four common overdependence patterns that emerge by adolescence and evolve throughout adulthood:

- *Helpless Overdependence: The Immature Pattern* Helpless overdependents maintain ties to others by exaggerating their vulnerability. They present themselves as weak and emotionally needy, and they often appear childlike and immature—easily frustrated and quick to cry. It is tempting to think of helpless overdependents as passive and "fragile," but in fact they are not. Their helplessness is a tool through which they "trap" other people into gratifying their unhealthy dependency needs.

- *Hostile Overdependence: The Controlling Pattern* Hostile overdependents maintain ties to others by intimidating them. On the surface, hostile overdependents appear to be in turmoil—barely holding themselves together, right on the edge of breaking down. When you look closely, however, it becomes clear that this surface appearance is deceiving: In reality, the hostile overdependent is very much in control. This control usually stems from some sort of implied or stated threat ("If you leave me, I'll kill myself!"), which is designed to exploit people's guilt and prevent them from ending the relationship.

- *Hidden Overdependence: The Subtle Pattern* Hidden overdependents behave in an overdependent manner, but oftentimes their dependent behavior is indirect—so much so it might not even be recognized as overdependence. Hidden overdependence can take many forms, from feigned illnesses to imaginary allergies. Whatever form it takes, hidden overdependence functions much like the other overdependence styles we've discussed: It traps people into remaining involved in an unsatisfying relationship they might otherwise end.

- *Conflicted Overdependence: The Unpredictable Pattern* Conflicted overdependents show inconsistent behavior, wavering between periods of extreme overdependence and superficial, short-lived episodes of autonomy. Conflicted overdependents can be especially difficult to deal with, because they are so unpredictable. Oftentimes the conflicted overdependent will show features of hostile overdependence during her "overdependent" periods and hidden overdependence during her "autonomous" periods.

From Healthy Dependency to Dysfunctional Detachment

Dysfunctional detachment—like destructive overdependence—is rooted in an individual's attachment style and early relationship scripts. Like overdependence, detachment evolves in stages, over time. Let's trace the evolution of dysfunctional detachment and the major detachment patterns that follow.

How Detachment Develops Over Time

An avoidant attachment style and got-to-go-it-alone script combine to produce dysfunctional detachment (see page 48). Again, this takes place in four stages:

1) *A Lack of Trust* The first stage in dysfunctional detachment occurs when the child develops the belief that other people are untrustworthy and unreliable—that they won't be there when needed. This is the core belief that underlies dysfunctional detachment, and it is present—consciously or unconsciously—in all detached people.

2) *Desire for Distance and Fear of Intrusion* To protect herself from pain and disappointment, the child who lacks trust begins to screen others out: He develops a *desire for distance* and *fear of intrusion*. Closeness and intimacy become uncomfortable—sometimes downright aversive.

3) *Shell-Building Behavior* The child's desire for distance and fear of intrusion combine to produce a pattern of *shell-building behavior*: She now spends much of her energy keeping other people at a distance.

4) *Disconnection From Others* Over time, the child's shell-building behavior causes him to "disconnect" from others—he spends more and more time in his own isolated universe, always in control, but never engaged with other people in a meaningful, satisfying way.

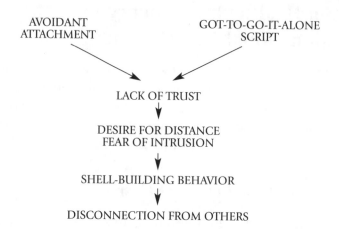

THE ROOTS OF DETACHMENT

As this figure shows, an avoidant attachment style and got-to-go-it-alone relationship script ultimately lead to a dysfunctional pattern of detached ("shell-building") behavior.

Dysfunctional Detachment Patterns

Just as each overdependent person expresses dependency needs differently, every detached person has his own unique way of seeking distance and solitude. And just as people can be overdependent in some areas but not others, they can be detached in certain areas (like romantic relationships) but not others (like friendships).

Researchers have identified four major dysfunctional detachment patterns:

- *Withdrawn Detachment: The Timid Pattern* Withdrawn detached people seem uncomfortable around others. They are socially anxious—so much so that oftentimes they cannot bring themselves to enter into social situations at all (instead they remain on the sideline, longing for the contact they secretly crave). Withdrawn detached people usually

UNDERSTANDING YOUR RESPONSES
TO OTHERS' DISCONNECTIONS

* * * * *

To recapture healthy dependency, you must understand your reflexive responses to others' disconnections, so you can change those responses and avoid relationship traps. By answering the following questions, you'll better understand your responses to overdependence and detachment in those around you. We'll go over your answers in Chapter 3.

For each scenario, choose the *one answer* that describes your most likely response.

When I feel as though someone is becoming overdependent on me, my instinctive response is to:

1) *do whatever it takes to help*—if they're leaning on me, there must be a good reason
2) *put some distance between us*—I don't want to encourage even more overdependence
3) *take charge of the situation*—if they're falling apart, someone else must take over
4) *lose respect for that person*—people should act like adults and take care of themselves, not look to others to bail them out

When someone I care about seems distant and detached, my instinctive response is to:

1) *try to draw them out*—I'm willing to go the extra mile to maintain the relationship
2) *look inward*—maybe I'm doing something that's causing them to withdraw
3) *look elsewhere*—if I can't get what I need in one relationship, I'll get it in another
4) *try not to think about it*—there's no point in worrying about what you can't control

THE GENDER QUESTION

* * * * *

People usually associate overdependence with women, and detachment with men, but our research confirms there's no truth to this myth. In 1995, we compiled and analyzed several decades' worth of published studies involving schoolchildren, college students, community adults, and psychotherapy patients—literally thousands of people overall, from every walk of life. The results were clear: Men are overdependent just as often as women are, and women become detached just as frequently as men.

The bottom line: We can't let gender stereotypes cloud our thinking. To understand self-defeating relationship styles, we must leave our stereotypes behind and learn to recognize signs of overdependence and detachment...wherever they occur.

surround themselves with a small number of familiar people who seem "safe" (family members, plus one or two other acquaintances), and they shut out everyone else.

- *Angry Detachment: The Aggressive Pattern* Angrily detached people barricade themselves behind a wall of hostility that keeps everyone at arm's length. At times, this hostility can shade over into suspiciousness—even paranoia—as the angrily detached person imagines that others are plotting against him. Angrily detached people can be frightening at times (and they do, on occasion, become abusive or violent). But it is important to remember that the angrily detached person's hostility is partly a defense: Unconsciously, they feel sad and lonely, and their wall of hostility helps keep these emotions under wraps.

- *Narcissistic Detachment: The Self-Centered Pattern* Narcissistically detached people use their imagined superiority as an excuse for avoiding genuine contact with people. By presenting themselves as smarter (or stronger, or better-looking) than others, narcissistically detached people are able to justify their detachment (after all, "lesser" people aren't worth their time). Like the anger in angry detachment, the narcissistically detached person's self-centeredness is a defense that helps keep underlying feelings of inadequacy out of conscious awareness.

- *Superficial Engagement: The Barely-There Pattern* Superficially engaged people may not appear detached at all. They typically have many ongoing relationships—sometimes a remarkably large number (which is actually a clue that these relationships are superficial). The superficially engaged person's social contacts usually center on some sort of common task (like work) or a shared interest (like sports), but beyond this, there's little emotional depth. Relationships with superficially engaged people can be quite enjoyable at first, but after a while, the person's inability to move beyond shared tasks and surface interests becomes more and more frustrating (especially in friendships and romantic relationships).

Anne: The Flaw in
Her Self-Assured Veneer

Anne displayed a confidence and self-assurance one rarely sees in beginning college students—especially when they've just arrived on campus. But here was Anne, in our first advising meeting, and she seemed completely, utterly in control. She claimed to have no worries—no concerns whatsoever about her adjustment to college. Her course schedule was meticulously planned (she needed little input from me), and her social life was mapped out in detail as well. Anne intended to join the college's most exclusive sorority, and she was certain she'd assume a leadership position there within a very short time.

I saw little of Anne during those first few weeks, and my mid-semester "How's it going" e-mail went unanswered. I spotted Anne once outside the dining hall, but she was immersed in a lively conversation with several women, and I didn't intrude.

> * * * * *
> **Challenges are what make life interesting;**
> **overcoming them is what makes life meaningful.**
> —JOSHUA J. MARINE

Early December brought fraternity and sorority rush—a taxing time for many first-year college students. On the Saturday of rush weekend, they learned whether they'd received "bids" from their fraternities and sororities of choice. Every year at least one or two of my advisees received disappointing news, and for many of them it was a defining life event—the first time these bright, high-achieving young adults had worked hard, put themselves on the line for something they wanted very much, and failed. Needless to say, this was hardly the outcome they'd hoped for; but for many students, the event became a growth experience, as they learned that they could survive rejection, tolerate disappointment, and move on.

It was a growth experience for many students, but not for Anne. When I arrived at work on the Monday after rush weekend, Anne was waiting outside my office. She said nothing, but her expression said it all. I invited her inside, and closed the door.

As Anne explained what had taken place, her voice was so soft I could barely make out the words. But it soon became clear what had happened.

Anne had indeed tried to join the college's most selective sorority, and she had indeed been turned down. A bit of questioning revealed the likely cause: Anne had been so confident of her acceptance that she hadn't bothered to go to the requisite pre-rush parties. She hadn't taken the time to cultivate relationships with the sorority's movers and shakers, and when her name came up for consideration, no one knew her. I offered this to Anne as a possible explanation, but she would have none of it. As far as Anne was concerned, the problem wasn't her, but the other sorority members. They had somehow failed to see what a valuable leader she would have been and what an important role she would have played in the group.

My efforts to challenge this interpretation were met with staunch resistance. Anne had no insight at all into her role in this process, and she clung desperately—defensively—to her own version of the event. It soon became clear that there was no point in rehashing the incident further. Anne was unable to see things any other way.

Anne left college at the end of the fall semester. The rejection had shaken her so deeply that she felt she could not return and face us again. Anne's narcissistic detachment—her self-assured veneer—had failed her for the first time, and the overwhelming feelings of shame and anger were too much for her to bear. Anne transferred to a university near her home and graduated with honors last spring.

Looking Ahead: Your Responses to Overdependence and Detachment

In Chapter 1, we identified the building blocks of healthy dependency. In Chapter 2, we traced the roots of overdependence and detachment and the different overdependence and detachment patterns—like Anne's—that can result. Now it's time to look more closely at how we react to overdependence and attachment in others. Think about it: How would *you* have responded if Anne entered your life? What would *your* reaction have been to her detachment, self-centeredness, and frustrating lack of insight?

Even when we struggle to change, people around us might not. How we respond to these people can have a powerful effect on our own efforts to learn and grow. In Chapter 3, we'll explore your reactions to overdependence and detachment in those close to you. The *Understanding Your Responses* test you took on page 49 will help you analyze these reactions. Once you understand them, you can begin to change them.

RELATIONSHIP GAMES
AND RELATIONSHIP TRAPS

Kathleen flipped the pages of the menu while she waited. She checked her watch: 12:15. It wasn't like him to be late. She closed the menu and rested it on the table, sipped her water, and watched the waiters moving back and forth across the room.

Kathleen was lost in thought when she felt a hand on her shoulder. She nearly jumped out of her seat.

"My God, Jason. You scared me."

"Sorry. The traffic was awful. I hope you weren't waiting long."

"Oh, no. No problem. I just got here a few minutes ago."

Jason took a seat across from Kathleen, opened his menu, and rubbed his chin while he scanned the pages. Kathleen pretended to read, but every few seconds she peeked over the top of the menu to see what Jason was doing.

Soon a busboy arrived with a basket of bread. The waiter came by and took their orders. Kathleen's water glass was refilled.

Then they were alone, and Kathleen began. She'd planned what she wanted to say.

"Jason, be honest, okay? You know Michael better than anybody. What do you think?"

"What do I think? How do you mean?"

"You know." Kathleen hesitated, laughed nervously. "What's your diagnosis?"

Jason smiled. He leaned back in his seat and spread his arms wide, resting his palms near the corners of the table.

"My diagnosis, huh?" Jason stared into space as he gathered his thoughts. When he spoke, he spoke slowly and chose his words carefully.

"Michael's a terrific guy—thoughtful, nice. In a lot of ways he's a great colleague."

"But?"

Jason smiled again, shook his head slightly. "Right. But." He shifted in his chair.

"I guess the problem is, sometimes he's too nice. He lets people take advantage."

"And?"

"How do you mean?"

"Isn't there more?"

"Well, to be honest, Kathleen, sometimes he gets on people's nerves."

Kathleen felt all the tension drain from her chest. So it wasn't just her. It happened at work, too.

"Go on," she said.

"Well," said Jason, "Like the other day. Worth is going around the table, people are reporting on their programs, and Michael, you know…he just sits there. It's like he doesn't know what he wants to say. And when he finally does talk he blurts out all this stuff, and…I don't know. People got annoyed. They were talking afterward."

"What did they say?"

Jason exhaled deeply. "Some people think Michael's holding the whole project back. They feel like he sort of corners them—almost traps them—into helping him shape his ideas. As if he can't take responsibility for his part of the deal."

Kathleen nodded.

"Then, after he's gotten all this feedback from everybody, he presents it as if it's his own. I think that's what bothers people most."

Kathleen said nothing, but looked over at Jason. She hesitated, then spoke. When she did, her voice was quiet.

"Um, you know what? He does the exact same thing at home."

"Really."

The words came out in a rush then, as Kathleen explained what had been going on between them, how Michael cornered her into making all the tough decisions, always being the bad guy, always taking responsibility. Then Kathleen told what had happened last week—how Michael had been unable to stand up to Kimberly, and the two of them waited up half the night, worrying and wondering.

Finally Kathleen ran out of steam. She was breathing deeply, her chest rising and falling.

"You know what's ironic about the whole thing?"

Jason spoke softly. "No, what?"

"When we first met, I loved how he was so gentle, sensitive, caring, and all that. That's what first attracted me to him. Now it drives me crazy."

The words stopped, and Kathleen found herself staring down at her plate. After a moment she looked up, across the table.

"Jason, I'm thinking of leaving him."

The Three Key Qualities of Healthy Relationships

Studies show that all healthy relationships have three key qualities. Be it lover or friend, parent or sibling, supervisor or colleague—if the relationship isn't characterized by *openness and honesty*, *empathy and caring*, and *security and trust*, it is not a healthy relationship.

Here's what you should look for:

- *Openness and honesty* Healthy relationships involve the open exchange of ideas and honest discussion of feelings—positive as well as negative (for many people, positive feelings are harder to talk about than negative ones).
- *Empathy and caring* Healthy relationships are those wherein both members care enough to try to understand how the other person feels and have empathy for what the other person is going through.

- *Security and trust* Healthy relationships are those wherein both people trust each other and feel secure enough to talk about troubling issues in a nonconfrontational, constructive way.

Relationship Games and Relationship Traps

Instead of being characterized by openness and honesty, empathy and caring, and security and trust, unhealthy relationships involve hurtful *relationship games* and harmful *relationship traps*.

Relationship games are power struggles—contests wherein each member of the relationship tries to extract as much as possible from the other person, while giving as little as possible in return. Relationship games are usually initiated by one member of the relationship, but over time the other person gets drawn further and further into the game, until both members become active players. Oftentimes, people are unaware that they're involved in a relationship game. The rules of the game are never discussed, and both partners play their parts unconsciously—reflexively—with old relationship scripts repeating themselves over and over in new situations.

Relationship traps are strategies used by people who play relationship games. They are designed to manipulate others into doing things they wouldn't otherwise do. Relationship traps typically involve one person exploiting the other person's emotional vulnerabilities, so the victim feels anxious or guilty if they refuse the "trapper's" request. As time passes, anxiety and guilt usually turn into anger and frustration: The exploited person realizes he has fallen once again for the same old trap.

As you might guess, overdependent and detached individuals set different relationship traps. Overdependent people try to trap others into *taking responsibility* and shouldering a burden the overdependent person would rather not carry. The person who deliberately exaggerates a minor illness to get extra loving care

57

from his spouse is setting an overdependent relationship trap. If the spouse falls into the trap, she may find herself taking responsibility for all sorts of household tasks that the overdependent person could easily handle himself (not just now, but during future illness episodes as well).

Detached people try to trap others into *giving up control* and letting the detached person decide how much closeness and contact will be allowed in the relationship. The person who grows distant and sullen each time her spouse tries to talk about personal issues is setting a detachment-based relationship trap. If the partner falls into this trap, he will gradually give up control and stop trying to talk about things that make the partner uncomfortable. Now important relationship issues will remain unexplored.

The games and traps we all experience are important because they bring us to one of the key challenges of healthy depend-

---

WHY OUR REFLEXIVE RESPONSES
DO MORE HARM THAN GOOD

* * * * *

In addition to keeping us enmeshed in unhealthy relationship games, our reflexive responses to overdependence and detachment cause us to:

- *Change in ways we don't like* Compromise can be good, but too much compromise to salvage a dysfunctional relationship is never a good idea. The longer the relationship lasts, the more likely we are to change in ways we don't like.

- *Blame ourselves for things we can't control* After enough time has passed, it becomes difficult to remember where relationship problems began. We may lose perspective and begin to see ourselves as the root of the problem.

- *Compromise other healthy relationships* Oftentimes our efforts to maintain a dysfunctional relationship cause us to put other healthier relationships "on hold," isolating us from important sources of strength and support.

ency: Even though you want to change, others around you might not. If you allow yourself to get caught up in relationship games, you'll spend so much energy trying to escape from relationship traps it will be difficult to move forward, learn, and grow.

Recognizing and Responding to Overdependence

The first step in changing your reflexive responses to overdependence involves recognizing the signs of overdependence in people around you. As Harvard psychologist Ellen Langer points out, when we respond reflexively, we respond *mindlessly*—without thinking about what we're doing. By becoming aware of our reflexive responses, we can respond *mindfully* instead of *mindlessly*: We can make deliberate choices about how best to act, instead of letting our behavior drift along on "automatic pilot," driven and directed by old, well-learned habits.

Signs of Overdependence

It's not always easy to know when one is falling into an overdependent relationship trap. Here's the key: Instead of looking *outward*, look *inward*—focus on how you feel when you are around this person and how you react when the person needs help. By looking inward, you can identify the three telltale signs that you've been caught in an overdependent trap: *feeling smothered*, *assuming responsibility*, and experiencing *creeping resentment* toward the overdependent person.

- *Feeling smothered* People use all kinds of terms to describe this feeling: strangled, suffocated, cornered, trapped...you name it. But the bottom line is, when you're involved in a relationship with an overdependent person, you feel boxed-in and controlled, as though you've lost your freedom. Don't ignore this feeling, because it's telling you something important. If you *feel* you've lost your freedom, you probably have.

- *Assuming responsibility* Sometimes it's hard to know when we're involved with someone who won't take responsibility until we discover that without realizing it, we've taken it all upon ourselves. It's a slow and subtle process, but if you wake up to find that you're shouldering all the "adult" tasks in a relationship, you've identified the second common sign that you're involved with an overdependent person.

- *Creeping resentment* Feeling smothered is unpleasant, and assuming responsibility wears you out after a while, so it's not surprising that the third key signal of an overdependent relationship is creeping resentment. If you find it increasingly difficult to hold your tongue—to stop yourself from telling the person to grow a backbone and get it in gear—you're experiencing creeping resentment, a sure sign that you're in a relationship with someone who's overdependent.

Reflexive Responses to an Overdependent Person

Most of the time, our reflexive responses to overdependence make things worse—they keep us enmeshed in relationship games and ensnared in relationship traps. Using the information from the *Understanding Your Responses* test you completed in Chapter 2 (page 49), let's take the next step: Which of the following best describes your typical reaction to overdependence in those close to you?

ROMANTIC PARTNERS AND BEYOND

* * * * *

As you read these descriptions, it's easy to focus on romantic relationships, but don't forget: We each have our own "response style," and sometimes we react in similar ways to overdependent and detached friends, colleagues, children, siblings...even our parents. The same principles that help you change your reflexive responses in love relationships will help you change your reflexive responses in other relationships as well.

SPREADING THE PAIN

* * * * *

Sometimes people who are overwhelmed by the demands of an overdependent lover, friend, or colleague use what we call the *spreading-the-pain* strategy to get a brief responsibility break: They foist the overdependent person off on others.

Needless to say, this strategy won't work in the long run. As people wise up to what's happening, they'll stop buying into the game. Unless you can find an endless supply of trusting souls, you'll eventually run out of people on whom you can dump the overdependent person. (Not only that, you'll have alienated a whole lot of people along the way by taking advantage of their good will.)

- *Codependency (Answer 1)* Some people respond to overdependence by taking on a nurturing, caregiving role. They are seduced by the person's neediness, and devote a great deal of time and energy to propping up the "weaker" member of the relationship. This nurturing role can become so comfortable that the codependent person begins to do things that encourage even more overdependence in their partner. They may baby the overdependent person, call attention to his weaknesses, even reward him (with increased affection) when he exaggerates his dependency. Now the overdependent and codependent members of the relationship are both trapped. Let the relationship games begin....

- *Counterdependency (Answer 2)* Instead of becoming codependent, some people respond by backpedaling—putting distance between themselves and the overdependent person. Most of the time, the counterdependent individual will withdraw emotionally; in romantic relationships, they may withdraw physically as well. This withdrawal can take several forms, including losing interest in sex, spending extra time at work, or throwing oneself into activities that exclude the overdependent person.

- *Authoritarianism (Answer 3)* Some people respond to overdependence by taking charge: If the overdependent person wants someone to take responsibility, by golly, they'll do it—with a vengeance. The authoritarian person then proceeds to make all the decisions, set the rules, and generally take control of the relationship. Needless to say, the authoritarian response only reinforces the overdependent person's sense of helplessness, rewards his passive behavior, and makes things worse in the long run.

- *Denigration/Devaluing (Answer 4)* Sometimes authoritarianism turns into denigration/devaluing: As the authoritarian person takes control of the overdependent person's life,

---

DENIGRATION: A WARNING SIGN FOR ABUSE

* * * * *

Abuse is a complicated problem with multiple contributing factors. No single event causes someone to become emotionally, physically, or sexually abusive toward another person. Abuse can be surprisingly subtle as well—difficult to recognize and easy to deny. It may creep up slowly, in tiny steps, until one day you wake up and realize that a serious problem has taken hold.

Studies show that denigration plays an important role in child, partner, and elder abuse. As the abuser belittles the other person in his or her mind, they begin to think that this person somehow "deserves" mistreatment. The stage is then set for abuse to begin. And denigration can be used to justify ongoing abuse as well: The more we see the other person in a negative way (weak, sick, lazy...whatever), the easier it is to rationalize abusive behavior and continue engaging in it.

If you find yourself denigrating your child, parent, or partner—tearing them down and belittling them in your mind—be on the lookout: You are at risk for becoming an abuser. And if you are abusing someone in your life—emotionally, physically, or sexually—don't let it continue. Get help. Call your local child abuse, elder abuse, or domestic violence hotline (all are listed in the *Human Services* section of the phone book).

their perception of the overdependent person changes, and they begin to belittle that person in their mind ("If he insists on acting like a child, I'm going to treat him like one...."). They see the overdependent person as inferior (wimpy, weak, sick, immature), and as denigration/devaluing increases, so does the possibility of emotional, physical, and sexual abuse.

Healthy Responses to Overdependence

Instead of responding reflexively to overdependence (and ultimately making things worse), you can learn to respond in ways that foster healthy dependency and create a better environment for everyone. Three strategies are useful here:

- *Reward autonomous behavior.* As pioneering behaviorist B. F. Skinner pointed out, we humans are just like other animals: We seek to maximize rewards and minimize punishments. To foster healthy dependency in an overdependent person, you can put Skinner's insight to use. First, *stop reinforcing overdependent behavior.* When the rewards stop coming, the relationship traps will disappear. At the same time, be sure to *reward autonomous behavior.* It doesn't take much— a kind word, a smile, a pat on the back. But whatever rewards you choose, use them consistently. Any time the overdependent person behaves independently, takes responsibility, or engages in growth-motivated help-seeking, reinforce him for doing this. You'll be surprised how quickly new behavior patterns begin to take hold.
- *Set limits—but be flexible.* No matter how careful you are in facilitating autonomy, the overdependent person will probably regress at some point, and begin to exhibit his old helpless ways. This can be frustrating, but don't overreact (sometimes a strong emotional response is just what the overdependent person is after). Instead of getting angry, hold your ground and set "flexible limits": Make it clear to the overdependent person that while they—not you—are

responsible for the choices they make, you're still there for them, ready and willing to help—up to a point.

- *Help the person find new ways to cope.* Remember that most overdependent people don't have much experience managing things without help—they haven't developed the healthy dependency skills they need to function independently. These skills will come with practice, but learning is a process that can't be rushed. In the meantime, be on the lookout for those moments when the overdependent person is genuinely struggling to find ways to do things on his own. When these opportunities present themselves, help the person by engaging in constructive problem-solving: Offer suggestions, tips, and practical advice—but always with the goal of helping the overdependent person learn new ways to cope. By doing this, you'll strengthen the overdependent person's growth motivation and help him develop strategies for managing things on his own.

* * * * *

**Life is a succession of lessons
enforced by immediate reward, or, oftener,
by immediate chastisement.**
—ERNEST DIMNET

Brian: A Counterdependent Therapist

We met Brian during our first week in graduate school, and we were both impressed (and more than a bit intimidated) by his quick wit, self-assurance, and grasp of complex psychological theory. Brian was a brilliant student, and he soon became a tremendous resource for the rest of us. Whenever we had a tricky research question or found ourselves lost in some vexing statistical problem, Brian was the first person we'd call. Most of the time, he was happy to oblige.

Brian excelled at the start of graduate training, earning straight A's his first year. But as time went on, and we shifted from classroom studies to hands-on clinical work, Brian's performance deteriorated. Rumors began to circulate that Brian—so knowledgeable regarding psychological theory—was having difficulty with his patients. The word among the students was that Brian overanalyzed everything during therapy sessions and couldn't connect emotionally. Patients were getting frustrated and giving up on treatment.

As we talked with Brian about his clinical struggles, it became clear that he had developed a counterdependent response to his patients' overdependence: Every time a patient began to rely on him, Brian withdrew. Brian's counterdependent style wasn't a problem when he interacted with other graduate students, but it was a serious problem in his clinical work. After all, many psychotherapy patients develop a pronounced dependency on the therapist. This is expected, and in some ways quite helpful (it keeps patients engaged in treatment and motivated to follow through). As you might guess, though, problems arise when a therapist cannot tolerate the patient's dependency, and when the therapist allows his reflexive responses to undermine the therapeutic relationship.

In Brian's case, his counterdependent style turned treatment from a growth experience into a harmful relationship game that repeated itself anew with each patient. Brian always started out by encouraging his patients to open up, as he had been taught to do. But when his patients did open up and start to reveal the details of their lives, Brian became anxious. Not knowing how to deal with his anxiety, Brian unconsciously engaged in various counterdependent strategies designed to keep his patients at a distance. He shifted the discussion away from emotional issues, subtly encouraged patients to talk in *thinking* rather than *feeling* terms, and even acted out (by coming late or cancelling sessions) when a patient's dependency became too much for him to bear. His patients ended up feeling trapped—encouraged to open up, but then punished for doing so. Not surprisingly, many patients grew frustrated and quit therapy.

65

Brian eventually left psychology, seeking a professional niche wherein he could use his intellectual talents while avoiding some of the emotional challenges that made him uncomfortable. Looking back on Brian's decision, it seems a shame: Rather than finding better—more therapeutic—ways of responding to his patients' dependency needs, Brian abandoned his chosen field. We'll never know how things might have worked out if Brian had taken a different approach, and learned to replace his reflexive responses to overdependence with new, more productive responses.

Recognizing and Responding to Detachment

The same basic principles that helped you avoid overdependence traps and relationship games can help you cope more effectively with people who are detached—people at the other end of the relationship spectrum. Detached people present a different set of challenges—distancing rather than clinging, shutting down rather than opening up—but your strategy will be the same. You must: 1) identify the telltale signs of detachment; 2) analyze your reflexive responses to these behaviors; and 3) replace these reflexive responses with healthier, more adaptive responses.

Signs of Detachment

As was true for overdependence, the signs of detachment are best seen by looking inward, not outward. Three signals that you are involved in a relationship with a detached person are *endless pursuit, emotional walling-off,* and *intimacy frustration.*

- *Endless pursuit* Do you always initiate the activity, order the tickets, and then make the dinner reservations, too? Have you ever tried *not* taking the initiative, just to see what would happen? When you stopped making the effort, did the relationship stop dead in its tracks? If you answered yes to any of these questions, take note: You may be engaged in the endless pursuit of a detached person.

- *Emotional walling-off* Emotional walling-off can take many forms, but the end result is always the same: You end up feeling shut out, as though there's some hidden, secret part the other person won't let you see. If your efforts to get closer invariably cause the other person to back away, you are experiencing emotional walling-off.
- *Intimacy frustration* The inevitable result of emotional walling-off is intimacy frustration. When you can't get close to someone, you can't connect, and when you can't connect, your intimacy needs go unmet. Some people become angry—conflict results. Others turn their anger inward and

ANGER AND DEPRESSION

* * * * *

Bottled-up anger (sometimes called *anger turned inward*) can make you depressed. Studies by neuroscientists and medical researchers confirm that when anger builds up and goes unexpressed, changes in body chemistry soon follow: Stress hormones flood the bloodstream, and serotonin levels decline in the brain. (Serotonin is a neurotransmitter that helps elevate mood, so too little serotonin means increased likelihood of depression.)

Unfortunately, studies of people's efforts to change their *anger turned inward* coping style have yielded discouraging results. University of Cincinnati researcher Goldine Gleser and her colleague David Ihilevich report that people who respond reflexively by bottling up anger find it almost impossible to stop this process on their own, even when they become aware of it.

If bottled-up anger is a problem for you or if you experience troubling bouts of depression (for *any* reason), you should talk to a physician or psychologist. They may be able to help you express your anger more productively and manage your mood more effectively. When you talk to a professional about problems with anger or depression, you're putting your healthy dependency skills to work—you're taking the initiative and seeking help to learn and grow.

beat themselves up for "doing something wrong" or "not being good enough" to get the closeness they crave.

Reflexive Responses to a Detached Person

Just as we develop reflexive responses to overdependence, we develop reflexive responses to detachment—and they inevitably cause more harm than good. Based on the *Understanding Your Responses* test on page 49, which of the following best describes you?

- *Overcompensation (Answer 1)* Some people respond to detachment by redoubling their efforts to connect. Although this is certainly understandable, it almost always ends up making things worse, not better. The detached person feels intruded upon, so he withdraws even further into his protective shell. The overcompensator feels frustrated and angry that her well-meaning efforts are met with such staunch resistance.
- *Self-deprecation (Answer 2)* Some people respond to detachment by looking inward—blaming themselves for the other person's distance, and wondering what they should do differently to "fix" things. This is a particularly problematic response because it feeds into the vulnerabilities of both members of the relationship. The self-deprecator ends up feeling bad about herself (guilty, inadequate), so she searches even harder to discover what she's doing "wrong." The detached person, sensing the other person's insecurity, becomes empowered, and sets even firmer limits on closeness and contact.
- *Displacement (Answer 3)* Some people find it easiest to look elsewhere for closeness. The primary risk here (at least as far as romantic relationships are concerned) is deceit: As the displacer finds emotional intimacy elsewhere, she may be tempted to seek sexual intimacy elsewhere as well. This sometimes signals the end of the initial relationship, but it can also lead to a lengthy pattern of deception and a complicated three-way relationship game where nobody really wins.

- *Denial (Answer 4)* Another common response to detachment is denial. Rather than confront the detached person (and deal with her own troubling feelings), the denier sweeps everything under the rug. She makes excuses, convincing herself that things are all right or that they'll get better with time ("As soon as the kids are in school, we'll have more time to spend together...."). Needless to say, denial does nothing to alter a dysfunctional relationship pattern. It's also unhealthy (as we'll see in Chapter 9) because over time, denying negative feelings can lead to increased stress and illness.

Healthy Responses to Detachment

Just as you learned healthier ways of responding to overdependence, you can learn better ways of responding to detachment. Three strategies are useful:

- *Test your perceptions.* Detachment can be subtle—so much so that you might begin to question whether you're misperceiving the situation or blowing things out of proportion. Here's where a bit of "reality-testing" can help. Seek out someone you know and trust, and discuss the problem with them. Describe the detached person's behavior— including how it makes you feel—and try to get a fresh perspective on things. You might discover that you *are* overreacting, and if this is the case, you need to look inward to see what's really wrong. (Are you asking too much? Not communicating effectively?) Or you might find out that your perceptions are accurate—that the other person's detached behavior is indeed out of the ordinary. If this is the case, you need to take action.
- *Seek support—but use it well.* There's a fine line between *healthy support-seeking* and *unhealthy displacement.* Healthy support-seeking is driven by growth motivation: It involves looking to others for advice and reassurance and using this advice and reassurance to deal more effectively with the

problems that confront you. Unhealthy displacement (which we discussed earlier in this chapter) involves seeking advice and reassurance to *avoid* problems instead of dealing with them. Bottom line: It can be useful to seek support elsewhere when you're involved with a detached person, but monitor your motives carefully, and be sure you're using this support in a constructive—not destructive—way.

HEALTHY DEPENDENCY
WITH UNHEALTHY PEOPLE

✳ ✳ ✳ ✳ ✳

One of the great challenges of healthy dependency is maintaining healthy connections with unhealthy people—friends with substance abuse problems, for example, or family members with untreated mental illnesses. Even though these connections can be very meaningful to us, they are fraught with relationship traps.

How to maintain good connections in these difficult, challenging relationships? You'll do best if you apply the three principles we discussed at the outset of this chapter:

- *Do not allow yourself to change in unhealthy ways.* It is tempting to do everything you can to rescue a hurting friend, but be careful: Sometimes help does more harm than good. Even with the best of intentions, it's all too easy to become an "enabler" (someone who inadvertently helps the person maintain his dysfunctional state by caring—and doing—too much).

- *Do not blame yourself for things you can't control.* People with addictions or untreated mental illnesses will change when they're ready. Sometimes they won't change at all. No matter how hard you try, or how much you care, you cannot force this process to occur.

- *Do not compromise other relationships.* When maintaining connections with troubled people, your other, healthier relationships are your safe haven—the place where you can get your own needs met and express your healthy dependency fully and completely. Whatever you do, do not let these relationships wither as you support a hurting friend.

- *Air your concerns.* While you seek advice and support elsewhere, you should also begin to deal directly with the problem at hand. Make time to discuss your concerns with the detached person (set up an appointment to talk if you have to). When you do raise the issue, be sure to present your concerns in a nonthreatening way. Don't blame the other person or yourself—just stick to the facts. Use concrete examples to illustrate your points. Try not to get defensive if the detached person disagrees at first (odds are, they will). And choose your talk time carefully. It's best not to do it when you're upset or tired—you're likely to say things you'll regret later on. If at all possible, try not to meet when the other person is frazzled (like at the end of a long day). If the detached person is tired or stressed, they will be in no mood to hear about your concerns, and your well-meaning efforts might end up making things worse, not better.

Looking Ahead: Healthy Dependency Across Situations

The core principles of healthy dependency apply to every relationship, but each relationship brings its own unique challenges—and its own unique opportunities as well. To lay the groundwork for growth and positive change in *all* your relationships, take a few minutes to complete the *Sketching A Roadmap* exercise on page 72. It will give you a sense of where you are right now and where you want to be in the future. We'll refer back to your "Relationship Roadmap" throughout the book, beginning in Chapter 4.

* * * * *
**The best time to hold your tongue
is the time you feel you must say
something or bust.**
—JOSH BILLINGS

SKETCHING A ROADMAP:
YOUR AGENDA FOR CHANGE

* * * * *

You bought this book because you want to change, and to do that effectively, you need a plan—a roadmap to guide your journey. By answering the questions below, you'll get a clearer sense of *how* you want to change and grow, and *where* you want to be in the future.

My three best qualities are:

1)

2)

3)

Three things I would like to change about myself are:

1)

2)

3)

The three best things about my most important relationship* are:

1)

2)

3)

Three things I would like to change about my most important relationship are:

1)

2)

3)

*Everyone is different, so don't feel inhibited. Your most important relationship might involve a lover, friend, sibling, child, parent, pastor, or colleague at work—it's completely up to you.

HEALTHY DEPENDENCY
IN LOVE

As she drove home that evening after talking with Theresa, Ellen thought about her husband James. She thought about her daughter Melissa and her son Steven. She wondered whether they felt the same way Theresa did. Did they want her to "open up," too?

As Ellen pulled into the driveway and eased the car to a stop, she saw lights on in the living room. James was sitting on the couch, reading a magazine, when something upstairs seemed to catch his attention. James's brow furrowed as he looked toward the hallway. A moment later Melissa's legs appeared as she came partway down the the steps.

Something was wrong. James was angry. He gestured toward the kitchen. Melissa came down the rest of the way. She stood in the hallway, pleading with her father. James shook his head, gestured again. Melissa's mouth twisted out of shape, her face contorted in frustration and anger. She turned and ran upstairs. James watched her go.

Ellen was surprised to discover that her heart was racing. Her palms were sweating as she gripped the wheel. She waited for a moment, let her breathing subside, checked her reflection in the rear-view mirror. Then she gathered her things and headed up the walk.

Ellen opened the front door, called out a greeting, but no one answered. She put down her briefcase and went into the kitchen. James was fussing over the stove, adjusting burners and peeking under lids.

"Hello," said Ellen. "How's everything?" She tried to sound casual—didn't want him to know she'd been watching.

"Fine," said James. He kissed her on the cheek.

Ellen waited for him to say more, but he didn't. He stirred one pot, then another.

"Everything okay?"

"Sure," said James. Then, "Why do you ask?"

"No reason. Just wondering. How are Melissa and Steve?"

"Fine. They're upstairs."

Ellen and James stood in the kitchen. Neither one spoke. After a moment, James turned back to the stove.

"Dinner should be ready in a few minutes, okay? Could you let the kids know on your way up?"

"Sure," said Ellen. She turned and left.

On her way past Melissa's room, Ellen stopped, then knocked. There was no answer at first so she knocked again, louder. This time there was movement inside.

Melissa opened the door and stood there. Her eyes were red. The desk was covered with papers and books. Clothes and CDs were strewn on the bed.

"Hi Mel. How's everything?"

"Fine."

"School was good?"

"Yup."

"Did practice go well?"

Melissa shrugged. "Okay, I guess."

Ellen hesitated. Should she ask about what she'd seen? She decided to hint instead.

"Dad okay? He looks tired."

"I don't know," said Melissa. "You'd have to ask him."

Ellen stood in the doorway, gazed at her daughter. Melissa stared back, blinked once, twice. Finally Ellen broke the silence.

"Tell your brother dinner's ready, okay? I'll meet you downstairs."

In her bedroom, Ellen exhaled deeply. She threw her jacket on the bed and went into the bathroom. As she looked in the mirror, she found herself getting angry. It was one thing at work—those were her employees—but here at home, too, with the people she loves? Her hus-

band and daughter have a screaming, crying fight, and neither one says a word about it. What's going on here? How much is she missing?

Poets tell us that love is something magical and mysterious, uncontrollable and unexplainable. When love blossoms, it brings life's greatest joy; when it withers, life's greatest sorrow. As William Shakespeare wryly observed, "The course of true love never did run smooth."

Psychotherapist Albert Ellis takes a less romantic, more down-to-earth view. The art of love, says Ellis, is largely the art of hard work and persistence.

Who's correct—the poet or the therapist? Both are, of course, but in different ways. The poet is right: Love is a mystery that springs from within, arrives when least expected, and abandons us cruelly just as quickly as it came. But Ellis is right, too. Wherever loves comes from, it takes hard work, persistence, and effort to sustain it.

In this chapter, we see how healthy dependency can enhance romance and deepen love. We explore the romantic obstacles that stem from destructive overdependence and dysfunctional detachment, and learn how healthy dependency can help us overcome these obstacles.

Love's Unique Challenges

Yale University's Robert Sternberg has been a leader in the scientific study of love. The key to love's power, says Sternberg, lies in the complex array of feelings and emotions that characterize romantic relationships.

Sternberg's studies show that love relationships are unique: They are the only human relationships that blend *intimacy, passion,* and *commitment* into a single, seamless whole. When we're in love, we reveal parts of ourselves no one else gets to see (intimacy). We feel physical longings that no one else can stimulate (passion). And we experience a unique sense of loyalty and shared purpose that no one else can evoke (commitment).

In an ideal world, every romantic relationship would reflect generous portions of all three qualities. But as most of us can attest, finding just the right balance of intimacy, passion, and commitment is quite a challenge. Young or old, rich or poor, we all face the same dilemmas as we strive to create that perfect, lasting love:

- *Blending intimacy and identity* When we're truly intimate with someone we love, we feel joined, merged—as though two individuals have literally become one. It's a blissful feeling, but a risky one as well. Here's the problem: Without a strong identity—without a firm sense of who we are and what we want out of life—it is easy to "lose oneself" in intimacy. As the psychoanalyst Erik Erikson pointed out, loss of identity in the throes of intimacy can be terribly frightening—so much so that we instinctively pull back to

---

ROMANTIC GOALS: EXTENDING
YOUR RELATIONSHIP ROADMAP

* * * * *

Everyone's relationship goals are different. Before you begin exploring yours, take a few minutes to look back at your *Relationship Roadmap* from Chapter 3. How does your romantic relationship fit in here? What do you especially *like* about this relationship, and what aspects of the relationship would you *change* if you could? Write your answers in the spaces below; they'll help you think more clearly about your romantic goals:

What I like best about my current (or most recent) romantic
    relationship is: _____

_____

_____

What I'd most like to change about my romantic relationship is:

_____

_____

_____

---

maintain our sense of self. Love becomes a painful tug-of-war where we're alternately drawn toward intimacy, then driven away when it gets too near. Needless to say, this creates a frustrating, unsatisfying situation for both partners.

- *Communicating honestly* Research findings are clear: One of the best predictors of marital success is honest communication. Couples who stay together share their thoughts and feelings openly, without holding back. They express negative thoughts and troubling emotions in nonjudgmental, noncritical ways, so disagreements don't escalate into fights. But couples who divorce do just the opposite: They let anger and resentment build up unexpressed, until finally these festering feelings burst forth in a hurtful, hateful cascade of resentment, blame, and recrimination.

- *Sustaining the passion* There's no faking passion: It's there or it isn't. And we can't "make" passion last through the years—it either does, or it doesn't. So what can we do to sustain this key element of romantic love? The trick is not to dwell on passion itself, but to focus instead on intimacy and honesty. When heartfelt intimacy and honest communication are part of your relationship, passion will remain strong all by itself—you won't have to chase it, or struggle to sustain it.

In the following sections, we explore the challenges that stem from overdependent love. We discuss strategies for turning your partner's overdependence into healthy dependency and techniques you can use to give your partner room to breathe if you—not your partner—are the overdependent one.

Overdependent Love

Overdependent love is driven by insecure attachment and a can't-make-it-on-my-own relationship script. The end result is a *suffocating lovestyle*—a smothering, controlling, hang-on-tight way of relating that eventually alienates even the most devoted partner.

77

OVERDEPENDENCE AND DETACHMENT IN THE BEDROOM: "BIRDS OF A FEATHER FLOCK TOGETHER" OR "OPPOSITES ATTRACT"?

* * * * *

Cupid's arrow strikes in the least likely places, and we don't always make "rational" choices when it comes to love. Are certain types of people more compatible than others?

Certain lovestyles mesh well together, while others are somewhat more challenging, according to a recent study of several hundred college-age romantic couples. Researchers Jeffrey Simpson and Steven Gangestad asked people to fill out questionnaires assessing their relationship goals, their perceptions of their partner, and their thoughts and feelings about the relationship itself. Here's the bottom line:

- *Overdependent-Overdependent* The good news in this case is that relationships between two overdependent partners tend to be strong on commitment. The downside of such relationships is shared insecurity: Two overdependent people have a way of bringing out each other's anxieties, yet their common fear of conflict prevents them from discussing problems openly. Resentments build up, responsibilities are avoided, and the end result may be a complicated array of self-defeating relationship games.
- *Detached-Detached* In some ways this is the trickiest combination because both partners have difficulty connecting emotionally. Romantic relationships involving two detached people can survive when both partners have outside interests to occupy their energy. Oftentimes problems arise at retirement, when two detached partners are finally forced to confront their inability to be intimate and communicate honestly.
- *Overdependent-Detached* Studies show that this combination can work surprisingly well because each partner brings a unique set of strengths to the relationship. These relationships are not without problems, of course: At times, the needs and goals of overdependent and detached partners conflict, and create considerable friction. Interestingly, evidence suggests that this combination of lovestyles works best when the woman is detached and the man overdependent, rather than the other way around. No one knows why, though—at least not yet.

The Suffocating Lovestyle

In the suffocating lovestyle, genuine intimacy is replaced by *self-centered intimacy*, honest communication is replaced by *ingratiating communication*, and passion is replaced by *insecure sexuality*. Let's take a closer look:

- *Self-centered intimacy* Overdependent people crave closeness, but their insecurity and fragile identity prevent them from managing the challenge of intimacy. Rather than relating to their partner as an equal, the overdependent person assumes a child-like role in romantic relationships, trapping the partner into the complementary role of pseudo-parent. The end result is *self-centered intimacy*: The partner is valued not for who they are, but for the security and protection they provide to the overdependent person.

- *Ingratiating communication* Because overdependent people see their partner more as parent than peer, they have trouble communicating honestly. They're too worried about jeopardizing the relationship. As a result, the overdependent lover adopts an *ingratiating communication style*: Every interaction is shaped by their need to strengthen ties to the partner and preserve the status quo. Although this can be gratifying in the short run (since the overdependent person goes out of his way to bolster the partner's ego), ingratiating communication eventually becomes tiresome, as its manipulative, relationship trap features become increasingly apparent.

* * * * *

Immature love says, "I love you because I need you." Mature love says, "I need you because I love you."
—Erich Fromm

- *Insecure sexuality* The overdependent person's insatiable need for reassurance turns sexuality from a joyful, spontaneous experience into a ritualized relationship game. The overdependent person is always on the lookout for signs of sexual difficulty ("Is anything different? Have I done something wrong?"). The partner, in turn, feels as if she must watch her every move to avoid making the overdependent person anxious. Now both people are so caught up in monitoring the situation that they cannot relax, unleash their inhibitions, and enjoy the moment. Passion inevitably fades under such challenging circumstances.

Coming Up for Air

By helping change your overdependent partner's suffocating lovestyle, you set the stage for intimacy, passion, and commitment to grow. This takes time, of course (change is never easy, nor quick), but three strategies are useful:

- *Provide targeted reassurance.* Reassurance can help the overdependent person gain confidence, but the trick is to use it wisely. In small doses, reassurance will help your partner gain confidence. In too-large doses, reassurance can become a crutch for an overdependent romantic partner— so gratifying that the person may begin to exaggerate her helplessness to ensure that the reassurance keeps coming. To avoid this, target your reassurance where it's needed most, and make your support contingent on your partner's continued efforts to master challenges on her own. When your partner's growth motivation is enhanced, there will be less need for your external reassurance to bolster it.
- *Create relationship space.* If you feel suffocated, you'll become angry, and you'll act impulsively ("mindlessly") rather than thoughtfully. To minimize this, make a concerted effort to create relationship space by spending some

time on your own or with other people. Encourage your partner to do the same—prod her a bit if you have to. Be forewarned: Your partner will likely become anxious at your efforts to create space, but this is one place where targeted reassurance will come in handy. Let your partner know that your efforts to create relationship space are not a sign of rejection or lost interest. If your partner gains confidence from hearing this, continue. If she doesn't benefit from being reassured, stop doing it. After time has passed, experience should teach your partner what words cannot: Even though things have changed, you're still there and the relationship remains strong.

- *Build confidence through clear communication.* It is important to let your partner know when you feel smothered, but *how* you communicate this is critical. Don't blame or overgeneralize (avoid terms like "You always..." and "I never..."). Present the issue as a shared problem that you can work on together. Try not to back off if your partner becomes tearful or angry—if you do, you'll risk being drawn into a new relationship game. Instead, persist in discussing the problem, firmly but gently. Take "time out" if you have to, so your partner can settle down. And be sure to communicate your belief that the relationship will strengthen—not weaken—if you get a bit of breathing room.

Letting your partner breathe

If you—not your partner—have a suffocating lovestyle, you need to find ways to be comfortable with your partner's autonomy. At the same time, you must find ways to behave more autonomously yourself, so you don't suffocate your partner. These tasks can be accomplished simultaneously when you focus on rebuilding the four key healthy dependency skills in the context of your romantic relationship.

Here's what you should aim for:

- *Try doing more things on your own.* Before you ask your partner for help, be sure you've given it your best shot. You'll feel better about asking if you've made a good, honest effort beforehand, and your partner will feel better about helping as well. Plus, if you've given it your best shot, both you and your partner will find it easier to separate the act from the person—you'll be less likely to confuse *asking for help* with *being helpless.* Be careful not to use one problem as an excuse for avoiding other challenges, or as a negotiating ploy to get help in areas where you don't really need it. Your best strategy is to decide ahead of time where help is needed most, and limit your requests to those situations.
- *Watch your language.* Don't trap your partner into rescuing you by using "babytalk" to create an aura of helplessness. When you *act* like a child, you *feel* like a child—and your partner will see you as a child as well. Be sure to monitor your nonverbals: Sometimes even when we choose our words carefully, our facial expression and body position signal fear and insecurity. You might want to practice asking for help in front of a mirror, paying particular attention to how you appear. If you don't like what you see, correct it.
- *Monitor your motives.* Think before you act, and determine whether you're asking for help to master new skills or whether you're secretly (or not-so-secretly) looking to be rescued by your partner. Try not to ask for help when you feel desperate: A breathless, panicky request is usually designed to avoid a challenge. Finally, wait before acting: If you're really seeking help to learn and grow, putting it off a bit won't hurt. And if you feel like you can't possibly wait another minute, take note: Your inner urgency is telling you that your request isn't based on growth, but on fear.
- *Plan your request.* Choose the time and place carefully. Ideally, your request for help should come at a low-stress moment (not when the kids are already late for school) and in a private place (not in a restaurant with friends at the table). If your partner chooses not to help, accept this

gracefully. Find out why your partner refused, and use this information to do better next time. Whatever you do, avoid emotional blackmail: Never guilt-trip, threaten, yell, whine, cry, or otherwise try to coerce your partner into helping. You might win in the short run, but you'll lose in the long run.

Detached Love

Like overdependent love, detached love undermines intimacy, passion, and commitment. But it does so in a different way—by causing those closest to us to withdraw. Notice how Ellen's detached relationship style caused her husband and daughter to distance themselves from her emotionally. Instead of opening up when conflict occurred, James and Melissa both shut down. They revealed to Ellen only the most superficial details, and kept her away from the intimate aspects of their lives.

Ellen's behavior illustrates the underlying basis of detached love: an avoidant attachment style coupled with a got-to-go-it-alone relationship script. These combine to produce the *arm's-length lovestyle*—a distancing, off-putting way of relating that squelches romance and squanders love.

The Arm's-Length Lovestyle

In the arm's-length lovestyle, genuine intimacy is replaced by *superficial intimacy*, honest communication is replaced by *guarded communication*, and passion is replaced by *faceless sexuality*. Let's break it down:

- *Superficial intimacy* The detached person's inability to trust other people means she invariably chooses identity over intimacy—independence and self-reliance over mutual trust and shared vulnerability. In a very real sense, the detached person doesn't know what it means to be intimate (she's probably never experienced it). Instead of leading to gen-

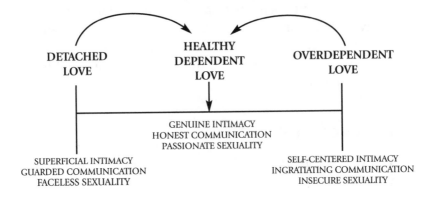

HEALTHY DEPENDENCY IN LOVE

To recapture healthy dependency in love, the overdependent person must overcome self-centered intimacy, ingratiating communication, and insecure sexuality. The detached person must move beyond superficial intimacy, guarded communication, and faceless sexuality.

uine intimacy, your partner's well-meaning efforts to connect will likely produce *superficial intimacy*. Even when personal issues take center stage, there's no emotional give-and-take, no sense of shared experience, and no feeling of partnership in life's journey.

- *Guarded communication* Because detached people are threatened by closeness, their communications tend to be guarded—even defensive. The detached person may make periodic attempts to talk about "relationship issues," but even then the focus tends to be on thoughts rather than feelings—observations rather than emotions. Such *guarded communication* prevents genuine intimacy from taking hold. It can also undermine both partners' efforts to communicate: The same relationship issues keep coming up time and again, with no real progress toward honest resolution.
- *Faceless sexuality* Making love with a detached person can sometimes be physically gratifying, but it is never emotionally satisfying. The irony here is that when the relationship

DEALING WITH IN-LAWS: THE PARENT TRAP

* * * * *

In-laws present different types of challenges, depending upon whether your partner is overdependent or detached:

- *The overdependent partner* If your partner is overdependent, you'll likely find yourself competing with his parents for power and influence. At times, the overdependent partner will turn to the parents—not you—for advice and support, so you end up feeling shut out. Worse, some overdependent people play the spouse and parents off against each other: They begin by seeking advice or support from you, only to undermine your efforts by immediately discussing the very same issue with their parents. Needless to say, sometimes you and the in-laws will offer contradictory opinions. Be careful here: It's easy to get sucked into a no-win, three-way relationship game.
- *The detached partner* If your partner is detached, you will probably be forced into the role of go-between, relaying messages (both subtle and direct) from spouse to parents, and back again. The pressure to assume this messenger role will be especially intense if one or both of your partner's parents are detached as well. In this situation, there will be an even stronger "pull" for you to mediate conflicts and resolve familial disputes. The rules of this relationship game may be hard to decipher, but make no mistake: The more fully you cooperate, the more deeply enmeshed you'll become, and the harder it will be to extricate yourself when you tire of your messenger role.

was just beginning, it's likely that lovemaking seemed unusually passionate and uninhibited; now it's become mechanical and oddly unemotional. Though this pattern might seem strange, in fact it's a predictable consequence of detachment. When there's little commitment, the detached person can relax and be sexually uninhibited, but when intimacy and commitment appear on the horizon, the detached person's need for distance increases and passion flies out the window.

Shrinking the Distance

By helping your detached partner open up emotionally, you can begin to shrink the distance that's opened up between you. It takes time to overcome an arm's-length lovestyle, but the following strategies will make your task easier:

- *Accept your partner's fear of intimacy.* We don't choose our feelings, and we don't choose our fears. Your partner's fear of intimacy may be frustrating to you, but getting angry won't change this (and it might even make things worse). Though it seems counterintuitive, the first step in helping your partner overcome a fear of intimacy is for you to accept it without question—no ifs, ands, or buts. Acceptance takes the pressure off both of you. Now you can approach the issue more rationally and with less pent-up anger and frustration. Your partner, in turn, will find it easier to confront a difficult situation without the added concern that you're angry or upset.

- *Acknowledge your own need for closeness.* Accepting your partner's fear of intimacy doesn't mean foregoing your own need for closeness. On the contrary, when you acknowledge and accept your partner's ambivalence, you create an environment wherein you can discuss, in a nonthreatening way, how your needs enter into the equation. Begin by explaining how you *feel* about what's missing from the relationship. Then tell your partner what you *want.* Be specific and concrete. "I'd like us to sit close together on the couch when we watch TV" is better than "I want us to be closer physically." Begin with small, manageable requests, and when the two of you make progress with these, move on to larger, more challenging changes. Don't rush things, and be prepared for the occasional setback. Progress is never smooth where relationships are concerned. It comes instead in fits and starts—two steps forward, one step back. If you can't tolerate the periodic "one step back," you'll never be rewarded with "two steps forward."

MANAGING BACKSLIDES

* * * * *

No matter how conscientious you are, you'll likely find that some old, self-defeating patterns re-emerge every once in a while. This is not at all unusual, and it is not a sign that you're doing something wrong. In fact, the occasional re-emergence of old patterns reflects a fundamental principle of the human mind: Changing old habits takes mental energy, and anything that saps this energy will turn *mindfulness* into *mindlessness* and cause well-rehearsed patterns to re-emerge temporarily.

Three experiences in particular tend to drain our mental energy, and make it hard to inhibit old, self-defeating habits:

- *Stress* Stress steals energy from both mind and body. When you're stressed, you divert mental and physical resources to dealing with whatever is bothering you. You feel anxious, jittery, worried, and pressured, and you "spend" a great deal of energy managing these unpleasant feelings—energy that might otherwise be devoted to strengthening your new way of interacting.

- *Fatigue* Fatigue, like stress, drains mental energy. When we are fatigued we must devote extra effort to planning simple tasks (like making coffee) that we usually perform almost without thinking. The energy we spend on planning these tasks is no longer available for other things. So don't be surprised if a sleepless night is followed by a temporary backslide and the re-emergence of old habits.

- *Distraction* It's difficult to focus your attention on two things at once. That's why you're more likely to make a mistake when you write out a check while talking on the phone—and why lecturing the kids while driving is an invitation to disaster. When you do two things at once, you can't do either well (psychologists call this the "divided-attention effect"). Because you're dividing your mental energy between two competing tasks, old patterns are likely to re-emerge.

- *Find common ground.* Relationship change involves compromise on both sides. Don't draw a line in the sand and tell yourself (or worse, your partner) that you'll settle for nothing less. If you're truly in love with a detached person and you're determined to make the relationship work, you'll need to balance your needs with her fears, and find ways to grow closer that satisfy both of you. You might not get everything you want exactly as you've pictured it, but you'll probably get a lot more than you would have without flexibility and compromise.

Romantic reconnection

If you—not your partner—have an arm's-length lovestyle, take note: Your relationship is at risk. To deepen love, you must reconnect. You must learn how to let yourself be emotionally vulnerable and allow your partner to help and support you. By practicing healthy dependency in the context of your romantic relationship, you can make letting down your guard less frightening and less intimidating:

- *Focus on the situation when you ask for support.* Find opportunities to ask your partner for help and support, and when you do, focus on those aspects of the situation that are prompting your request. You'll be less likely to confuse *asking for help* with *being helpless*—and less likely to beat yourself up about it. You can also put help-seeking in perspective by recalling past instances when you faced similar kinds of challenges, and met them on your own. You'll be reassured by the knowledge that you haven't lost your ability to go it alone—you're just choosing to take a different approach to strengthen the relationship and gain new skills that will serve you well in a variety of situations.
- *Reframe the request.* You'll feel better about asking for help if you reframe the request in your mind: Rather than thinking of asking for help as a sign of weakness, think of it as a strategy for connecting with your partner—something that

will benefit both of you. And rather than thinking of receiving help as a sign of vulnerability, think of it as a sign of strength. After all, for you, being vulnerable is more frightening than being independent. By asking for help, you're taking on a new challenge and doing something that you find difficult (even if others don't).

- *See reconnecting as growth.* Most of us associate growth with increased self-reliance (a vestige of our childhood years). For the detached person, the opposite is true: Growth means *reconnecting*, not *disconnecting*. When you think this way, it will be easier to see asking for help as a sign of maturity—you can begin to rewrite your old got-to-go-it-alone relationship script. And it will be easier to see how asking for help reflects your emerging growth motivation: Reconnecting is a way of learning new skills, strengthening your relationship, and challenging yourself emotionally.

- *Take a Zen approach.* If asking for help from your partner feels awkward to you, begin by taking a Zen approach: Instead of *asking* for help, *offer* it. Offering help is another way of growing closer, and it sets the stage for your partner to reciprocate. By accepting your partner's overtures, you'll gain practice in receiving help and support. The whole process will become less frightening, and it will be easier to ask for help on your own—honestly and directly.

Judy and Bennett:
No More Dueling Dependencies

When Judy and Bennett came to us for marital therapy, they identified their core problem as mutual jealousy and insecurity. No matter how much reassurance they offered each other (and believe us, it was a *lot*), the same issues kept coming up time and again. Judy and Bennett were worried that their marriage was being permanently damaged by this near-daily rehashing of the same old relationship problems.

ROMANCE PAST AND PRESENT

* * * * *

Most of us have had one or more romantic relationships in the past, and we know that these "shadows in the bedroom" can potentially lead to conflict in our current romantic relationship—even if old lovers are long gone. This issue presents very different challenges, depending upon whether you (or your partner) are overdependent or detached.

The Overdependent Challenge

For the overdependent person, a key challenge of past romance is jealousy. Most overdependent people are insecure to begin with, and the image of a partner's past lover can sometimes be too much to bear. If your partner is overdependent, be forewarned that talking about past relationships may lead to near-irrational bouts of jealousy and envy, along with endless (and fruitless) comparisons with your past lover. High school and college reunions can be high-risk jealousy times if you are in a romantic relationship with an overdependent person.

If you are overdependent, make a concerted effort not to overreact to your partner's past loves. Put the past relationship in perspective: Your partner has chosen to be with you, not them. Don't bring up the issue repeatedly, seeking constant reassurance that the old relationship is over (or that this relationship is somehow "better" than the one that came before). Instead, think of this as an opportunity to build your healthy dependency skills by finding ways to manage your insecurity, and accept the fact that there have been—and will be—other important people in your partner's life.

The Detached Challenge

For the detached person, a key romance challenge is monogamy. Detachment expert Martin Kantor has found that extramarital affairs are surprisingly common among detached people, in part because such affairs allow the detached person to be physically intimate without having to risk emotional intimacy and the vulnerability and commitment that come with it.

If your partner is detached, be aware of their need for space: Move slowly and cautiously as you reconnect, so you don't drive your partner away. Tolerate backslides (they're sure to occur) and recognize your partner's desire for distance and control. Remember that healthy dependency involves relationship flexibility—*how* and *when* you reconnect are important, too.

If you are detached, take care to monitor your motives and behaviors within and outside the relationship. It may be tempting to seek "intimacy-free" physical closeness elsewhere, but ask yourself: Is it really worth jeopardizing your current relationship and all that goes with it?

Oftentimes therapists find that a couple's presenting complaint is just a cover for some deeper, more troubling issue, but in this case Judy and Bennett were right on the mark. Their marriage was indeed being compromised by intense, shared insecurity. Bennett's concerns revolved around Judy's past loves: Despite her repeated assurances, Bennett was convinced he could never live up to Judy's early sexual experiences. Judy's insecurity centered on her perceived intellectual flaws: Never having graduated from college, Judy had convinced herself that she was less intelligent and interesting than Bennett's colleagues at work, and therefore less worthy of his affection.

Judy and Bennett not only brought some measure of insight to marital therapy (a very helpful thing), but they were also genuinely devoted to each other and committed to making the marriage work. This provided a firm foothold that allowed us to help

* * * * *
If you love somebody, let them go.
If they return, they were always yours.
If they don't, they never were.
—Anonymous

Judy and Bennett move beyond their "dueling dependencies," and rebuild both partners' healthy dependency skills in the context of their romantic relationship.

We began by trying to help Bennett overcome his insecure sexuality. We encouraged Judy to provide targeted reassurance, rather than working overtime in the bedroom to bolster Bennett's fragile sexual ego. We used role-playing exercises to help Bennett communicate honestly with his wife during their sexual encounters. This included being open and direct in asking Judy to do things that pleased him sexually, and also being direct in offering to please Judy in ways she found fulfilling. To short-circuit Bennett's "I'm-not-worthy" sexual game, we agreed that he must not follow lovemaking with requests for reassurance and that he must take special care to monitor his nonverbals so that his body language and facial expression did not communicate insecurity and put Judy on the spot.

At the same time, as we were working to help Bennett overcome his sexual insecurity, we tried to help Judy move beyond her perceived inadequacies as an intellectual partner. We began by encouraging Judy to create some relationship space—in her case, by taking an adult education class at the local community college. She enrolled in a literature course, did extremely well, and acquired a circle of friends with whom she could spend time outside the home. As Judy helped her classmates wrestle with difficult course material, she became more confident, and was able to ask others for help without feeling "dumb." Judy began to see intellectual help-seeking as a sign of growth, and her emotional synergy was strengthened: Now she could *ask for help* without *feeling helpless*.

Judy's academic success helped her gain confidence in her intellectual abilities and healthy dependency skills—confidence that no amount of reassurance could ever have provided. Judy's newfound self-assurance enabled her to be more spontaneous and passionate in the bedroom: Not only did she find sexuality with Bennett more fulfilling, but Bennett—sensing Judy's deepened pleasure—became more confident and self-assured as well.

Looking Ahead:
The Healthy Dependent Friend

Can the same strategies we use to create healthy dependent love be applied to our friendships as well? Yes and no. The more psychologists study the ingredients of good friendship, the more they understand that friendship brings its own special benefits—and its own unique challenges as well.

The pleasures of friendship may be different than those of love, but they are no less important. In Chapter 5, we'll discuss how you can use your healthy dependency skills to strengthen and deepen friendship, and we'll explore strategies you can use to improve relationships with friends who may be overdependent or detached.

HEALTHY DEPENDENCY
IN FRIENDSHIP

"Michael? Are you busy?"

"Jason, good to see you. Please, come in."

"Do you have a moment?"

"Of course. Have a seat."

"Thanks. I'm sorry to interrupt. I know what a busy time this is."

"Not at all. What can I do for you?"

"Michael, I need to talk with you about something."

"Sounds ominous."

"Sort of. Not really. I mean, we've been friends for a long time, and I feel like I ought to be the one to fill you in."

"What is it? What's going on?"

"Well, let me ask you. Have you heard the rumblings around here lately?"

"Rumblings?"

"You know. About the project?"

"To tell you the truth, Jason, I haven't heard anything. What's up?"

"Michael, please don't be offended, okay?"

"Um...okay."

"All right, here's the thing. You know how yesterday, at the afternoon meeting, Andrea sort of...snapped at you? Told you to stop pestering her and all? Remember?"

"Well, sure. But you know how Andrea can...."

"Michael, it's not just Andrea."

"How do you mean?"

"I mean, she happened to say it during the meeting, but other people have been saying the same thing behind your back. When you're not around."

"People are talking?"

"Yes."

"About me?"

"Michael, I'm afraid so."

"What are they saying?"

"Well, pretty much what Andrea said. People think you're too dependent on them—that you nag them for ideas and suggestions and such...."

"Wait a minute. I thought we were supposed *to lean on each other. I thought we were a team."*

"Michael, we are. But right or wrong, people think you're asking too much of them. People think you're not pulling your weight."

"Wow. Jason, I had no idea."

"I know. That's why I wanted to talk to you about it."

"Well, I appreciate it. What do you think I should do?"

"Maybe you need to talk to some people. Mend some fences. That sort of thing."

"Right. You're right. That's what I need to do. Oh, hey, Jason?"

"Hm?"

"You're a good friend."

"Forget about it, Michael. I'll see you at the meeting."

The Lebanese poet-philosopher Kahlil Gibran once wrote:

> *Your friend is your needs answered....*
> *For without words, in friendship, all thoughts,*
> *all desires, all expectations are born and shared,*
> *with joy that is unacclaimed.*

More than eighty years after they were first written, Kahlil Gibran's words still ring true. Many long-time friends are so intimately familiar with each other's hopes and wishes, feelings and fears, they can literally communicate "without words." Such inti-

---

UNDERSTANDING YOUR FRIENDSHIP GOALS

* * * * *

Just as you began Chapter 4 by taking a look at your romantic goals, let's begin Chapter 5 by outlining your friendship goals. What do you especially *like* about your most important friendship? What features of this relationship would you *change* if you could? If you write your answers in the spaces below, they'll help you think more clearly about your long-term friendship goals:

What I like best about my most important friendship is:

_____

_____

Here's what I'd like to change about my most important friendship:

_____

_____

---

macy is one of the great joys of friendship, but it can also lead to problems if two friends become enmeshed and lose themselves in the relationship.

Hence, the key challenge of healthy dependent friendship: Staying connected while still maintaining your unique identity, distinct and separate from your friend. In this chapter we discuss strategies for healthy dependent friendship—ways that you can shrink the distance with detached friends and gain some breathing room with friends who are overdependent.

Four Types of Friendships, Four Distinct Challenges

When researchers ask people to describe the most important qualities they look for in a friend, two words come up time and again: *tolerance* and *dependability*. From our teens through our eighties and beyond, we want friends who are nonjudgmental—

> * * * * *
> **A friend is one who knows us, but loves us anyway.**
> —JEROME CUMMINGS

friends who will tolerate our idiosyncrasies without question or complaint. And we want friends we can rely on in good times and bad—friends (like Jason) who will stand by us through thick and thin and put themselves on the line when the chips are down.

In some ways, all friendships are very much alike, but there are important differences as well. Psychologists classify friendships into four categories: *lifelong friendships, short-term friendships, intermittent friendships,* and *context-specific friendships.* As we'll see, each type of friendship brings a unique opportunity to use your healthy dependency skills.

Lifelong friendships: Avoiding overdependence

Lifelong friendships can be as intense as romantic relationships. Like romantic partners, lifelong friends describe themselves as having a special "bond" or "connection," and studies show that lifelong friends are, in fact, unusually well-attuned to each others' feelings and needs. Surprising though it may seem, many lifelong friends report levels of relationship satisfaction that equal—or even exceed—those of their most important romantic relationships.

That's the good news. Here's the bad news: When lifelong friendships become too intense, they can shade over into enmeshment. Some lifelong friends get so comfortable around each other that they avoid nurturing other relationships. They exclude other people from their social network, and spend more and more time alone together. Because of this, a key challenge of lifelong friendship is avoiding "friendship overdependence." You must learn how to *depend* on a friend without becoming *dependent* on him.

Several strategies are useful here:

- *Use your friend as a sounding board, not a crutch.* The difference can be subtle, but it comes down to growth motivation. Begin by taking a good, hard look at *how* you use your friend's advice. If you turn to your friend merely to provide excuses and rationalizations, then you are using this person to avoid responsibility. However, if you turn to your friend for honest, forthright feedback about dealing with life's problems, then you are using this person as a sounding board, not a crutch. The key is to see whether your friend's advice ever challenges you a bit—even makes you anxious or uncomfortable. If it does, that's good: Your friend is pushing you forward, not holding you back, and the relationship is helping you learn and grow.

- *Make a conscious effort to widen the circle.* There's nothing wrong with finding comfort in closeness, but to avoid friendship overdependence, you must make a deliberate effort to bring others in (not all the time, but once in a while). Be forewarned that the first few times a new person is introduced into your relationship, this person may seem like an intruder. Their presence will inhibit your well-rehearsed friendship banter, and make the entire interac-

THE FRIENDSHIP CONTRACT

* * * * *

For friendship to thrive, friends must meet each other's needs. Researchers Michael Argyle and Monica Henderson identified several rules that are part of most people's unspoken "friendship contract." According to this contract, friends are supposed to:

1) Provide emotional support.
2) Trust and confide in each other.
3) Give honest advice.
4) Pitch in and help in times of need.
5) Be tolerant of each other's friends (even the creepy ones).

tion more effortful and inhibited. You can avoid becoming resentful of this by using connection-based thinking to separate the *act* from the *person*: Recognize that changing circumstances—not your new friend—are causing these uncomfortable feelings. Recognize, too, that such feelings are a normal response to altering a longstanding relationship pattern, and they usually diminish with time.

- *Don't think of friendship as a zero-sum game.* One reason we feel threatened by new people is that we tend to think of friendship as a "zero-sum game." We convince ourselves that each person only has a finite amount of friendship to give, so any goodwill that is directed toward others must somehow detract from our relationship. There's no evidence whatsoever to support this belief (since when did friendship come in finite quantities?). By and large, the opposite is true: New friends mean new connections, new opportunities, renewed relationship vigor, and a fresh perspective.

Short-term friendships: Healthy termination

Some friendships last for decades; others may last for only a few weeks or months. Sometimes circumstances throw two people together, then separate them just as friendship begins to take root. Graduation from college, a transfer at work, a move to a distant part of the country—these and other circumstances can turn a deepening friendship into a *short-term friendship*.

Premature separation can be painful, but it need not shatter the connection you've forged. To reshape your friendship and help it grow, you must both engage in a process called *healthy termination*. You must accept the fact that the friendship as it currently exists is coming to an end. Only then can you reinvent your relationship in light of your new circumstances.

Several strategies can facilitate this reshaping process:

- *Mourn your loss, then move forward.* Even a brief friendship can have a profound impact, and pretending otherwise will only make your transition more difficult. If you discover that you're trying to talk yourself out of feeling bad—that you're making excuses to convince yourself the relationship wasn't that big a deal—you may be in "termination denial." It's better to let yourself be sad (or hurt or confused or angry) and mourn your loss deeply and completely. If you fight off troubling feelings, they'll persist even longer, and you'll end up obsessing about the past instead of looking ahead to the future. When you do begin to move forward—however long it takes—use relationship flexibility to facilitate change. Don't think of a *changed* relationship as a *ruined* relationship. Focus on strengthening the connection you still have, instead of ruminating about the one you've lost.

- *Set realistic friendship goals.* A key symptom of termination denial is setting unrealistic friendship goals ("We'll talk on the phone every day!"). Early on in the process, this is normal—it's a way of softening the blow and coping with a painful loss. Though this kind of thinking is helpful at the beginning, as time goes on it's important to become more realistic. Allow your interactions to evolve naturally, until the mode and frequency of communication both feel right. For some friends, this means daily e-mails; for others, the occasional telephone chat. For still others, holiday cards are enough.

- *Understand the power of long-distance friendships.* Sometimes we expect too much from a long-distance friendship, but sometimes we expect too little. Researcher James Pennebaker has found that long-distance friendships can have powerful positive effects on our health and well-being because they give us a unique opportunity to unburden ourselves of negative emotions in a "safe" context. In a groundbreaking study of this unburdening process,

* * * * *
Friendship is like money, easier made than kept.
—SAMUEL BUTLER

Pennebaker found that recently widowed women who shared their feelings with long-distance friends had a more optimistic outlook—and significantly fewer health problems—than widows who kept their feelings to themselves. The bottom line: Face-to-face contact isn't needed to reap the benefits of friendship. All it takes is a willingness to open up and talk about the goings-on in your life.

Intermittent friendships: Periodic reconnecting

Even more complicated than short-term friendships are *intermittent friendships*—friendships that must be renewed periodically, then interrupted again as circumstances change. Perhaps you encounter someone once or twice each year at a professional meeting or conference. When you're together, you enjoy each other's company immensely, but between meetings, you have little or no contact.

A key challenge here is *periodic reconnecting*. Unlike friends who see each other frequently, intermittent friends are sometimes surprised to discover they've grown in very different directions between contacts. This need not signal the end of the friendship, but it does require an active approach to reconnecting each time you renew the relationship.

Several strategies are useful here:

- *Bring each other up to date.* The greater the time between friendship renewals, the more you need to work at rekindling the connection. If the time between contacts is substantial (months or years rather than weeks), take time to fill each other in regarding changes in your lives. If you don't, you may find you've lost the common language and shared experience that make friendship so rewarding. This filling-in process also provides a unique opportunity to gain perspective: Not only can your intermittent friend provide you with a fresh take on old problems, but the act of describing what's been happening in your life—the mere act of putting thoughts into words—actually deepens your

101

understanding of where you've been and where you're headed.

- *Understand your friendship goals.* Relationship flexibility is key here. An intermittent friend is not the best person to turn to when you need extensive hands-on help (for example, in recovering from a serious illness). To avoid confusion and resentment on both sides, you need to decide what you can and cannot realistically expect from your intermittent friend. At some point you should sit down and map out your friendship goals: What do you want to *get* from this relationship? What are you willing to *give* in return? How *intimate* do you want this relationship to be? What parts of your life would you rather keep *private*?

- *Structure your activities to meet these goals.* Once you have some idea of your goals for this relationship, you should structure your activities accordingly. You can decide whether you want to see each other more frequently (through the occasional weekend visit), or whether the events that throw you together periodically provide the right amount of contact. You can decide whether you want to include your intermittent friend in formal family occasions (like weddings), or whether it's best to keep these things separate. Whichever way you go, remember that as circumstances change, your relationship goals may change as well. Somewhere down the line, you might need to adjust your behavior to accommodate changing needs.

Context-specific friendships: The boundary problem

In some ways the most challenging friendships are those that arise in specific contexts—at work, for example, or through involvement in a therapy group or charitable organization. Most of us have had such *context-specific friendships*—friendships wherein we encounter a person in one (and *only* one) setting. As a result, we've been forced to confront the "boundary problem":

Should we invite this person into other parts of our life, or would it be better to just see them in the usual setting, where we're certain we get along well?

There is no easy, ready answer to this question. Sometimes we attempt to broaden the friendship, only to discover that outside the initial context, the relationship just doesn't work—for whatever reason, this person doesn't mesh well with other aspects of our world. Sometimes we make the opposite choice and maintain a firm friendship boundary. While this may seem the safer route, the primary risk here is regret: Somewhere down the line, we may wonder whether we unintentionally stunted the growth of what could have been a deeper, more fulfilling relationship.

From a healthy dependency perspective, context-specific friendships are particularly tricky to manage, but several strategies can make your task easier:

- *Let the friendship evolve naturally.* Circumstances change, and what might have started out as a good choice can later become a poor one. Perhaps you decided to set a firm boundary, but after a while you discover that you really enjoy spending time with this person, and you want to interact in other contexts. Or you may find that broadening the friendship really wasn't a good idea, and you'd rather limit your interactions to certain specific settings. As your goals change, you must be willing to use your relationship flexibility, and try a different approach.

- *Be alert for backlash effects.* Although rebuilding friendship boundaries is possible, it can also be risky. Sometimes we experience the "backlash effect": We actually find ourselves resenting the person we had once hoped to become closer to ("I never really liked her all that much anyway...."). The backlash effect is nature's way of helping us re-establish boundaries: By becoming resentful, we find it easier to distance ourselves from this person. The trick is to manage the backlash effect—to moderate it so it doesn't destroy the relationship. Connection-based thinking will help you here: Remind yourself that you're frustrated with the *situation,* not the *person*. And remember: You might never recapture the old way of relating, but over time you can establish a new comfort zone.

- *Manage your own friendship boundaries.* It's easy to see when someone else is violating our boundaries, but harder to know when we are the one doing the violating. Remember that just as you are trying to decide how intimate you want to be with your context-specific friend, she is doing the exact same thing. Try to be sensitive to ways you might be violating friendship boundaries without realizing it. And if you're not sure, ask. By bringing the issue out into the open, you'll make it easier for your friend to tell you what level of contact she's comfortable with at this time. Plus, you'll create a situation where you can discuss your comfort level more openly as well.

Nancy and Trina: An Unusual Intermittent Friendship

Nancy and Trina had been friends since third grade, and even though their lives had taken very different paths in recent years, they remained close. After college, Nancy had given up her old, raucous ways, as she became increasingly devoted to her career as a management consultant. Nancy planned her life carefully—relationships included—and she approached every new challenge with quiet resolve. To Nancy, life's obstacles were just problems waiting to be solved—nothing less, nothing more.

Unlike Nancy, Trina had never quite outgrown her old ways. She couldn't seem to settle on a single career path, and she changed jobs frequently. Trina's life was punctuated by a series of brief, intense romances, each of which followed a similar pattern: Trina would meet someone and become intensely involved, throwing herself headlong into the relationship. Eventually each romance ended—usually with considerable fireworks—and after a while Trina would repeat the entire sequence over again with a new person.

Because Trina became so intensely involved with each new ro-

mantic partner, her relationship with Nancy evolved into an unusual kind of intermittent friendship. When Trina was between
romantic partners, she and Nancy spent a great deal of time together, just like they used to. But when a new romance started
up, Trina literally disappeared, and Nancy might not hear from
her for weeks—sometimes months. Then, without warning,
Trina would reappear, and the two friends would resume their
relationship.

Trina came to one of us for therapy because she was unhappy
with the costly emotional toll of her many failed romances. Little did she (or we) know that the focus of therapy would soon
shift, as Trina came to realize how much she admired Nancy,
and how important their relationship really was.

Although we began therapy by helping Trina focus on rebuilding healthy dependency in the context of her romantic relationships, it soon became apparent—even to Trina—that her
dysfunctional sexual relationships were just a symptom of some
deeper concern. As she spoke about the goings-on in her life,
Trina returned again and again to her relationship with Nancy.
Trina admired her friend, idealized her, and emulated her. Not
surprisingly, Trina also harbored a fair amount of resentment toward Nancy. She envied her friend's career success, her quiet
calm, and her ability to deal with life's challenges as a mature
adult.

Being around Nancy gave Trina great joy, but it frightened her
as well, since deep down inside Trina felt she could never have
those qualities she so respected in her friend. And as she spoke
about this, Trina realized something important about herself:
She didn't run back to Nancy to escape her failed romances, but
plunged into romance when her ambivalent feelings regarding
Nancy came too close to the surface.

Once Trina recognized this, the rest was (comparatively) easy.
Instead of dwelling on romance, we helped Trina explore her complex feelings toward Nancy, and rebuild her healthy dependency
skills in the context of this important relationship. We helped
Trina explore her friendship goals, her romantic goals, and the
tension between the two. As therapy began to wind down, Trina

even asked Nancy to sit in on a session, so she could talk to her friend about changes she'd made, and changes she hoped to make as time went on. Two weeks after that, therapy ended.

We didn't hear from Trina for quite some time, but a year ago a letter arrived. Trina had moved to the midwest, and her relationship with Nancy had turned into a long-distance friendship. They spoke frequently and e-mailed each other between phone calls to fill each other in on the details of their lives. Though their friendship had changed, the two women remained close. Included with the letter was one of Trina's wedding pictures—a photo of Trina arm-in-arm with her maid of honor. Nancy's smile was as wide as Trina's.

Reconnecting with the Overdependent Friend

Picture this: As part of a psychology experiment, you agree to complete a series of personality tests and carry a small pocket diary with you for the next four weeks. In this diary, you jot down brief descriptions of your social interactions at predetermined times each day—112 descriptions in all. At the end of the investigation, you return your completed diary so it can be analyzed by the researchers.

We really did conduct such a study several years ago, and the results were published in 1998. When we analyzed these diary entries, we discovered something important about dependency and friendship. Healthy dependent people in our study were able to ask their friends for help and support in a direct, appropriate manner, and more often than not, they got the help they needed. Healthy dependent people also *offered* help and support to friends in a way that strengthened the relationship, and left the friend feeling good about what they'd received.

A different pattern emerged for those participants who were destructively overdependent. These people *hinted* at needing help instead of asking directly. They offered help to their friends very rarely, and when they did, the offer usually came with strings attached. As a result, overdependent people's interactions were strained and awkward, with misunderstandings, miscommunications, and missed signals on both sides.

The moral of the story: Even if you bring healthy dependency to all of your relationships, certain friendships will require special effort on your part. When someone you care about is overdependent, building new connections begins with changing old ways. Until your overdependent friend breaks some unhealthy habits and alters some self-defeating relationship patterns, truly satisfying friendship can never be achieved.

The first step in reconnecting with an overdependent friend is identifying the signs of friendship overdependence. Once you've "diagnosed" the problem, you can deal with it more effectively.

THE EVOLUTION OF FRIENDSHIP

* * * * *

University of Minnesota researcher Willard Hartup finds that as we grow, we use different criteria to select our friends. Friendship evolves in three distinct phases:

- *Phase 1: Convenience* Children begin to form friendships around age three, and at that point, friends are chosen largely on the basis of convenience. Proximity is paramount, and children are more likely to spend time playing with the child next door than the one down the block.
- *Phase 2: Value* As childhood blends into adolescence, our friendship criteria shift, and we choose friends based on what they can do for us. We value comfort and mutual trust, but this sometimes conflicts with our adolescent desire to affiliate with popular, high-status peers (so we too can be part of the "in group").
- *Phase 3: Mutuality* As adolescence gives way to adulthood, we focus more on the internal qualities of potential friends (sense of humor, interests, attitudes, and moral values). Our emphasis on mutuality deepens as we move from middle to late adulthood, when shared values, common interests, trust, and dependability become even more important.

Signs of friendship overdependence

Insecurity, possessiveness, and *overidentification*—these are the key signs that you're involved with an overdependent friend.

- *Insecurity* The symptoms of insecurity are many and varied. They can range from endless requests for reassurance (which never seem to help) to frequent phone calls with no real purpose (other than to make sure you're still there). Whatever form they take, the symptoms of friendship insecurity always reflect an underlying lack of self-confidence and shaky self-esteem. When it comes time to help your friend change her insecure behavior, it will be important to remember this. Understanding the roots of friendship insecurity makes it possible for you to deal with the issue rationally, rather than emotionally.

- *Possessiveness* When insecurity is part of a relationship, possessiveness usually follows. On some level, the insecure friend is convinced they're not worthy of your attention, and they are certain you'll eventually lose interest and move on. When the possessive friend feels threatened, her first response may be to build a protective wall around you, and try to bar other people from your life. The suggestion of bringing another person along on an outing is met with staunch resistance (and a barrage of flimsy reasons why it's not a good idea). Keep in mind that no matter how obvious this wall-building seems to you, your friend may well be completely unaware of their behavior and its impact. As a result, he may be shocked—and deeply offended—if you try to raise the issue.

- *Overidentification* We've all had it happen at one time or another: A day or two after you buy new shoes or a new jacket, your friend shows up wearing the exact same thing. The experience can be humorous or creepy, depending on your mood, but one thing is certain: When this imitative behavior becomes too intense, it's a symptom of a deeper relationship issue. Make no mistake: We all model our behavior after people we admire (which is why children imitate their parents and adolescents dress like rock stars). Problems arise when identification shades into *over*identification—when the boundary between two people becomes blurred. If you begin to feel as if your every move is being shadowed, and your friend is identifying with you in an unhealthy way, then it is time to deal with the issue.

Creating space within the relationship

Once you've identified the telltale signs of friendship overdependence, you need to take the next step: You must avoid getting enmeshed in unhealthy friendship games and ensnared in friendship traps. Three strategies will be helpful here:

- *Manage insecurity/abandonment fears.* To help your overdependent friend manage his insecure behavior, look beyond the behavior and focus on its cause. Since you know that shaky self-esteem and fear of abandonment are at the root of the problem, try to react in ways that bolster your friend's self-confidence, and reassure him that you're not going to abandon him. Instead of getting angry when your friend gets clingy, focus on how frightened your friend must be feeling. Chances are he has lost touch with his growth motivation—he has no sense of moving forward, but is obsessed with preserving the status quo. All your friend can see is that he must hold on tight—and the more nervous he gets, the tighter he clings. It's your job to help him see that distance doesn't equal danger—that even if the relationship changes, you'll still be there.
- *Set limits and maintain boundaries.* Having empathy doesn't mean giving in to your friend's fears or jumping in to rescue him every time he gets anxious. On the contrary, empathy should form the context for creating space within the relationship. When you focus on your friend's feelings rather than his off-putting behaviors, you can begin to set limits

(gently) and maintain boundaries (firmly). If phone calls get too frequent, let your friend know you're too busy to talk—but be sure to communicate this kindly, not angrily. If you feel intruded upon, let your friend know you're feeling overwhelmed and you need some room for yourself. Don't overjustify or explain how you're feeling in painful detail—that would simply set the stage for a power struggle. Just say your piece and let it stand. And don't be surprised if your initial efforts to create relationship space result in increased insecurity. This is a natural response from an overdependent friend, but it's also a critical point in the evolution of the relationship: If you don't hold the line here, all your efforts will be undermined, and any progress you've made will be undone.

- *Encourage healthy individuation.* It will be easier to create relationship space if you encourage healthy individuation at the same time as you set limits on your friend's insecure behavior. Encouraging healthy individuation can take many forms, but the goal is always the same: To help your friend make new connections, develop new interests, and feel stronger and more autonomous because he no longer relies on one or two people for all his emotional support. Encouraging healthy individuation requires that you actively discourage overidentification (be honest—tell your friend it makes you uncomfortable) and steer your friend toward activities where he can form new connections (lectures, classes, charities, community groups). When these two things occur in tandem, your overdependent friend can begin to develop an identity of his own, separate from you.

Reconnecting with the Detached Friend

While the main challenge of overdependent friendship is managing your friend's *insecurity*, the key challenge of detached friendship is dealing with issues of *control*. Because detached people have trouble with trust, they often engage in subtle

THE FRIENDSHIP GENDER GAP

* * * * *

British psychologist John Archer has found that in Western societies, friendship patterns differ across gender. Most male-male friendships are *activity-based*—men tend to do things that allow for companionship without too much emotional closeness. Female-female and female-male friendships, on the other hand, are more often based on *self-disclosure* (shared feelings and confidences). Emotional connection comes more easily here.

It's tempting to conclude, based on these data, that men's friendships tend to be detached, while women's edge toward overdependence. Archer cautions against such an interpretation, however. He points out that the friendship gender gap—while real—is not huge. Men may share fewer emotional experiences than women do, but they'll still share some private thoughts with same-sex friends they know and trust. Women may be more open than men are emotionally, but their friendships include a fair amount of interest-based companionship as well.

The more we learn about gender and friendship, the more it becomes clear that our similarities outweigh our differences. Not only is the friendship gender gap smaller than one might guess, but studies suggest that it's shrinking as well. As traditional gender roles blur, gender differences in friendship grow smaller with each passing year.

games designed to keep control over the relationship. Your detached friend may be completely unaware of these games—they usually reflect decades-old, well-rehearsed relationship scripts. Your job is to avoid getting caught up in a control game while helping your friend feel comfortable enough to let down her guard bit by bit.

The friendship issues may be different when your friend is detached, but the process of bringing healthy dependency into your relationship is pretty much the same: You must first diagnose the problem by identifying the telltale signs of friendship detachment. Then you must confront the problem head-on.

Signs of friendship detachment

The signs of friendship detachment can be subtle, but if you know where to look, they're easy to spot. *Hidden hostility, endless pursuit,* and *friendship power plays*—these are the things you should watch for.

- *Hidden hostility* Detached people are ambivalent about friendship: They want desperately to connect, but when they begin to get close, they find the experience anxiety-producing and stressful. No surprise, then, that you're likely to get mixed messages from a detached friend. On the surface, they seem to accept your overtures and invitations, but lurking just below the surface may be hidden hostility. More often than not, this hostility is expressed indirectly, in the form of cutting remarks or passive-aggressive behaviors (like showing up late or cancelling at the last minute). Whatever form it takes, hidden hostility is a sign of friendship detachment.

- *Endless pursuit* One way detached people manage troubling feelings is to force those around them into the role of "pursuer." If you find yourself in this role, you may feel that the friendship is "unbalanced"—that you're more invested in the relationship than your friend is and that you work harder to maintain it. In certain respects, these perceptions are correct (if you didn't make the effort, the relationship might wither). But there's another, less obvious part of this dynamic: Your detached friend—so mistrustful of others—is testing you to make sure you'll go the extra mile. Each time you renew your pursuit, your detached friend is temporarily reassured that you aren't going to abandon her. The feeling never lasts, though, which is why the pursuit game must be repeated many times over (Freud called this the "repetition compulsion"). The irony here is that most people eventually tire of the pursuer role, so the detached person is in fact abandoned frequently. The detached person creates a self-fulfilling prophecy which ends up confirming her deepest fears.

APPROACH-AVOIDANCE CONFLICTS

* * * * *

If you've ever wanted to ask someone out on a date, but feared the embarrassment that would follow rejection, you've been in an approach-avoidance conflict. In this situation—as in all approach-avoidance conflicts—you feel simultaneously drawn toward something (the person you desire) and afraid of it (What if they laugh in my face?). It's an unpleasant feeling because whichever way you go, you risk losing something valuable (self-esteem if you are rejected, a potentially rewarding relationship if you give in to your fear).

Try to understand that for the detached friend, every social interaction involves an approach-avoidance conflict—a conflict between wanting to connect (approach) and fearing they'll be hurt if they let down their guard (avoidance). With this in mind, you may be able to cope more effectively with the detached person's ambivalence. When you reframe their behavior in this way, it seems less confusing and less frustrating.

It's been more than fifty years since Rockefeller University's Neal Miller and his colleague John Dollard first described the dynamics of *approach-avoidance conflicts*. But much of what they said in 1950 still holds true today.

- *Friendship power plays* Endless pursuit is the most common way detached people maintain a sense of control, but there are others. Any time your detached friend gets you working hard to structure activities, be aware that a friendship power play is probably underway. The signs of a power play can be subtle, but they usually involve rejecting each suggestion you offer (every restaurant is unacceptable; every movie sounds boring). The key to identifying a friendship power play is to focus not on what your friend *does*, but on how you *feel* when he does it. If you find yourself frustrated at your inability to come up with the "right" activity, and obsessing like crazy to find a better idea, you've been the target of a power play, and are trapped in a struggle for control.

113

Breaking through the barrier

To reconnect with your detached friend, you must find ways to avoid detachment-related friendship traps and the control games that come with them. Three strategies are useful:

- *Deal with hidden hostility.* There's only one way to deal with hostility that's expressed indirectly: Bring it out into the open. When your friend makes a cutting remark, let him know you're hurt by what he said. When your friend cancels abruptly or shows up late, tell him this bothers you. Don't be surprised if your friend is genuinely surprised to hear these things—he may well be completely unaware of his hidden hostility and the manner in which it's expressed. One key to dealing with hidden hostility is to avoid overanalyzing the meaning or appropriateness of the behavior: Simply tell your friend it bothers you, and you don't want him to do it anymore. Don't get drawn into a debate about whether the behavior is "really" hostile (in fact, don't even use the term). This is one of those situations where feelings rule, and no elaborate explanations are required: If the behavior makes you uncomfortable, that's good enough.

- *Refuse to engage in control games.* One reason to avoid debating the "meaning" of behavior is that it opens the door to a new control game: It allows your detached friend to focus on convincing you to accept something you don't like, instead of looking inward at his self-defeating pattern. The more completely you disengage yourself from these kinds of control games, the easier it will be for you to break through the barrier and begin to reconnect. So once you've identified the dynamic, take steps to short-circuit it. Stop making restaurant suggestions if every one is unacceptable. Don't try to structure activities if every one is flawed. Instead, put the responsibility on your detached friend, and encourage her to invest some energy in structuring the relationship. Your friend will likely resist this at first, but if you can just get her started (and be supportive of her early, clumsy efforts), this can become a real growth experience. It will enable your friend to gain confidence, and enhance her relationship flexibility at the same time.

- *Shift the balance of power.* As you bring hidden hostility into the open and extricate yourself from harmful control games, the balance of power will begin to shift. You'll no longer feel like a "pursuer," and you won't have to put the lion's share of effort into structuring the relationship. Ironically, as your detached friend begins to give up power, her self-confidence will actually increase: She'll learn through experience that it's safe to give up some control, that it's okay to trust you (you won't run away), and that it's possible to feel secure in a more balanced, healthy relationship.

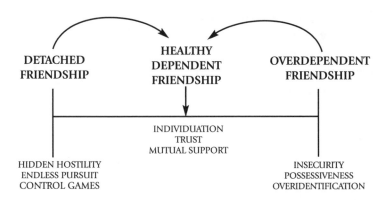

HEALTHY DEPENDENT FRIENDSHIP

As this figure shows, healthy dependent friendship is characterized by individuation, trust, and mutual support. Reaching these goals requires different strategies, depending upon whether your friend is overdependent or detached.

Looking Ahead: From Romance and Friendship to Parents and Siblings (or out of the Frying Pan, into the Fire)

Family relationships have all the emotional intensity of the most passionate romance and the well-rehearsed intimacy of the deepest friendship. Little wonder, then, that family relationships seem even more "loaded" and "energized" than our other relationships. When Thanksgiving rolls around, and we're trapped in the house with Brother, Sister, Mom, and Dad, our defenses fade and underlying tendencies become more pronounced. Old patterns replay themselves in the most primitive, stunning ways. The stage is set for overdependence to blossom and for detachment to strengthen and tighten its grip.

There's no question about it: Family gatherings are high risk times. Even if you've made great progress in strengthening your healthy dependency skills, family interactions are the situations where backslides are most likely to occur.

Using healthy dependency to improve family relationships is a challenge, but it is one you can master if you approach the situation calmly and deliberately. In Chapter 6, we look at healthy dependency in the family, and review strategies for reconnecting with siblings, parents, and others.

6

HEALTHY DEPENDENCY
IN THE FAMILY

Ellen checked her watch: 4:10. She looked around the room. People were thumbing documents, chatting quietly, waiting for the meeting to begin. At 4:15, Andrew arrived—out of breath, hair disheveled, tie thrown over one shoulder. "Sorry," he said. "I didn't realize how late it was."

Ellen waited, said nothing, and one by one the faces turned toward her. She cleared her throat. The meeting began.

She started by running through the most recent quarterly figures. Then she turned the floor over to Regina, who outlined tomorrow's proposal. When Regina had taken her seat, Dave filled everyone in on the upcoming trade show in Phoenix. There were the usual jokes—and the usual excuses—as they debated who would make the trip to represent the company.

Finally it was Ellen's turn again, and she talked about her plans for the next product season. She passed around a summary of her marketing strategy, and she began to go through it point by point. She had just started on Point Three when there was a knock on the door. Theresa leaned in.

"Sorry to interrupt," Theresa said, smiling weakly. "Ellen, your mother's on the phone."

There was silence, then hushed nervous laughter at the far end of the table.

Theresa continued, "She says it's important."

The laughter stopped.

Ellen felt her face flush red. She looked down at her watch—she wasn't sure why—then back at Theresa, who still stood in the doorway.

"Tell her I'll call her as soon as we're done. Fifteen minutes tops, okay?"

Theresa nodded and closed the door.

Ellen finished her outline—Points Four, Five, and Six—and after that there were questions, and then the meeting was over.

When Ellen returned to her office, she saw the long list of unread e-mails on her screen, and the pile of folders on the corner of her desk. Ellen sighed, rubbed her eyes, leaned back in her chair. She decided that before she started in on all this, she'd better return her mother's call.

She dialed the number and the phone rang seven, eight times. No answer. She hung up, waited a moment, and redialed. Still no answer. She made a mental note to try back as soon as she'd made a first pass through the other messages.

Forty minutes later Ellen's phone rang again. It was Michael. His voice was panicky—hurried, shrill. The words came so quickly Ellen could barely keep up, and she had to ask him to slow down so she could understand what he was saying.

Michael took a deep breath and started over from the beginning. Their mother was in the emergency room. She had started to feel nauseous—dizzy and weak—so she'd gone into the bathroom in case she got sick. That's when it happened: She had stumbled on the rug, fallen into the side of the tub, and broken her hip. They were preparing her for surgery right now.

Hurry over, urged Michael. Please come as soon as you can. We need you here.

Ellen grabbed her things, rushed out the door, and explained the situation to Theresa while they waited for the elevator. When she got to the lobby Ellen hailed a cab and gave the driver the address. They lurched out into rush hour traffic.

The cab crept across town in fits and starts. Even though it was cold Ellen lowered the window and fanned her shirt to let in some air. She settled back in her seat and tried not to notice how slowly they were moving.

As they inched along 57th Street, Ellen had a strange, creeping feeling. At first she couldn't identify it, but then suddenly it emerged, turned from feeling to idea, and Ellen grasped the door handle to steady herself. My God, she thought, what if that phone call...what if her mother had been calling to ask for help when she started feeling sick? Was it possible that by not taking that call, she had caused this to happen? And now, what if....

Ellen sat in the cab, silently urging it forward, when all at once it hit her: These problems she'd been having, the silences, the miscommunications—they weren't caused by James or Melissa. They weren't the fault of the people at work. For the first time in years Ellen's vision cleared, and she grasped an honest, troubling truth about herself.

The problem isn't anyone else, she realized. The problem is me.

There's no escaping one's family. They affect us in ways that we can't always see, and their hold on us remains powerful to the end. Even when we're grown, we're still our parents' children. And no matter how accomplished we become, we never stop being someone's big sister or little brother.

Ellen doesn't realize it yet, but she's lucky. She just learned an important truth about herself—a truth that will help her recapture the healthy dependency that's eluded her all these years. For Ellen, positive change is about to begin, as she reconnects with those who've known her best: her family.

The Family System: Roles, Alliances and Power Centers

In 1976, pioneering family therapist Jay Haley outlined the fundamental principles of *family systems theory*—a framework for conceptualizing families as dynamic, evolving systems. Haley pointed out that to understand how a given family functions, you must not only understand each *individual* within the group, but you also need to know how those individuals *fit together*—how they interact and influence each other.

Haley's family systems theory is key to enhancing healthy

119

dependency with parents and siblings, because it allows us to understand the forces that foster overdependence and detachment within the family. Let's begin by looking at four principles of family dynamics, as systems theory explains them:

- *Family roles* Over time, each person develops a unique role within the family. These roles do not evolve by chance, but in response to events that take place within the group. Some family roles are easy to identify ("Strong One," "Selfless Caregiver," "Sensitive One," "Troublemaker"), but other roles are harder to pin down. Once in place, family roles fit together into a complex, interlocking system, so changing one person's role disrupts all the others.
- *Hidden alliances* Family members form alliances that not only meet individual needs, but also help preserve the status quo and maintain each person's role. Some alliances are obvious (Mom and Dad allied against a misbehaving son). Other alliances are hidden—sometimes so deeply that even those involved are unaware of them. For example, a hidden alliance may develop between an alcohol-abusing mother and her stoic, selfless daughter: Though both people claim to be unhappy with the situation, their alliance benefits each of them (albeit in different ways). Mother gets to express some unacknowledged anger by abrogating her parenting responsibilities, while Daughter gets to lose herself in caregiving tasks that protect her from frightening adolescent challenges (like her burgeoning sexuality).
- *Power centers* Roles and alliances combine to produce power centers within the family—spheres of influence that have a particularly strong impact on everyone's behavior. Power centers can be subtle and hard to spot. Drinking Mom and Selfless Daughter are a good example of a power center: Not only is the daughter unconsciously invested in maintaining her mother's drinking (so she won't have to confront other difficult issues), but Mom's drinking helps maintain other family roles as well. Perhaps it provides an excuse for Dad to detach emotionally and throw himself

into his work. Perhaps it draws attention away from Son's behavior problems, so he's free to act out with his peers.

- *Resistance to change* Because family roles are so tightly interlocked, they can be very resistant to change. Once family members find ways of relating to each other that are predictable and familiar, they tend to choose the devil they know over the one they don't, and cling to their established roles even if the resulting relationships are far from ideal. Thus, a key principle of family systems theory: *When one family member begins to shift, other family members will work to undermine that shift and preserve the status quo.* This is why— as Jay Haley pointed out nearly three decades ago—to help an individual change and grow, one must first understand how that change will affect other people within the family.

Healthy Dependency with Parents

Just how important is healthy family dependency? Consider the results of a recent investigation involving 2,302 sibling pairs from the National Institute of Child Health and Human Development. In this ethnically and geographically diverse sample, healthy family dependency was associated with increased family cohesion and decreased conflict. Healthy family dependency also produced some noteworthy spillover effects to other areas (like better school adjustment and decreased risk for depression).

Healthy family dependency is powerful indeed—all the more reason to look carefully at ways we can improve our relationships with parents and siblings. Let's begin by exploring strategies that foster healthy dependency between adult children and their parents.

The unique challenges of parental relationships

From a healthy dependency perspective, parental relationships are particularly complex. Because we all went through a prolonged period of dependence on the parents during our first few

121

> * * * * *
> **The family you come from isn't as important
> as the family you're going to have.**
> —RING LARDNER

UNTANGLING YOUR FAMILY'S
ROLES AND ALLIANCES

* * * * *

Before you can change old behavior patterns, you must think about your family from a systems perspective. The following four steps will get this process underway.

Step 1: List every member of your immediate family (parents, step-parents, siblings, step-siblings), including yourself. (Leave out your children though—they present a different set of issues which we'll take up in Chapter 7.)

_____ _____
_____ _____
_____ _____
_____ _____

Step 2: Think about each person's *relationship style,* and make a mark on the chart below for each person (put each person's name or initials next to their mark):

._____._____._____._____._____._____.

Dysfunctionally   *Healthy*   *Destructively*
Detached   *Dependent*   *Overdependent*

Step 3: Describe, in 2–3 words (but no more), each person's *role* within the family:

Person   Role

_____ _____
_____ _____
_____ _____

Step 4: List any *alliances* (hidden or otherwise) you can identify among members of your family, and briefly describe (a few words if possible—a sentence at most) the key features of that alliance:

Alliance   Key Features

_____   _____

_____   _____

_____   _____

_____   _____

Now take a moment to look back on what you've written. You'll probably discover some things about your family you hadn't seen before. It's a good idea to keep this information handy as we discuss overdependence and detachment with parents and siblings.

years of life, we all have long relationship histories that must be overcome before healthy dependency can be achieved.

The situation becomes even more complicated because a second dynamic, very different from the first, eventually comes into play. During adolescence, most of us deliberately distance ourselves from our parents. This is normal and an important part of establishing one's independent identity. But this adolescent distancing process leaves behind a second relationship history—a "residue of detachment"—that must be dealt with before positive change can take place.

Bottom line: Before you can develop a healthy dependent relationship with your parents, you must first confront the overdependence and detachment issues that are a part of all parent-child relationships.

Overcoming overdependence: Relating as equals

To overcome overdependence on the parents, we must revise longstanding parent-child *roles*, break apart *hidden alliances* that undermine change, confront *resistance* (both ours and theirs),

---

CHANGE-RESISTANT FAMILIES
AND FLEXIBLE FAMILIES

* * * * *

All families resist change, but some resist it more forcefully than others do. Researchers distinguish between *change-resistant* ("locked-in") families and those that are more *flexible* ("adaptable").

Not surprisingly, studies show that flexible families function more effectively than change-resistant families: They communicate more openly, are more satisfied with their relationships, and have a greater number of positive and supportive interactions. Studies also indicate that family flexibility predicts success in individual family members, even outside the group. People in flexible families have happier marriages, higher levels of job satisfaction, and better physical and psychological health.

---

and set in motion a new *individuation process.* Let's take a closer look at each step:

Overdependent parent-child roles The signs of overdependence are usually straightforward: If you seek your parents' approval for every decision, can't make a move without checking first, or ask for advice about even minor things (like everyday purchases), you have assumed an overdependent role. Sometimes the signs are less obvious, so be on the lookout: If you find yourself exaggerating minor illnesses (yours or your children's) or hinting at financial difficulties so your parents will bail you out, you are showing some common *indirect* signs of parental overdependence.

Strategy: To revise an overdependent role, you must divert energy from maintaining the status quo, and invest that energy in growth motivation. Begin by monitoring your motives carefully: When you have the urge to seek approval or ask for help, stop and think about *why* you are doing this. If you genuinely need your parents' support, then fine—go ahead. But if you're asking for help because you're afraid to take responsibility, then don't repeat the same old game. Look for better ways to deal with the

BEYOND THE "TYPICAL" TWO-PARENT FAMILY

* * * * *

Although we discuss overdependence and detachment from the perspective of the two-parent family (for simplicity's sake), the same principles apply to single-parent and blended families as well. There are differences, of course, but from a healthy dependency perspective, the particular combination of players is less important than how those players interact. Here's what you need to know:

- *Early parental loss is a risk factor for overdependence* British researcher John Birtchnell has found that the early death of a parent increases the likelihood that a child will become overdependent. But parental loss—while significant—has only a moderate effect: Many children who suffer the early death of a mother or father end up showing healthy dependency, without a trace of overdependence.

- *Separation and divorce are risk factors—not death sentences* Parental separation and divorce increase the likelihood that children will become overdependent or detached, but studies show it's not always the divorce that hurts—sometimes the pre-divorce conflict has greater negative effects. If separation and divorce occur while a child is young, overdependence is the more likely outcome; if these events occur close to adolescence, detachment is more likely.

- *As far as healthy dependency is concerned, blended families are like any other* From a systems perspective, blended families have roles and alliances that are just like those of any other family. Though the "blending process" can be rocky (especially if it comes on the tail of a divorce), once a blended family settles in, the usual rules apply.

- *Nontraditional lifestyles make little difference* The research findings are clear: Children are no more likely to be overdependent or detached when they are raised by a same-gender than a mixed-gender couple. In certain ways, same-gender couples may even have an advantage, because these parents tend to be particularly sensitive to the messages they send their children about healthy dependency.

challenge at hand—ways that strengthen your autonomy, build your self-confidence, and chip away at your overdependent role.

One effective strategy is to use relationship flexibility to get support from others (not your parents). To facilitate this process, reframe the situation: You're not helpless, but are choosing to ask for help in an adaptive, appropriate way. When you combine relationship flexibility with this kind of connection-based thinking, you'll not only break some old unhealthy habits, but you'll strengthen your healthy dependency skills at the same time.

Overdependent family alliances If you are overdependent, be forewarned: One or both of your parents may be unconsciously invested in maintaining this pattern. Oftentimes parents derive great satisfaction from being needed, and are reluctant to relinquish their caregiving role. If this is the case, you may be involved in a hidden alliance with one or both parents—a tacit agreement that as long as you fulfill your part of the bargain (never making a move without their approval), they'll fulfill theirs (by rushing in to rescue you whenever the going gets rough).

Strategy: Take charge of the situation. Begin by asking yourself: What *payoffs* am I getting for relating to Mom and/or Dad in this way? What are the *costs* of this overdependent alliance? If it helps, make a list—a written comparison of costs and benefits. Sometimes this makes the tradeoffs easier to see.

Once you've examined both sides thoroughly, take the next step, and ask yourself: On balance, do the payoffs that come from this alliance outweigh the costs? If your answer is no, then you're ready to change. If your answer is yes, you might not be.

Overcoming resistance in overdependent parent-child relationships When you begin to extricate yourself from an overdependent relationship with one or both parents, be prepared for resistance to emerge. This resistance will usually come from the parent who benefits most from your overdependence, and it will likely take the form of actions designed to pull you back into your old role ("Why didn't you *tell* me you were going to buy that? Your father could have gotten you a much better deal!").

As you can see, resistance (in this case, a heavy dose of infantilization with a sprinkling of guilt thrown in for good measure) *always* has as its goal the reinforcement of current interaction patterns and maintenance of the status quo.

Strategy: To counter resistance, bring it out into the open. Let the resistant parent know how their actions make you feel (but communicate this calmly, not angrily). Use connection-based thinking to separate the act from the person, so you can see resistance for what it is: a frightened parent's reflexive attempt to preserve the safe and familiar. When you remind yourself that old relationship patterns are hard to break—especially those that have been in place for decades—it will be easier for you to approach the issue rationally. And don't be surprised if, in response to your feedback, your parents form a new alliance aimed at squelching your autonomy. This is a good example of how changing one part of the family system causes shifts to occur in other areas.

The parent-child individuation process *Individuation* is the formal term for establishing an identity separate from one's parents. Although we tend to think of identity formation as something that takes place during adolescence, University of British Columbia researcher James Marcia found that this is not always true. Since the mid-1960s, Marcia has followed a group of former SUNY-Buffalo college students through adulthood, tracking their personal, relationship, and work histories. Marcia discovered that identity formation is a lifelong process. Setbacks, victories, births, deaths—these and other life transitions can reawaken our identity struggle many times as we move through adulthood. Marcia's findings apply to all of us, but for the overdependent person, they boil down to a single, simple truth: No matter when in life it occurs, identity begins with individuation—first finding and then firming the boundaries between you and your parents.

Strategy: Individuation takes place in three steps. You must first *identify and inhibit your overdependent behavior*. Then you must *counter your parents' resistance* to your changing role. Finally,

A REVERSAL OF ROLES:
WHEN A PARENT IS OVERDEPENDENT ON YOU

* * * * *

It's relatively easy to tell when you are overdependent on a parent, but how can you tell if one or both parents are overdependent on you? Many of the usual danger signals will occur (approval-seeking, checking, obsessive help-seeking), but these signs may be harder to spot, since they don't fit with our expectations and stereotypes.

Needless to say, parental overdependence does occur, and it tends to increase as parents enter late adulthood (we'll have much more to say about this in Chapter 10). How to manage "reverse overdependence" when it becomes a problem? Three steps:

- *Focus on motivation.* If your parent is asking for help out of genuine need, consider giving it (or working with them to find other ways to get what they require). If your parent is asking for help merely to avoid a challenge, then don't reinforce this behavior. Instead, try to set limits, so your parent can begin to find ways to do it on their own (you might have to help them get started with this, if they don't have much experience in adaptive help-seeking).

- *Bring things into the open.* If "triangulation" (indirect, manipulative communication) is taking place, make explicit the effects this dynamic has on you. If Dad's vivid descriptions of Mom's minor illnesses make you feel guilty, tell him. If Mom's hand-wringing tales of Dad's depression bring you sleepless nights, tell her (and follow it up by showing him how to get help appropriately).

- *Persist, but do it kindly.* It is important that you let your parents know when overdependence is harming your relationship, but be sure you say this gently (not harshly), and choose the time and place carefully (in private for sure, and not in the midst of a family crisis). It might take several tries before your parent can accept that he's communicating in a manipulative way, but eventually, he probably will.

you must *make a conscious effort to bring healthy dependency into the relationship.*

Though this is quite a challenge, the strategies you used to introduce healthy dependency into your romantic relationship will be useful here as well. As we discussed in Chapter 4, you can begin the individuation process by *doing more things on your own.* Be sure to *watch your language* as you interact with your parents (no babytalk!), and *monitor your motives* carefully, especially around Mom and Dad. Finally, during those times when you genuinely need help, *plan your request* so you don't fall back into old helpless habits and behave in ways that reinforce your overdependent role.

Reconnecting after detachment: Reinventing the family

Once you know how to deal with parental overdependence, you can apply many of the same principles to the detachment situation. A parallel process is involved: You begin by updating dysfunctional *roles*, then undo *hidden alliances* that undermine change. By confronting *resistance* wherever it occurs, you create a situation wherein *reconnection* can take place.

Detached parent-child roles As every adolescent knows, detachment brings power. The more one keeps family members in the dark, the more motivated they become to reach out to us—tolerating our idiosyncrasies and accommodating our quirks so we don't drift even further away. The power that comes with a detached family role can make it difficult to give up that way of relating. After all, change will weaken your position relative to others in the family, and leave you more vulnerable to emotional hurts and slights.

Strategy: As with changing an overdependent role, the first step here is to weigh costs and benefits. Sometimes the costs are hard to see (after all, one symptom of detachment is trouble focusing on feelings). So as you examine the impact of your detachment, take special care to notice the negatives. Think about times you've been hurt or disappointed, and see whether your detachment played a part in this. Honesty is key: For some people, detachment from the parents is genuinely painful (a sure sign they're ready to change). For others, change is too risky—too frightening. They're not yet ready to give up the power detachment provides.

Detached alliances within the family Oftentimes families deal with an adult child's detachment by shifting one parent into the role of "communicator." When this occurs, the other parent withdraws—interactions with the detached child become infrequent and superficial. The communicator (the more engaged parent) relays information back and forth between the detached child and the isolated parent. Notice that two interlocking alliances have now been formed. One involves the detached child and the communicating parent (who may cherish the connection that's developed between them). The other alliance involves the two parents: The communicator has acquired considerable influence (since all information now flows through her), while the isolated parent is able to "disengage" and avoid the risks that come with emotional contact.

Strategy: You can undo both alliances by shifting your communication pattern. First, identify which parent has become the communicator (they're usually easy to spot). Then, begin directing some of your communications to the more isolated parent. Move slowly at first, since disrupting alliances can be painful. Begin with mundane communications (like goings-on at work), then move gradually to more personal communications with greater emotional heft.

Be prepared for resistance to emerge as you move forward—it almost always does in this situation (we'll discuss how to deal with resistance in a moment). And whatever you do, be sensitive to everyone's emotional responses—especially those of the more isolated parent. If this parent seems uncomfortable with your new way of interacting, slow down—even back off temporarily—until they relax enough for you to move forward again.

Overcoming resistance in detached parent-child relationships
Each family member resists relationship shifts in his or her own
way. For the detached adult child who's not ready to change,
resistance may take the form of implied (or even stated)
threats: If you push too hard I'm gone, so lay off. For the more
engaged parent, resistance means selective communication: She
will choose which tidbits to pass along, never giving away too
much, and being careful to maintain the influence that comes
from exclusive access to key information. For the isolated parent,
resistance involves distancing himself with renewed vigor when
the reconnection process begins—losing himself in his work
perhaps or in other activities that exclude family members.

Strategy: If your more engaged parent begins to manipulate
information in hurtful ways, don't call her on it (at least not at
first). Instead, take steps to reduce her anxiety. Spend time alone
together, talk on the phone, go shopping…whatever. Let your actions tell her that even though you're re-engaging with the other
parent, your relationship with her is as important as ever. Reassurance takes time, and it might involve some setbacks along the
way, but be patient. It's worth it.

When the more isolated parent resists by backing off, ease
up—but not completely. The trick here is to manage your parent's comfort level while you show him (through quiet persistence) that you're serious about communicating, and you're not
giving up. If possible, avoid being drawn into a discussion of
what's happening. In this situation, actions speak louder than
words, and overanalyzing your behavior is not likely to be helpful. Once your disengaged parent realizes things are going to
change no matter what, he'll find ways to accommodate the shift.

Parent-child reconnection This can only begin in earnest when
two things happen. First, the detached child must genuinely
want to reconnect with the parents, and must be willing to take
the emotional risks necessary to do so. Second, the communicating parent must be willing to give up some influence to facilitate the reconnection process. Ironically, once this process is
underway, it is usually undermined more forcefully by the com-

municating parent than by the disengaged parent. Given this dynamic, reconnecting may require bringing the communicating parent's ambivalence out into the open.

Strategy: If your efforts to reassure your communicating parent behaviorally aren't working, then—and only then—should you talk with her about her fears. How does she interpret your changing behavior—what does she make of it? What does she imagine will happen if you reconnect with the other parent? Will she be actively excluded? Ganged-up on? Ignored?

A one-on-one discussion can be helpful in correcting misperceptions, and allaying misplaced fears. As with other heart-to-hearts, choose the time and place carefully (a quiet spot during a low-stress period), and be prepared for sadness, guilt, and anger to emerge (this doesn't always happen, but it might). It's best if you leave the isolated parent out of the initial discussion—three people with three sets of competing concerns is too much to manage this early in the process. You can always have some three-way talks later, once change is underway.

Healthy Dependency with Siblings

Some people have fond sibling memories—images of closeness, intimacy, late-night secrets shared, and unwitting babysitters mercilessly tormented. Other people have very different memories—eaten worms and stolen boyfriends, public ridicule and humiliation, and the hopeless, helpless feeling that they'd never live up to a sibling's high standard in their parents' critical eyes.

No question about it: Sibling relationships bring unique joy—and a special brand of horror as well. Sometimes both, in the very same relationship. No wonder so many people have ambivalent, conflicted feelings about their brothers and sisters. Who else has witnessed first-hand our most soaring successes and flat-footed failures, time and time again?

Sibling relationships involve different challenges than parental relationships and different strategies for change. Let's explore the sister-brother bond and techniques you can use to overcome sibling overdependence and detachment.

Overcoming overdependence: Finding your niche

By focusing on *dysfunctional roles, hidden alliances,* and *resistance,* we set the stage for sibling individuation to occur.

Overdependent sibling roles In an overdependent sibling relationship, one sibling (most often the younger one) adopts a *pseudo-child role,* while an older brother or sister assumes the role of *pseudo-parent.* In childhood, these roles can be adaptive, especially during difficult, stressful times. In fact, a classic study of World War II orphans by Anna Freud and Dorothy Burlingham showed that this kind of intense sibling bonding can be critical to surviving a traumatic event like early parental loss. (More recent investigations have shown that intense sibling bonding can also help children survive the trauma of divorce.) Bottom line: A pseudo-parent/pseudo-child sibling dynamic can be adaptive during stressful childhood periods, but when this dynamic persists through adolescence and beyond, problems usually ensue.

Strategy: The first step in overcoming an overdependent sibling role is *insight*—knowing when adaptive bonding is shading over into destructive overdependence. Begin by focusing on the effect your sibling relationship has on your other relationships. Do you find yourself excluding other people—even potential romantic partners—because you're afraid they'll disrupt your special bond with brother or sister? Do other people comment—even joke— about how close you two are (not just once in a while, but all the time)? If you answered yes to either of these questions, you've probably assumed an overdependent sibling role.

Overdependent sibling alliances When siblings adopt pseudo-parent and pseudo-child roles, they invariably form a strong alliance (though not necessarily a hidden one) and detach from other family members (emotionally if not physically). A symbiotic relationship results: Now *both* siblings are dependent on each other—they just show it in different ways. The pseudo-child's overdependence usually resembles the *Immature Pattern*

133

DOES BIRTH ORDER MATTER?

* * * * *

The myths are many: First-borns (we're told) are natural leaders, while the youngest will always be the baby of the family. Only children? Well, legend would tell us it doesn't bode well....

Is there any truth to these myths? According to the research findings, there's some—but not much. Birth order expert Frank Sulloway has found that first-borns are indeed overrepresented in visible leadership positions (U.S. Presidents, corporate CEOs), but there is no evidence that first-borns are at increased risk for detachment. Other studies confirm that (as legend holds) last-borns are indeed treated with special care—parented by siblings as well as Mom and Dad. Still, a half-dozen studies of American and Asian families produced unanimous results: Last-borns may be somewhat more overdependent than other siblings, but many last-born children don't show any overdependence at all. Birth order matters, but no more—and no less—than other family characteristics.

And what about that lonely only child? Is there any evidence that he will turn out differently from the child next door who's been blessed (or cursed) by a house full of siblings?

The answer to that one is a firm *no*. While only children have a slightly harder time adjusting to day care and nursery school, studies also show that most only children find their social niche within a fairly short time. By the time they reach adolescence, personality differences between only children and children with siblings have largely disappeared.

we discussed in Chapter 2 (helpless, weak, emotionally needy). The pseudo-parent's overdependence fits the *Controlling Pattern*, with one important difference: Instead of manipulating the pseudo-child through intimidation, the pseudo-parent maintains the other sibling's submissive position by undermining her efforts to develop a sense of autonomy and independent identity.

Strategy: If the first step in overcoming sibling overdependence is insight, the second step involves setting limits on your behavior. The pseudo-child must recognize when he is deliberately exaggerating his weakness and vulnerability, and once he recognizes it, he must stop doing it. The pseudo-parent must be sensitive to the ways she undermines her submissive sibling's autonomy, and when she has identified her controlling behaviors, she must take steps to change them. Whenever she has the urge to step in and protect the submissive sibling, the pseudo-parent should ask herself: Am I doing this to *help*, or am I doing it to maintain *control*? Am I doing this out of *love*, or out of *fear*? It may be difficult to answer these questions honestly, but honest self-scrutiny is a prerequisite for change.

Overdependence-based resistance in sibling relationships Although both siblings will be invested in maintaining the status quo, resistance takes different forms depending on one's role. The pseudo-child resists change by *escalating*—exaggerating his vulnerability more and more until it finally produces the desired effect (that is, trapping the dominant sibling into caregiving). The pseudo-parent resists change by becoming even more overprotective and infantilizing the pseudo-child (thereby increasing her control).

Strategy: Two strategies are useful for overcoming this overdependent resistance: *self-monitoring* and *self-control*. Since the pseudo-child knows her resistance will take the form of exaggerated vulnerability, both siblings should be on the lookout for this and identify it when it occurs. Since the pseudo-parent knows she'll react with increased overprotectiveness, both siblings must agree that when they see this, they'll say something. It takes practice to identify these patterns, but if you persist, you'll discover the telltale signs in yourself and your sibling. In the end, it comes down to growth motivation: If you want your relationship to change in positive ways, you both need to work at it and support each other's efforts.

Sibling individuation For overdependent siblings, individuation involves letting go and allowing a bit of space into the relationship. This can be tricky for both siblings—pseudo-parent and pseudo-child alike. Oftentimes the sibling individuation process begins when the pseudo-child develops his first serious romantic relationship. The pseudo-parent senses that she is being pushed aside in favor of another caregiver—an experience not unlike that of actual parents who "lose" their children through marriage. As is true for actual parents, the pseudo-parent's challenge is to let go gracefully, and give the pseudo-child room to develop his new relationship. At the same time, the pseudo-parent must begin to develop an identity of her own that does not center primarily on caregiving.

Strategy: It's one thing to tell yourself you'll let go; actually doing it is another matter. Your best approach is to adapt the individuation strategies that help heal romantic relationships, and use them here as well. Step 1: Make a deliberate effort to *do things on your own* without your sibling. Step 2: *Watch your language* (and your nonverbals) so you don't unintentionally reinforce old relationship patterns. Step 3: *Monitor your motives*—act out of growth, not fear. Step 4: *Plan your requests for help and support.*

The process can sometimes be difficult and slower than you'd hoped, but rest assured: When mindful decision-making replaces mindless habit, unhealthy sibling overdependence will gradually give way to healthy sibling dependency.

Reconnecting after detachment: Healing old wounds

In certain ways, reconnecting after sibling detachment is easier than overcoming sibling overdependence. After all, there is a natural tendency in most Western societies for brothers and sisters to drift apart after adolescence, then rediscover each other as they mature. Detachment becomes problematic when old wounds cause resentment to build up to the point that two siblings can no longer relate to each other in any sort of constructive way. When this happens, an active approach to sibling reconnection is needed.

Detached sibling roles The most common form of sibling detachment is *sibling rivalry*—an endless, fruitless competition for the parents' attention and favor. Many years ago, psychotherapist

MASOCHISTIC SIBLINGS

* * * * *

Most overdependent sibling relationships follow the pseudo-parent/ pseudo-child dynamic, but sometimes sibling overdependence gets expressed in a *masochistic* way. A masochistic sibling dynamic usually occurs when one sibling is clearly perceived as the parents' favorite, and the other sibling protects herself by refusing to compete. The favored sibling adopts a *Good Child* role, and the other sibling takes on a *Bad Child* role, with masochistic (self-punishing, self-defeating) features.

Though a masochistic sibling role may seem strange—even irrational—this role actually brings two rewards. First, it precludes failure in comparison to the favored sibling (after all, one cannot lose if one refuses to compete). Second, it provides a focal point for underlying anger that would otherwise be directed at the parents. As Freud pointed out more than seventy years ago, we usually find it easier to loathe ourselves than to (consciously) hate our parents for rejecting us.

Alfred Adler speculated that rivalry plays a role in virtually all sibling relationships. According to Adler, sibling rivalry is a natural outgrowth of identity formation, as each sibling seeks a unique niche within and outside the family. But sometimes the rivalry becomes so intense it persists for decades, distorting— even destroying—the lives of both siblings.

Strategy: Because longstanding rivalry eats away at both siblings (not to mention their spouses and other family members), it is important that you take action when you become aware of such a rivalry. If you feel as though you are competing with a brother or sister, and this competition is affecting you in negative ways, raise the issue with your "rival." Talk about it (preferably one-on-one) in a private place (no restaurants, please) and at a quiet (low-stress) time. Only do it when you're prepared to discuss the problem in a constructive (not vengeful or vindictive) way. And be prepared for a troubling insight to emerge from your discussion, because it almost always does: You're likely to discover that other family members have played a key role in keeping the rivalry alive.

Detached sibling alliances When siblings compete, they ally with parents and other family members, splitting the family into two camps: *us* and *them*. Researchers Clare Stocker and Lise Youngblade have found that parents (and other siblings) play a key role in this "family splitting" process, choosing up sides that reflect their own conflicts and concerns. When a family member joins one camp or the other, they are expected to support the sibling with whom they've allied, and help that person rationalize their behavior by blaming the rival for tension and conflict. The alliance evolves into a harmful relationship game.

Strategy: If you are part of a sibling rivalry, do not draw other family members into it. If they are already involved, take steps to distance them from the conflict. Stop seeking them out to rationalize your actions and justify your feelings. If they do this on their own (which they might, out of habit), don't reinforce the behavior. Change the subject, tell them you don't want to talk about it…whatever it takes to let them know you want to put the rivalry behind you. You might feel as though you're giving up power by doing this (especially if your rival maintains strong ties with her allies), but there's no other way to break apart the alliances that are maintaining a dysfunctional family dynamic. By giving up power in the short run, you'll feel better in the long run.

Detachment-based resistance in sibling relationships If you've read this far, you won't be surprised to hear that family members who ally with one or the other sibling can become strongly invested in maintaining the rivalry. After all, one payoff for being a loyal ally is reciprocal loyalty and support. Equally important, a rivalry can become the centerpiece of the family, distracting attention from other problems within the system (in this respect, sibling rivalries often represent power centers). Consciously or unconsciously, family members usually sense the risk involved in letting a rivalry die: They'll have to deal with other problems they've been able to ignore until now.

Strategy: Even as you work toward change, be sensitive to resistance from other family members who seek to preserve their established roles. In this situation, resistance is rarely subtle: It almost always takes the form of an ally prodding you toward increased anger and resentment—fanning the flames of the rivalry. The irony here is that the same statements you once perceived as supportive ("Can you believe what she said yesterday?") now seem hostile and destructive. Don't become angry, though, or lash out at the prodder. They haven't yet realized the rules have changed, and they're acting out of habit—it's how they thought you wanted them to behave.

Your best bet now is to stay the course and continue to use the strategies we discussed for undoing hidden alliances: Change the subject, ignore the prodding, and stop reinforcing the behavior. If you keep at it, resistance will fade (though this may take some time).

Sibling reconnection Sibling reconnection is largely a matter of establishing a new interaction pattern that works for both of you. Don't expect to become best friends right away (or ever, for that matter). Overcoming sibling detachment is a slow process, and it's not always a steady one. Be prepared for a two-steps-forward-one-step-back dynamic to occur as you work toward your mutual comfort level.

Strategy: Once you've talked openly about your rivalry, don't keep bringing up the topic. Obsessing over past hurts won't help at this point—moving forward will. Let behavior (not talking) teach both of you how to be around each other in a mutually supportive way. Make a point of spending time together—first in situations that are not too intense (like dinner with spouses), then in more emotional contexts (like family gatherings). Bring healthy dependency into your interactions by asking for and offering help when opportunities arise. Begin with small things, move on to bigger ones, and use trial-and-error to correct your mistakes. As healthy dependency becomes an integral part of your relationship, the residue of detachment will eventually disappear.

Sharon: From Sibling Rivalry to Identity Distortion

We once knew a student named Sharon who was unable to take pleasure in success. The irony was, she was remarkably success-ful—a terrific writer, accomplished athlete, and active member of several campus organizations. Sharon worked as our research assistant during her junior and senior years, so we got to know her well. And to our surprise, every attempt to recognize her accomplishments—to congratulate her on a good game, or com-pliment her on a good grade—produced the exact same re-sponse: A shrug of the shoulders and a murmured, "Not bad."

We never pressed Sharon on her odd reaction—we didn't want to probe or make her feel uncomfortable. Over time, how-ever, clues began to emerge that said a lot about Sharon and why she had so much difficulty finding joy in her triumphs.

The first clue emerged just before Spring Family Weekend of Sharon's junior year. We knew Sharon's family was coming to visit—mother, father, and older sister Elizabeth—so we asked if they'd be stopping by the psychology department to chat. Sharon's response was revealing: "No!" she said, just a little too quickly, and the look on her face—a mask of sheer horror—told us in no uncertain terms that we'd wandered into forbidden ter-ritory. We let the matter drop.

The next clue emerged during the following semester. Sharon had just been voted to the All-Conference field hockey team, and when we congratulated her, we got the usual reaction: Shrugged shoulders, downcast eyes, and a murmured, "Not bad." This time we asked why she seemed so blasé about what seemed to us (both confirmed non-athletes) a remarkable achievement. Again, Sharon's response was revealing.

"It's okay," she said. "Elizabeth made All-State, you know."

"Still, this is quite an honor."

Sharon shrugged her shoulders. "Not bad," she said quietly, and her eyes drifted away.

At home that evening, as we thought about Sharon's response, we finally began to understand. Sharon was unable to see success in herself because all she could focus on was her sister. True, Elizabeth had been something of a legend at the college: All-State in softball and field hockey, twice President of the Student Senate, Phi Beta Kappa…the list went on and on. So perhaps from Sharon's point of view, nothing she did could possibly compare to the mountain of honors bestowed upon Elizabeth. In Sharon's mind, she was forever destined to be Elizabeth's younger, less successful sister.

No wonder Sharon's accomplishments brought her so little joy. She was so caught up in sibling rivalry that her self-image—her very identity—had become twisted and distorted. She was unable to see herself as others saw her—bright, accomplished, attractive, successful. Instead, she viewed every action as she imagined her family would view it: Good (but not good enough), worthy of acknowledgment (but not celebration), never more than second best.

Sharon went on to a successful career as a school psychologist, but she never returned to campus for an alumni gathering, and we eventually lost contact. Sharon never felt quite right about her time here, and she dealt with her sorrow by detaching from all of us. She simply couldn't see herself as truly successful—even when she, too, graduated with honors, and our work together resulted in a published paper that was very well-received.

We sent her copies of the paper, but never got a response. We can imagine her reaction though, and it makes us sad to think about it.

"Not bad," she must have murmured, with her eyes downcast. Not bad, she must have thought, but not good enough.

Looking Ahead:
The Healthy Dependent Parent

In 1986, family researcher Virginia Fu examined the intergenerational transmission of healthy and unhealthy dependency. By analyzing interaction patterns in 150 grandmother-mother-child "units," Virginia Fu found that over time, relationship styles are passed along through a kind of learning process. The healthy dependent grandmothers modeled healthy dependent behaviors, and rewarded their daughters for exhibiting these behaviors; the daughters, in turn, modeled and rewarded healthy dependent behaviors in their own children. And a similar process occurred for destructive overdependence: Overdependent grandmothers rewarded and reinforced overdependence in their daughters, after which the daughters—now mothers—did the same thing with their own children.

You already know (from Chapter 2) some of the factors that cause young children to "disconnect," and become destructively overdependent or dysfunctionally detached. To be a healthy dependent parent, you must take the next step and learn techniques that will foster secure attachment and an others-will-be-there-for-me relationship script in your own children. That's what we'll discuss in Chapter 7.

THE HEALTHY
DEPENDENT PARENT

The last two weeks had left Michael drained. Every morning he was up at 5:30, off to work an hour later, and from work he headed straight to the hospital to spend an hour with his mother. He was lucky if he made it home by eight most nights for a quick dinner with Kimberly. Kathleen was in the midst of a huge crunch at work, so she rarely got home before ten these days. By the time Kathleen trudged down the hall to their bedroom, Michael was usually asleep, or close to it.

But even as Michael slept, his worries tormented him. He tossed and turned, dreamed frightening dreams, and woke each morning with gritty eyes and a gnawing feeling that he couldn't quite put into words. A part of Michael somehow knew that things had changed between him and Kathleen—that their relationship was nearing an end. But even though a part of Michael knew this, another part of him refused to believe it.

It was Tuesday. Michael sat at the kitchen table, waiting for the oven timer to go off. When it did, he dragged himself to his feet and turned down the heat. He called out for Kimberly, but heard no response. He headed upstairs to get her.

Kim's door was ajar, and as Michael approached he could see his daughter stretched out on her bed, feet in the air, books and papers spread out in front of her. He knocked and poked his head in. Kim smiled, pulled herself into a sitting position. She took off her head-phones. Her smile faded and her brow furrowed.

"Dad, you look terrible."

"I do?" Michael was startled by his daughter's bluntness, but that was Kim—she said what she thought.

"Yeah, you really do. You look like you haven't slept in days."

"Well, that's not too far from the truth."

Kim looked intently at her father as he stood in the doorway. He seemed different somehow—not just tired, but fragile, frail. Kim suddenly felt protective, almost maternal. It was a strange feeling. She'd never experienced anything like it before.

"Come in, Dad." Kim got up and removed the books from her desk chair. She patted the cushion. Michael went over and sat down. He exhaled slowly as he deflated into the seat.

"How's Grandma?" Kim was back on her bed.

"Not too bad. The doctor says she'll be ready to come home in a day or two. Probably Friday."

"That's good."

"It might take her a while to get back on her feet though. A couple of months at least, they say."

"Oh." Kim paused. "Well, it'll be okay. I'll help, too."

"Yes." Michael nodded absently. "It'll be okay." He was picturing the house with his mother in it, camped out on the couch downstairs, learning to maneuver again, struggling with the walker.

Michael shook his head to clear the scene. He looked at his daughter.

"Kim, can I ask you something?"

"Sure, Dad. What is it?"

"Am I...a good father?"

Kim laughed abruptly, then caught herself—put her hand over her mouth—when she saw the expression on her father's face.

"You're serious," she said.

"Yes, I am. I really want to know."

Kim looked down at her feet, then back at her father. She started to talk, but stopped and bit her lip. When she finally spoke she chose her words carefully.

"Dad, you're a great father. You always listen to what I have to

say—really listen, you know—and that means a lot. Some of my friends never talk to their fathers at all."

Michael nodded slowly.

"And I've always felt like you really…I don't know…respect me. You don't just tell me what to do for no reason. We talk about it. There's give and take."

Michael smiled, looked away.

"Kim, can I ask you something else? Be honest, okay?"

"Sure, Dad."

"Do you ever wish I was…stronger?"

"Stronger?"

"Yeah. You know, firmer. About rules. About setting limits and all. That sort of thing."

"Huh. I hadn't really thought of it like that." Kim pursed her lips, tilted her head. "Now that you mention it, I guess I do. I mean, sometimes I push the envelope a little. I know that. It's not that I don't want to go out with my friends and all, but…I don't know…it's weird. Sometimes I almost wish you'd tell me no." Kim paused. "Does that make sense?"

Michael nodded.

"I mean, it would feel good—protective, like—if you let me know when I was pushing too hard." Kim looked away, then back at her father. "I wish you'd do that sometimes."

Michael gazed at his daughter, looked into her eyes, and he didn't know what to say. They sat in silence for a moment, then Michael got slowly to his feet. He walked over to where Kim sat, and he gave her shoulder a squeeze. Kim looked up and smiled.

Kathleen didn't get home until eleven that night, but this time Michael wasn't in bed. When Kathleen walked in and saw her husband sitting alone at the kitchen table, she knew something was wrong.

"Kathleen," said Michael, "we need to talk."

If only all children were as open as Kim—able to let us know how they feel, what they think, and what they need. But in the world of adolescents, Kim is the exception, not the rule. Most of the time, we don't get such clear feedback. We never quite know how we're doing as parents, so we watch and listen—nervously, expectantly—hoping we've done the right things.

It might not work in every family, but for Michael, a one-on-one talk with his daughter was just what he needed. Michael had suspected that his difficulties at work might be spilling over into his homelife, and now he knows his suspicions were correct. Michael is finally ready to change—to bring healthy dependency into *all* his relationships. And he started by clearing the air with his daughter.

Are You a Disconnecting Parent?

It doesn't matter how many books you read or how much advice you get: You can't possibly anticipate every parenting challenge that lies ahead. So instead of obsessing, take the long view. Assume that unexpected obstacles will come along, and have in mind a strategy that will help you overcome these obstacles—whenever they occur.

Our framework for healthy dependent parenting requires that you do three things: *Know the research, know your child,* and *know yourself.* When you know the research, you'll have the intellectual tools you need to be a good parent—you'll know which parenting behaviors lead to healthy dependency, and which behaviors promote destructive overdependence or dysfunctional detachment. When you know your child, you'll be sensitive to her strengths as well as her limitations, and you can act in ways that help your child recapture the healthy dependency that lies hidden inside her.

In a sense, knowing yourself is the most important (and most difficult) task of all. Only by knowing yourself can you acquire the *emotional* tools you need to be a good parent—the insight and self-awareness that allow you to connect with your children, and help them grow.

The best way to know yourself is to be objective about your parenting beliefs and behaviors, so before we begin, take a few minutes to complete the Parenting Style Test on page 148. When you're done, we'll examine the parenting practices that place children at risk for destructive overdependence and dysfunctional detachment. If your Parenting Style Test responses indicate that you engage in some of these practices, we'll help you change them.

Behaviors that foster overdependence

Psychologists have conducted dozens of studies of overdependence-fostering parents during the past thirty years. In some of these investigations, researchers observed parent-child dynamics in the home. In others, parents and children interacted in the laboratory (playing games, solving puzzles), and their behaviors were recorded on film for later analysis. These investigations took place all over the world—from Britain and Belgium to India and Japan—but they produced remarkably consistent results. Three parenting behaviors, alone or in combination, lead to overdependence in children:

- *Overprotectiveness* The single strongest risk factor for childhood overdependence is parental overprotectiveness. Overprotective parents coddle their child and discourage him from taking on challenges. Although the overprotective parent's goal may be to protect the child from failure or hurt, parental overprotectiveness sends the child a not-too-subtle message: *You are weak, we are strong, and the way to get by is to let us make decisions for you.* The child who receives these messages develops a habit of looking to the parents for protection and guidance—a habit that eventually gets transferred to other surrogate caregivers (supervisors, friends, romantic partners) when the child becomes an adult.
- *Authoritarianism* The second strongest risk factor for childhood overdependence is parental authoritarianism. Authoritarian parents set rigid rules, and enforce those rules with an iron hand. The child has little freedom to make his own decisions, and as a result, he never develops a sense of

147

WHAT KIND OF PARENT ARE YOU?
THE PARENTING STYLE TEST

* * * * *

To raise a healthy dependent child, you must understand your *parenting style*—your characteristic way of relating to your children. By answering the following questions, you can get a good sense of your approach to parenting and the changes you'll need to make to bring healthy dependency into your relationship.

For each statement, circle the number corresponding to how well that statement describes you. When you're done we'll tally your score and assess your parenting style.

Statement   *Rating*

                                        1   2   3   4   5   6   7

                                    Not at all   *Very true*
                                    true of me   *of me*

1) It's important to protect your
   child from failure, even if it means
   she tries fewer new things.   1   2   3   4   5   6   7

2) The best approach to parenting is
   to set firm rules; children need
   guidance to learn how to behave. 1   2   3   4   5   6   7

3) You must always push a child
   forward—otherwise they'll
   never leave the nest.   1   2   3   4   5   6   7

4) Too much affection spoils a child;
   it's better to hold back so the
   child will grow strong.   1   2   3   4   5   6   7

5) It is important to be selective
   about your child's friends; children
   pick up bad habits from the
   wrong people.   1   2   3   4   5   6   7

6) It's best not to let your child
   know when you're angry—
   he won't understand, so keep
   it to yourself.   1   2   3   4   5   6   7

7) It is important to let your child
learn by doing, even if that means
he'll fail at some things.   1   2   3   4   5   6   7

8) You should make a point of asking
your child for help sometimes,
even if you have to stretch the
truth to do it.   1   2   3   4   5   6   7

9) Parents should deliberately ask
each other for support in front
of the children, so they witness
the give-and-take.   1   2   3   4   5   6   7

Your Parenting Style

To determine your parenting style, add up your ratings for Statements 1–3. This is your *Overdependence Score*. Now add up your ratings for Statements 4–6. This is your *Detachment Score*. Finally, add up your ratings for Statements 7–9. This is your *Healthy Dependence Score*.

Your highest score represents your typical parenting style; the higher the score, the more committed you are to that way of relating. If you obtained comparable scores on two (or all three) dimensions, that means you combine features of different parenting styles in interactions with your children. This is a very common experience: Many parents show a mixture of parenting behaviors rather than one "pure" style.

As we learn about parenting practices that foster overdependence or detachment, you'll want to keep your test profile handy, so you can check your own behavior against what the researchers have found.

* * * * *

**How many hopes and fears, how many ardent wishes
and anxious apprehensions are twisted together in the
threads that connect the parent with the child!**
—Samuel Griswold Goodrich

PARENT-CHILD INFLUENCE IS A TWO-WAY STREET: HOW CHILDREN SHAPE THEIR PARENTS' BEHAVIOR

* * * * *

We tend to think that parents mold their children, not the other way around. But developmental psychologists have long known that parent-child influence is a two-way street. Children shape their parents' behavior in at least three ways:

- *Temperament* In 1984, child development experts Alexander Thomas and Stella Chess published a groundbreaking study of infant behavior. They found that as early as two weeks after birth—long before any real learning takes place—infants show distinctive, persistent patterns of responding. *Easy babies* are mellow but alert, relaxed but curious. Parents enjoy handling these babies, and give them extra love and attention. *Difficult babies* are just the opposite: Moody, edgy, and easily upset. As a result, parents learn to treat these babies gingerly—as if they were time bombs that might go off at any time. *Slow-to-warm babies* are calm but guarded. They don't show much reaction to their parents' overtures, as if they were off in their own world. Most parents eventually spend less time trying to connect with these distant, unresponsive babies.

competence and self-control (what child development experts call *self-efficacy*). Though at first glance authoritarian and overprotective parents seem very different, when you look beneath the surface you'll discover that the message they send their children is exactly the same: Do what we say, and things will be fine. Can you think of a better way to create a can't-make-it-on-my-own relationship script in your child, and set the stage for a lifetime of overdependence?

- *Premature independence pressure* Overprotectiveness and authoritarianism harm the child by infantilizing him. Premature independence pressure—forcing the child to take on challenges he's not yet ready to handle—has the opposite ef-

- *Attachment style* Remember the three attachment styles we discussed in Chapter 2? Would it surprise you to learn that *easy babies* tend to become *securely attached*, while *difficult babies* become *insecurely attached*, and *slow-to-warm babies* develop an *avoidant attachment style*? This makes sense when you hear it, and it is precisely what the data show. The route from temperament to attachment occurs via a three-stage process: The baby's temperament evokes a predictable pattern of parental behavior, which leads to a particular attachment style. Once formed, the child's attachment style begins to affect how her parents treat her, and the two-way influence is strengthened and renewed.
- *Sibling carryover* The third way that children shape their parents' behavior is through experience—what researchers call the *sibling carryover effect*. Parents hone their parenting skills on their firstborns, and for better or worse, their initial experiences carry over to later-born children as well. If the first baby was easy, the parents approach their second child with certain expectations. Ditto if the first baby was difficult or slow to warm. The sibling carryover effect confirms that not only do we affect how our parents treat us, but our brothers and sisters had a hand in this, too. Our family role, so it seems, begins to take shape even before we are born.

fect: It virtually ensures that the child will fall on his face and fail. As a result, the child feels bad about himself (embarrassed and ashamed). Over time, he learns to doubt his abilities. The pressured child comes to believe that it's safer not to try than to push himself and take risks. The inevitable result: Insecurity, self-doubt, and destructive overdependence.

Behaviors that foster detachment

There are fewer studies of detachment-promoting parental behaviors than overdependence-fostering behaviors, but while the data may be less plentiful, the conclusions are just as clear: Three parenting patterns—*emotional denial, hidden hostility,* and *isolationism*—place children at risk for detachment.

- *Emotional denial* Emotional denial (also known as *intimacy refusal*) occurs when parents are distant and withdrawn. They may go through the motions of being affectionate (like saying "I love you" and kissing goodnight), but beneath these surface displays there's no real connection—no genuine, heartfelt exchange of warmth and caring. The child comes to believe he's not worthy of his parents' love. Because emotional denial usually stems from detachment on the part of one or both parents, the parents may be completely unaware of the problem. After all, to a detached parent, superficial intimacy seems normal—it's part of most (maybe all) of their relationships, and probably has been for as long as they can remember.
- *Hidden hostility* Hidden hostility can take many forms, from rejecting behaviors (like ignoring important events in the child's life) to ego-busting comparisons with other children ("Your brother never would have brought home grades like these"). Hidden hostility often occurs in tandem with emotional denial, but it can also occur on its own, without these other patterns. However it gets expressed, hidden hostility always sends a clear message: It tells the child he's not worthy of a parent's attention, and doesn't deserve their love. The child's natural response is to disconnect from others and harden his protective shell.
- *Isolationism* Isolationism occurs when children are discouraged—either subtly or directly—from developing close relationships with other children. Like emotional denial and hidden hostility, isolationism sets the stage for detachment, but it does so in a different way: Isolationism teaches the child that other people can't be trusted—that it's best to keep to oneself and do things on one's own. The end result: The child internalizes a got-to-go-it-alone relationship script—the core of dysfunctional detachment.

UNDERSTANDING DEVELOPMENTAL NORMS

* * * * *

Being a healthy dependent parent requires that you know a bit about developmental norms—average ages at which children reach cognitive, physical, and social milestones. Your best bet here is to get hold of a good, parent-friendly manual of developmental norms, and keep it close at hand as your child grows. Keep in mind that there are wide variations in children's growth rates, so don't panic if your child reaches a particular milestone less quickly than you'd hoped. And remember, there are important cultural differences in development as well: Your child's growth might not match that of a "typical" North American child, and in most instances that's okay.

From a healthy dependency perspective, a few key facts are worth noting:

- *Childhood dependency is normal, especially early on.* All children start out dependent, so it's important to aim for that healthy middle ground: Don't reinforce dependency, but don't try to make it go away too soon.
- *Dependency conflicts are a part of growing up.* No matter how hard we try to be clear and consistent, our children usually receive some mixed messages about dependency. These mixed messages can create *dependency conflicts*—confusing, ambivalent feelings about giving and getting help. School is a major source of dependency conflicts: Children are told to be passive and conform ("Listen to your teacher!") at the same time they are told to move forward and take risks ("If you don't try new things, you'll never learn"). There's no need for you to explain these mixed messages. As your child matures cognitively, these messages will reconcile themselves in her mind through a process called *integration*.
- *Adolescence is a time of peer group dependency.* As adolescents detach from their parents, they usually transfer their dependency to members of a peer group (or "clique"). This is part of the normal transition to healthy, mature dependency later in life. If your child affiliates with a destructive "outsider" clique, you should talk to him about the importance of choosing friends wisely. But don't be too picky here: Even if you wish your child had affiliated with a different set of peers, let it go unless the group he's with is affecting his behavior in some significantly troubling ways.

153

Fostering Growth in the Overdependent Child

To help rebuild your child's healthy dependency, you need to know the telltale signs of childhood overdependence and detachment. Let's begin with overdependence.

Symptoms of childhood overdependence

Some symptoms of childhood overdependence are obvious; others are more subtle. Here are three things you should look for:

- *Exaggerated help-seeking* The most obvious sign of childhood overdependence is exaggerated help-seeking (for example, your child whines that he's "stuck" and can't get his sweater on, when all he needs to do is push his arm through the sleeve). Often theatrical and overdramatic, exaggerated help-seeking displays quickly turn into screaming tantrums if you try to hold the line. The reason: These displays are designed to make sure you're still willing to play the rescuer role and rush in at the first sign of distress. Any indication that you're no longer buying into the game—that the old, familiar trap isn't working anymore—will be very upsetting to the overdependent child and likely to produce an emotional escalation.
- *Low self-esteem* The signs of low self-esteem vary from tearfulness and withdrawal to harsh self-criticism and self-denigration. Oftentimes low self-esteem begins with quiet moping, and only if you probe will you uncover the self-loathing that underlies your child's sadness. The overdependent child may belittle herself in any number of areas—intelligence, appearance, athletic ability, social skills—but to get to the heart of the matter you must move downward through the layers. Underlying your child's harsh self-assessment is a negative self-image, and underlying her negative self-image is a helpless core. Your child

CHILDHOOD DEPRESSION

* * * * *

Until relatively recently, mental health professionals thought that very young children could not become depressed (*sad*, yes; *depressed*, no). We now know that children as young as two can develop diagnosable (but fortunately, treatable) depression.

Diagnosing depression in preschool children can be tricky, in part because pediatricians don't always think to look or ask. Beyond this, the symptoms of depression take a different form in younger children, which can make them hard to recognize. If you think your child might be depressed, tell your doctor. And if the doctor doesn't take your concerns seriously, see a child psychologist or psychiatrist instead.

In addition to the usual symptoms of depression (sadness, tearfulness, feelings of worthlessness), here are some child-specific symptoms you should be aware of:

- *somatic complaints*—persistent aches and pains that have no medical basis (sometimes called "masked depression")
- *increased irritability/crankiness*—often expressed as whininess or tantrums
- *loss of appetite*—a significant decrease from your child's usual appetite level
- *social withdrawal*—loss of interest in friends
- *anhedonia*—loss of interest in things that used to give your child pleasure (hobbies, sports, etc.)

feels powerless to control her life and her world, and her sadness and self-criticism are hidden cries for help—less obvious than exaggerated help-seeking, but no less serious.

- *Immaturity* Some children maintain an overdependent position within the family by *regressing*—displaying immature, age-inappropriate behaviors (like thumb-sucking). Immature behaviors usually increase with stress, so don't be surprised if they become more pronounced when your child is challenged (like at a birthday party where you aren't there to protect him). In one study of this issue, personality researcher Laura Fichman found that overdependent children—boys and girls alike—regressed when sent to sleep-away camp for the first time. They displayed a range of immature behaviors (from whining to bedwetting) that alienated other campers and angered the counselors. *School refusal* (formerly known as *school phobia*) is another classic "immature" sign of childhood overdependence. If you've ever witnessed first-hand a school-refusing child's temper tantrum when Mom or Dad tries to drop him off at the start of the day, you know how effective it can be in intimidating and controlling the frightened, embarrassed parent.

Coping and changing: Beyond Overdependence

The strategy you use to cope with your child's overdependence should be tailored to how it is displayed. You might need to use multiple interventions if your child shows more than one overdependence pattern (or if she shifts to a second approach when the first one stops working). Three strategies are useful:

- *Set limits on inappropriate help-seeking.* Two techniques, used together, will help you set limits effectively. First, stop reinforcing your child's inappropriate help-seeking. Second, reward any appropriate help-seeking overtures your child makes. When you do these things in tandem, the frequency of inappropriate help-seeking will gradually decrease and the frequency of appropriate help-seeking will increase. But don't expect progress to be perfectly smooth. On the contrary, your child will probably escalate her inappropriate help-seeking efforts when you begin withholding rewards. When this occurs, ignore it. If you reward your child's escalations with extra attention, you will encourage her to replace mildly inappropriate help-seeking strategies (like whining) with even more inappropriate strategies (like screaming and threatening).

- *Bolster self-esteem.* Bolstering your child's self-esteem begins within the family, but it must not end there. You can help by complimenting your child on her successes (even the minor ones), and pointing out her strengths and skills (even if you have to stretch the truth a bit). A pat on the back, a smile, a well-timed "Good job"—these may seem like minor things, but to the insecure child, they're nuggets of gold. Once you've gotten the process underway, it is important that positive feedback start to come from outside the family as well, so look for places where your child can flourish. Arrange play dates and sleep-overs with some of your child's mellower, less competitive peers—companions who'll build your child up, and let her take the lead. Encourage your child to become involved in low-pressure activities where she can relax and succeed (think art classes, not sports). Let teachers know how much your child appreciates it when her good work is recognized (and if your child would rather this feedback come in private—not in front of her classmates—let the teacher know this, too).

- *Extinguish immature displays.* When you set limits on your child's exaggerated help-seeking, she may regress and begin to display more immature behaviors. Try not to get angry, but instead use connection-based thinking to separate the *act* from the *person* (your child is behaving this way because she's frightened of losing your support). Implement the same strategies you would use to deal with exaggerated help-seeking: Ignore the immature displays, and reinforce appropriate behavior. Talk to your spouse (and older siblings if there are any) about what you're doing. That way you can all respond consistently and bolster each other's efforts. And no matter how conscientious you are, be prepared for every parent's nightmare: the dreaded grocery store temper tantrum. Most overdependent children try this at least once when you stop responding to their initial attention-getting efforts, and the grocery store temper tantrum can be terribly intimidating. Hold your ground,

BUILDING YOUR CHILD'S HEALTHY DEPENDENCY SKILLS: A STEP-BY-STEP GUIDE

* * * * *

There's more to healthy dependent parenting than simply avoiding overdependence and detachment. Healthy dependent parenting also means building your child's healthy dependency skills, so she can connect with other people, giving and getting good help along the way. University of Illinois researchers Karen Clark and Gary Ladd have found that when parents reinforce healthy dependency in their children, the children show growth in a variety of areas—not just family relationships, but also peer interactions and school adjustment.

Here are some techniques you can use to help your child recapture the four key healthy dependency skills:

- *Connection-based thinking* When your child asks for help appropriately, reinforce this behavior. Help her separate *asking for help* from *being helpless* by letting her know that leaning on others is an important part of all relationships. Explain that you and your spouse/partner ask each other for help all the time, and give your child concrete examples to make the message stick. When your child recounts instances in which she asked a teacher, friend, or other (appropriate) person for help, compliment her on this. Encourage her to offer help as well as receive it.
- *Emotional synergy* You can make it easier for your child to feel good about giving and receiving help if you challenge some cultural stereotypes. If your child believes that asking for help reflects immaturity, weakness, or failure, explain the difference between adaptive (growth-promoting) and maladaptive (challenge-avoiding) help-seeking. If your child feels bad when she asks for help, take advantage of this "teachable moment": Encourage her to explain how she's feeling and why. Don't belittle or discount her feelings, but gently point out that there are other ways to feel when receiving help: cared-for, connected, even strong (because she took the initiative and asked). Use yourself as an example to illustrate these responses.
- *Growth motivation* Forty years ago, British pediatrician D. W. Winnicott coined the term *holding environment* to describe a family wherein parents are available and welcoming, but not control-

158

ling and intrusive. By creating a holding environment within your household, you'll provide your child with a *secure base*—a safe haven from which she can venture out to explore the world and take risks. A holding environment will help your child develop growth motivation—the desire to forge ahead and try new things, with the security of knowing she can return to her safe haven if she feels overwhelmed.

- *Relationship flexibility* The best way to teach relationship flexibility is to model it yourself—with your romantic partner, other siblings, and your child. Let your son or daughter know that there are times when it's good to ask for help, and times when it's best to do things on your own. Help your child see that giving and getting help go hand in hand—you can't have one without the other. And show your child that it is important to give and get help with a variety of people (not just one). Practice this flexibility within your family, and explain what you're doing and why.

ignore the stares, and gently but firmly take your child away from her audience to a more private place where you can allow the tantrum to run its course.

Reconnecting with the Detached Child

To reconnect with a detached child, you must understand the symptoms of childhood detachment and strategies you can use to help your child cope and change.

Symptoms of childhood detachment

The symptoms of childhood detachment are more frightening than those of childhood overdependence. After all, we expect children (especially young children) to be a bit helpless and clingy, so some degree of overdependence seems normal. The symptoms of detachment—*isolation, conduct problems, a negative identity*—are more noticeable and more troubling.

- *Isolation* As they move into adolescence, most children distance themselves from one or both parents. That's normal. But when children detach from their peers as well—when they suddenly seem to have no friends at all—it's time to be concerned. Peer isolation is particularly worrisome because it is both a *symptom* of underlying detachment and a *cause* of new behavior problems. It's a symptom because the isolated child is telling you he doesn't feel right around his peers—doesn't trust others, doesn't fit in. It's a cause of new problems because the child who spends all his time alone deprives himself of the benefits of social interaction. Make no mistake: Isolation by itself doesn't cause a child to develop later social and emotional difficulties, but it is an important early warning sign.

- *Conduct problems* Conduct problems—behavior problems—are a second key symptom of childhood detachment. Research confirms that detached children act out their anger in a variety of ways, and these patterns differ for girls and boys. Girls tend to *internalize* anger—bottle it up, channel it inward, and exhibit self-punishing behaviors (like dysfunctional eating or mutilative "cutting"). Boys tend to *externalize* anger—channel it outward, express it directly, and engage in more overtly destructive behaviors (like fighting or vandalism). Whatever form they take, conduct problems are a signal that your child is angry—at himself, at other people, and probably at you as well.

- *A negative identity* Some detached children cope by taking on a *negative identity*—a self-image centered around antisocial behavior. When this happens, the detached child becomes alienated from mainstream society and devoted to a group of like-minded people who both support and help shape his belief system. In the past, taking on a negative identity usually meant joining a gang, or a cadre of drug-abusing peers. In recent years the Internet has created a world of new negative identity opportunities. Now the detached child can link up with any number of web-based groups who are ready and willing to validate his belief that

THE DETACHED CHILD: WHEN IS HE AT RISK?

* * * * *

Most detached children do not act out their anger, but recent episodes of schoolyard violence involving detached children and adolescents are enough to send parents into an absolute panic. If you believe your child may be at risk, don't try to handle the situation yourself. Talk to your child's guidance counselor or school psychologist, or arrange to see a psychologist or psychiatrist who specializes in conduct disorders. It's hard to know when to worry these days—even good kids dress like street thugs and zombies—so try to find a reasonable middle ground. Don't overreact, but don't delay either.

Here are some of the danger signs you should look for:

- *A persistent pattern of bullying/victimization* Many children who become violent have been victimized repeatedly by schoolmates—ridiculed, ostracized, made to feel unwanted or inferior.
- *Preoccupation with revenge* A persistent pattern of bullying/victimization may cause the child to become preoccupied with revenge: He spends more and more time thinking about ways to get back at his tormentors and "even the score."
- *Sudden withdrawal/lack of communication* Sometimes children shut down and withdraw shortly before they act out revenge fantasies. The best indicator of this is a sudden, sharp decrease in communication.
- *Obsession with violence and death* Many children who act out violently are obsessed with death. This can show itself in different ways: A fascination with the Internet or video game violence and a sudden, disturbing change in clothing or appearance are common.
- *Violent fantasies in notes or on film* A surprising number of imminently violent people leave written or filmed records of their fantasies and plans.
- *Physical evidence of preparation for violence* Revenge fantasies can be quite detailed, and it is common for people who are serious about their plans to prepare carefully ahead of time. If you see *any* physical evidence of preparation for violence (weapons, bombs, poisons…anything), intervene immediately—contact law enforcement officials right away.

others can't be trusted and don't understand him. Racist organizations, religious cults, political fringe collectives—these and other "outsider" groups can be too tempting for the angry, isolated child to resist.

Coping and changing: Reconnecting with others

As with childhood overdependence, how you approach your child's detachment depends upon how it is displayed. Three steps are involved:

- *Overcome denial.* The first step in reconnecting with your detached child is accepting that he or she has a problem. Parents—quite understandably—tend to see childhood and adolescent difficulties as temporary ("It's just a phase...."). Oftentimes that's true, but if your child shows signs of persistent peer isolation, conduct problems, or a negative identity, it's *not* just a phase. In this situation, it is important that you intervene before the problem gets worse. So don't let others' doubts undermine your confidence in your own perceptions (denial is often a collaborative effort). If you are worried and your spouse is not, make your case as you would for any other important family issue: Muster your evidence, make a list of key points, set up a time to talk in private, and follow through as soon as you can.
- *Take charge.* Once you've decided to intervene, don't delay. Create a plan of action and implement it. If your child shows signs of peer isolation, talk to him about your concerns (if he refuses, insist). If your child has conduct problems (either internalizing or externalizing), get help—from a psychologist, school counselor, or some other mental health professional. If you see worrisome signs of a negative identity, investigate thoroughly (and don't be shy—nosiness is a strength in this situation). Then do whatever it takes to disconnect your child from his destructive new support group—and do it quickly, before he drifts even further away.

162

- *Follow through.* Interfering with a detached child's self-destructive behavior brings a predictable three-stage response: *anger* (you're taking away something the child "owns" and values—a part of his identity), *resistance* (you're forcing him out of an established role), and *withdrawal* (when all else fails, detached people pull away). This three-stage response will probably occur no matter how you intervene, so your best strategy is to expect it and not be thrown by it. Stick with your plan, get the emotional and professional support you need to follow through, and be patient. Odds are your persistence will pay off eventually, and when it does, your child will change. You might have to deal with some unresolved parent-child issues at that point, and you might hear (or say) some angry, unpleasant things. There's no easy way to navigate these rough waters, but you must: If you don't work through the underlying issues that set the stage for your child's behavior problems, they'll still be there, contaminating your relationship for years—even decades—to come.

Overcoming denial, taking charge, and following through might seem like a tall order—make no mistake, reconnecting with a detached child can be a challenge. But it's worth the effort. Studies show that detached children—even those with significant conduct problems—can overcome their early difficulties and develop healthy dependent relationships in adulthood. No matter how challenging the situation may seem, take heart: With understanding, persistence, patience, and strength, you *can* make a difference in your detached child's life.

Kara: Adolescent Detachment and a Negative Identity

When we first met Kara and her parents, it was clear who held the power in this family. Kara, without question, was completely in control. Her parents hung on her every word, flinched at her every gesture. Kara's parents were frightened, intimidated—and

HIDDEN PARENTING AGENDAS

* * * * *

Know yourself. It's one of the key principles of healthy dependent parenting. Sometimes knowing yourself means facing up to some unpleasant truths, so here's one: No matter how well-meaning you are, your family relationships may be compromised by one or more hidden agendas.

Hidden agendas usually reflect a family role we're reluctant to give up and hidden alliances that help maintain this valued role. From a healthy dependency perspective, two hidden agendas are particularly important. Some parents become unconsciously invested in squelching their child's autonomy and fostering overdependence. Other parents collude to encourage detachment.

- *Squelching autonomy* Consider a study by McGill University researchers Richard Thompson and David Zuroff, in which overdependent mothers watched their adolescent daughters play a computer game, receiving false feedback about the daughter's performance throughout the session. Mothers had the opportunity to "coach" while their daughters played, giving suggestions, hints, and so forth. The surprising result: Overdependent mothers who thought their daughters were performing well actually gave the daughter *unhelpful* advice and *critical* feedback! Only when they were told the daughter was performing poorly did the overdependent mothers offer support and reassurance. These overdependent mothers had a hidden agenda: *Make sure my daughter fails, so she'll always need her mom.* When Thompson and Zuroff followed up with a similar study of mother-son pairs, they found the exact same thing. To the overdependent mother, an incompetent child is a safety net that ensures her valued role will be maintained.

- *Colluding in detachment* Just as parents can unconsciously foster their child's overdependence, parents may collude to maintain a detached child's distance. Sometimes this occurs when a parent (usually the mother) develops a strong bond with one of her children, and doesn't want another child to interfere with this "special" relationship. The parent engages in various detachment-fostering behaviors—emotional denial, hidden hostility—that keep the intruding child at arm's length. Now the stage is set for a complicated set of roles and alliances to form. The rejected child may assume a negative identity, and once this happens, the favored child becomes invested in maintaining her sibling's "outsider" role. At the same time, the parent and favored sibling form an alliance aimed at maintaining the rejected child's negative position. The favored child benefits because her "Good Girl" role is secure; the parent benefits because her special relationship with the favored child is protected.

no wonder. The more we heard about Kara's behavior, the more frightening it seemed.

Kara had been a model daughter—well-behaved, popular, good in school—until last fall. When her family relocated, Kara began ninth grade in a new school. She seemed isolated, friendless, an outsider for the first time. And all of a sudden, without any warning, Kara embraced the outsider role…with gusto.

She began dressing completely in black. She dyed her hair black as well (it had been red before), and applied black polish to her fingernails. Kara began to spend more and more time on the Internet, and when her father checked her browser bookmarks, he was horrified to discover links to web pages dealing with witchcraft, sorcery, violence, and death. The last straw came when Kara's English teacher called her parents in for a conference and handed them Kara's latest essay: It was a detailed, graphic description of her own bloody suicide.

That's when Kara's parents brought her in for treatment.

We decided that before we worked with the entire family, we needed to begin meeting in separate sessions with Kara and her parents. One of us met with Kara's parents, the other met with Kara herself, and we promised everyone that no information would be passed along without their permission.

As we learned more about Kara, we discovered that her detachment wasn't new—it had been there for years, but expressed more subtly. As Kara described it, her earlier "Good Girl" role had developed in response to her parents' hidden hostility.

Whenever she ran into difficulty—in school, with friends, or anywhere else—her parents blamed her, hinting that if only she tried harder, she'd succeed. In a familiar environment, Kara had indeed worked harder—as hard as she needed to escape her parents' criticism. But now, in a strange place with no support system, Kara found her parents' demands overwhelming. She did a 180-degree turn, and instead of keeping her parents at bay by being good, she kept them at a distance by being bad. Kara's message to her parents was clear and effective: If you think this is scary, you ain't seen nothin' yet. Stay out of my way or things will get worse—a lot worse.

No wonder Kara's parents were so frightened. And no wonder Kara was so angry.

We began by teaching Kara's parents about limits, letting them know that criticism—even implied criticism—would only drive their daughter further away. We talked to them about the importance of being available, but not intrusive (Winnicott's "holding environment"). And we role-played responses to various situations that might arise—failing test grade, bizarre new hairstyle, nose-ringed boyfriend, awful tattoo—so her parents could replace their reflexive relationship-wrecking reactions with healthier relationship-building responses.

At the same time we were helping Kara's parents cope and change, we were working to help Kara grow beyond her present unhappy situation. Since Kara was showing a pattern of internalizing (self-punishing) behavior, we helped her find ways to express her anger more directly. First, we encouraged her to do this in therapy. Since Kara aspired to be a writer, we asked her to put her thoughts on paper as well—then we helped her edit them so they communicated her feelings clearly and constructively.

* * * * *

**We never know the love of the parent
till we become parents ourselves.**
—HENRY WARD BEECHER

The final step in therapy came when we brought Kara and her parents back together so they could talk openly about their relationships. When Kara's parents read her essay, they were genuinely moved, understanding for the first time how much their words had hurt their daughter. And her father's tears seemed to shake something loose in Kara as well: She was finally able to see how much her detachment hurt her parents and how sad they were at being excluded from her life.

Unleashing years' worth of pent-up emotions allowed Kara and her parents to find healthier ways of relating, both within and outside the family. Kara began to acquire a circle of friends, and her frightening behavior dropped away. Family interactions became happier and more relaxed. Kara's mother started to work outside the home again, for the first time since Kara was born.

Kara's parents divorced a few years after they left therapy, but Kara reports that she has maintained good relationships with both of them. And she just published her first story in her college's literary magazine. We have to admit we were a bit nervous when she sent us a copy. But it's about baseball, of all things.

Looking Ahead: Healthy Dependency at Work

It is hard to believe, but true: The exact same skills that strengthen family relationships will help you connect with colleagues at work. After all, work relationships—like family relationships—involve *power differentials* (some people have more influence than others do). Coworkers—like family members—take on roles, form alliances, and manage the flow of information to strengthen their position within the group. If you've ever been called on the carpet by a supervisor, you surely recall that terrible feeling: All of a sudden you're five years old again. And if you've ever had to mediate personal conflicts among subordinates, perhaps you remember thinking: I didn't sign on to be everybody's parent!

To bring healthy dependency to work, we'll apply the same basic techniques we've used before, tailoring our strategies to accommodate the demands of different professional relationships (boss, colleague, mentor, subordinate). As Ellen and Michael are just now discovering, trouble at work usually spills over into the home, and difficulties at home almost always interfere with work. If you don't develop healthy dependency in both arenas, you won't succeed in either one.

HEALTHY DEPENDENCY
AT WORK

For the first few days, Ellen tried to put the incident behind her, but she just couldn't get it out of her mind. She was haunted by the image of her mother that first night—face swollen and bruised, body bound in a thick, heavy cast, IV dripping in a steady rhythm, tubes and monitors everywhere.

During the first couple of days after the accident, Ellen stopped by the hospital after work. She quickly gave that up, though. She was just too tired—too anxious to get home—by the time she loaded up her briefcase at the end of a twelve-hour day. She tried coming over during lunch, but that didn't work either. She was too rushed, too distracted by a morning's worth of unreturned phone calls and half-finished projects. Finally, she stopped by on her way into work, and to her surprise, that went well. Her mother was most alert early in the morning, and Ellen had a ready excuse for leaving when she got uncomfortable.

And Ellen got uncomfortable nearly every day. Her mother was cranky and angry much of the time—frustrated at being immobilized, frightened of what the future might hold. Ellen was concerned that her mother might never recover completely, and she felt terribly guilty about this. But mostly Ellen worried about missing more and more time at work, falling further and further behind as her mother's rehab dragged on.

Ellen began to salve her worries by calling Theresa from the hospital each morning before she left for the office. Ellen felt more connected to her normal routine when she did this, and she figured Theresa could fill her in on any emerging problems that would require her attention that day.

The first time Ellen called, there really was an emergent situation: a crisis brewing over a missed proposal deadline. Ellen was annoyed, but she was surprised to discover she was also faintly pleased. She was gratified that a problem awaited her attention—a problem only she could solve.

On the second day, Ellen called at 9:15, and Theresa told her everything was fine, under control. Take your time, Theresa said. No hurry to get here.

It was the same the next day, and the day after that, and as the days stretched on, Ellen grew increasingly ambivalent about her morning phone calls to Theresa. She was glad things were going well at the office. She just wished things weren't going quite so well without her.

Ellen thought about this on her way across town one day, pondering her ambivalence and trying to make sense of it. She was creeping through a knot of traffic just west of Third Avenue when she was struck by a sudden impulse. It was such a strange impulse—so new to Ellen— that she didn't know what to make of it.

She drove on across town, but the impulse remained, so as she waited to make a left onto Broadway, Ellen gave in to this strange feeling and reached behind the seat for her cellphone. She hit the speed dial, and the phone rang twice before someone picked up.

"James?"

"Ellen? Are you okay? Is anything wrong?" James sounded stunned to hear her voice, which bothered Ellen a bit, but she pressed on.

"No, everything's fine. I just had an idea."

"What's that?"

"Let's go out to dinner tonight."

"Tonight? On a Wednesday?"

"Yeah. Why not?" Ellen tried to sound casual.

"What about Melissa and Steven?"

"Don't worry about it. I'll call Judy right now. She'll be at practice anyway. She'll pick them up."

"Well, all right," said James, but he sounded uncertain, even a bit suspicious. "Ellen, are you sure?"

"Absolutely. It'll be fun. I'll make a reservation somewhere. Meet me at the office at seven?"

"Okay. Seven at your office. Fine."

Now it was Ellen's turn to be suspicious. "James, are you okay? You sound...funny."

"No, I'm fine. I mean, I'm just wondering."

"Wondering what?"

"Ellen, what in the world has come over you?"

"To tell you the truth, James, I'm not sure. But I'm not going to fight it. I kind of like it."

There was a long pause at the other end of the line, then James's voice came on again.

"You know what, Ellen? Whatever it is, don't fight it, okay? I kind of like it, too."

It seems ironic that it took a crisis to get Ellen moving, but this sort of reaction isn't all that uncommon. Change is difficult—risky, too—and oftentimes it takes an event like this to shake us out of our old habits. Her mother's accident forced Ellen to take a hard look at herself and her priorities. Ellen has finally faced up to her detachment and the negative impact it's having on her life. Now maybe—just maybe—she's ready to take the next step, and turn insight into positive change.

In this chapter, we discuss healthy dependency at work. We begin by looking at some important parallels between family dynamics and organizational dynamics, then examine the unique healthy dependency opportunities of career relationships.

* * * * *

**Not everything that is faced can be changed,
but nothing can be changed until it is faced.**
—JAMES BALDWIN

YOUR ORGANIZATIONAL RELATIONSHIP STYLE

* * * * *

Everyone has their own way of relating to an organization, and many factors affect your *organizational relationship style*, including your beliefs about work, your first work experiences, your career aspirations, and the nature of the company with which you are affiliated. Remember that organizational roles don't always parallel other life roles: Some people are detached at work, but not at home; others are overdependent with family members, but not with colleagues.

To get a sense of your organizational relationship style, take a few minutes to answer the following questions about your current (or most recent) work experience. When we explore the dynamics of healthy career dependency, these answers will help you understand where you are right now, and where you want to be in the future.

What I like *most* about the company I work for is:_____

_____

_____

What I like *least* about the company I work for is:_____

_____

_____

My *ideal boss* would have the following characteristics:_____

_____

_____

My *ideal colleague* would have the following characteristics:_____

_____

_____

My *greatest joy* at work is:_____

_____

_____

My *biggest problem* at work is:_____

_____

_____

The Corporate Family

Toward the end of Chapter 7 we noted that in certain ways, companies are like families. In his 1993 Award Address to the American Psychological Association, management expert Harry Levinson put it even more bluntly: "All organizations," argued Levinson, "recapitulate the family structure of the culture in which they are embedded."

What does it mean to say that today's companies "recapitulate family structure"? To answer this question, we must explore the dynamics of the modern organization, and look below the surface. Let's examine three key parallels between *family* and *company*:

- *Roles and alliances* Everyone within an organization has an *explicit role*—the formal role they've been assigned by the company (accounts manager, payroll supervisor, public relations director). Each person also has an *implicit role*—a hidden role—which can be just as important as their explicit role. "Rabble-Rouser," "Good Soldier," "Office Mom," "Ruthless Climber"—these are just a few of the implicit roles that emerge within organizations. As in families, people within organizations form alliances that preserve their roles, further their goals, and help them acquire power and influence. Some of these alliances are out in the open; others are hidden and hard to identify.
- *Communication pathways and organizational politics* There are two basic forms of communication within an organization. *Vertical communication* flows across levels (for example, from manager to subordinate). This type of communication is dictated largely (though by no means exclusively) by a company's *organizational structure*—the formal setup of explicit roles and responsibilities within the system. *Horizontal communication* flows within levels (for example, between two team members). This type of communication is determined largely by *organizational politics*—the underlying "who-knows-who" dynamic that drives day-to-day life

in most companies. Hidden roles and alliances are a primary determinant of horizontal information flow.

- *Organizational dependency and organizational detachment* Some people assume an overdependent or detached role within any organization. People in an overdependent role come to rely on the company for more than just a paycheck: To the person in an overdependent role ("Good Soldier," for example), the company is a key part of their identity. They are highly invested in maintaining their link to the organization, and if this connection is severed, sadness and depression will result. People in a detached role (like "Rabble-Rouser") may also be secretly dependent on

OVERDEPENDENCE AND DETACHMENT IN THE WORKPLACE

* * * * *

As this table shows, when people assume an overdependent or detached role within the organization, they harm themselves and their colleagues in a variety of ways.

	The Overdependent Colleague	The Detached Colleague
Typical hidden role	Good Soldier	Rabble-Rouser
Surface behavior	Insecure/ Anxious	Distant/ Self-Involved
Feeling toward the company	Weakness/ Vulnerability	Discontent/ Alienation
Relationship with supervisors	Timid	Guarded
Effect of disappointment	Sadness/ Depression	Anger/ Hostility

the company, just as detached family members are secretly dependent on other family members. But in contrast to the overdependent person, the detached person relates to the company by pushing it away and keeping it at arm's length. Don't be fooled by this surface behavior: Though he might not admit it (even to himself), the detached person is also highly invested in the organization—he just expresses it in a different way. The detached employee will be just as hurt as the overdependent employee if the organization lets him down, but his response is likely to be anger rather than depression.

Four Modes of Healthy Career Dependency

Roles, alliances, and communication patterns tell us how families and organizations are alike. Families and organizations also differ in many ways, and one of these differences has to do with how healthy dependency is expressed. Organizational relationships involve different healthy dependency opportunities than family relationships do, and different risks as well.

As we'll see, healthy career dependency requires considerable relationship flexibility. To thrive in the modern workplace you must tailor your behavior to fit each relationship and find ways to deal with multiple, conflicting relationships simultaneously.

Let's begin by looking at the four major modes of healthy career dependency:

- *Leadership: Connecting Downward* There are leaders at every level within an organization—people who (regardless of their assigned role) are looked to by others for guidance and inspiration. Being a good leader doesn't mean giving orders and expecting that everyone will comply. On the contrary, effective leadership involves actively *connecting downward*—gaining and maintaining people's loyalty, confidence, and respect. To do this, you must behave in ways

175

that make others want to follow your example and further your agenda.

- *Followership: Connecting Upward* Everyone knows it takes certain skills to be an effective leader, but sometimes people are surprised to learn that being an effective follower takes skill as well. Followership is not a passive process—far from it. Effective followership means actively *connecting upward*. It means trusting other people enough to follow their lead, but still having the self-confidence to voice your opinion—constructively, respectfully—when it conflicts with the majority view or that of a supervisor.

- *Collegiality: Constructive Interdependence* Researchers who study organizational dynamics have identified two key qualities that make for effective collegiality: *teamwork* and *trust*. Teamwork means putting the good of the group ahead of personal gain. Trust (in this context) means believing that your efforts will be recognized and rewarded. Teamwork and trust lead to *constructive interdependence*—healthy dependent collegial relationships and the kind of selfless collaboration that results in good, creative work.

- *Mentorship: Facilitating Growth* Effective mentorship means *facilitating growth* in the person whose career you're guiding. Like good parents, good mentors are invested enough in the relationship to take joy in their mentee's achievements, but secure enough to let the mentee "own" their successes fully and completely. Good mentorship also requires that the mentor maintain firm boundaries, avoiding enmeshment and conflicts of interest. As we'll see, when the boundaries between mentors and mentees blur, growth ends and manipulation begins.

Leadership

Once you recognize that effective leaders lead by inspiring—not commanding—it is easy to see how healthy dependency is critical to good leadership. By taking the time to connect downward, you turn coercion into collaboration, and intimidation into

TURNING ORGANIZATIONAL OVERDEPENDENCE INTO HEALTHY CAREER DEPENDENCY

* * * * *

If you find yourself in an overdependent organizational role, you must move beyond this role before you can bring healthy dependency into the workplace. Here are a few tips to get you started:

• *Get some of your dependency needs met elsewhere.* Sometimes the problem isn't that you're too dependent, but that you're trying to get too many dependency needs met in one place. So spread it around a bit. Deliberately seek guidance and support from people not affiliated with your organization (like colleagues at other companies). Not only will you develop healthier work relationships, but by seeking support from colleagues who work elsewhere, you'll be building your networking skills. Next time your colleague needs advice about a problem, perhaps she'll come to you.

• *Be realistic about career risks.* It's okay to be anxious about doing a good job (at moderate levels, anxiety sharpens mental focus and increases our motivation to do well). But if you're *overanxious*—if you're paralyzed with fear about messing up—take time to look critically at your career vulnerability. Remember that in this litigious society, firing (or even demoting) someone involves legal risk on the company's part. Remember, too, that hiring and training a new employee is an expensive proposition. Sometimes people do get downsized out of jobs (but you can't really control that anyway). So ask yourself: What are the odds that I'll make a mistake that would literally get me fired?

• *Act mindfully.* Overdependence becomes a career-killer when you alienate colleagues and supervisors. This usually occurs when you act impulsively—when you get so worried that you seek help from others in a desperate, panicky state or bug people repeatedly for reassurance and support. When you have the urge to seek help from co-workers, slow yourself down. Ask yourself whether you're seeking help to avoid challenges (bad) or to learn and grow (good). If you're about to ask for help for the wrong reasons, don't do it—it's not worth it. But if you're asking for help out of growth motivation, then go ahead. It's an opportunity to get the support you need and build healthy dependency skills at the same time.

OVERCOMING ORGANIZATIONAL DETACHMENT: FROM UNHEALTHY ANGER TO HEALTHY CAREER DEPENDENCY

* * * * *

Organizational detachment can be even more destructive than organizational overdependence because it usually comes with a good dose of bottled-up anger and resentment. If you have assumed a detached role at work, here's how you can begin to replace unhealthy anger with healthy career dependency:

- *Focus on the negative impact of your anger.* Sometimes people actually enjoy being angry—they revel in their resentment, and feel righteous indignation about all the wrongs they've suffered. When we allow ourselves to wallow in anger like this, we lose sight of the negative impact our anger may be having on our career (not to mention our personal and family life). So take the time to explore the negative impact of your anger—on yourself, your coworkers, your children, and your spouse. When you take a close look at anger's negative effects (make a written list if you have to), it becomes easier to see how the costs outweigh the benefits. Knowing how anger hurts you won't cause you to change, but as James Baldwin pointed out, it is a necessary first step.

- *Understand the roots of your discontent.* Sometimes we're genuinely angry at an organization, but sometimes we direct anger at supervisors and others because it's easier to be mad at them than at the people we're actually angry at (a process known as *displacement*). So ask yourself: Is your discontent at work a reflection of problems at home? Does it stem from unrealistic goals you picked up from your parents ("Make CEO by age thirty or you've really screwed up")? When you understand the roots of your discontent, you'll learn something important about yourself, and you can begin to channel your anger more constructively.

- *Change your behavior—the feelings will follow.* If all else fails and you still feel resentment toward the organization, try changing your behavior. Act more collegial and more pleasant. Chat by the coffeemaker, or ask people to lunch. Sometimes by changing our behavior, we change the way others see us and treat us. The work environment becomes more pleasant—and less stressful—and the anger may dissipate all by itself.

admiration. When leaders connect with subordinates through their actions as well as their words, they promote mutual respect and a positive work environment.

Four strategies will help you connect downward and become a better leader:

- *Setting goals* Effective goal-setting requires that you *communicate clearly* and *accommodate peoples' psychological needs*. To *communicate clearly*, you must articulate the long-term goals of each new initiative (so people know what they're working toward), explain how each person's efforts contribute to these goals (so people see how they fit into the big picture), and acknowledge the difficult aspects of the task (so no one feels misled when frustrations arise). To *accommodate peoples' psychological needs*, you must set realistic—achievable—goals. This usually means breaking each long-term goal into a series of incremental sub-goals that contribute to the overall effort. When large-scale projects are broken down in this way, employees receive reinforcement as each sub-goal is met, and are reminded regularly how their individual efforts contribute to the group's collective work.

- *Enhancing motivation* Breaking large goals into sub-goals is one way to keep people motivated. A second useful strategy is to create a reward structure that is perceived as being equitable. When employees feel they are not being treated fairly, organizational detachment results, and productivity declines. Ironically, while rewards must be reasonably generous, it is also important that leaders not place too much emphasis on monetary carrots and sticks. Studies show that overemphasizing monetary issues has the paradoxical effect of decreasing worker motivation and commitment (in part because workers become more focused on the rewards than on the work itself). By rewarding people's efforts equitably but without fanfare, you will enhance their growth motivation: People feel connected to the organization (since the company is treating them well), and invested in doing good work for its own sake (that is, for intrinsic rather than extrinsic reasons).

179

- *Solving problems* Effective leadership requires considerable relationship flexibility, especially when it comes to problem-solving. By creating an environment wherein people can collaborate productively, you encourage healthy dependency among team members. By periodically stepping out of your leadership role to "get your hands dirty" and help solve problems alongside subordinates, you connect with people at different levels within the organization. You also reinforce a sense of teamwork and collaboration, and gain credibility by demonstrating that you are willing to take on the kinds of challenges that everyone else must confront in their day-to-day work.
- *Leading by example* Reaching out to employees—asking for their input and advice—is an invaluable leadership tool. This is one of those areas where actions speak louder than

---

BRAINSTORMING

* * * * *

One of the most effective problem-solving strategies is *brainstorming*—encouraging everyone to contribute ideas freely within a group, with no critical evaluation until everybody's had their say. When you find yourself in a leadership role, you'll want to encourage colleagues and subordinates to brainstorm anytime a vexing problem presents itself. A. F. Osborne —who first popularized the technique more than forty years ago—advises brainstorming groups to adhere to four basic rules:

- *Rule 1: No criticism.* Postpone judgment until all ideas are on the table.
- *Rule 2: Let it flow.* Generate as many ideas as possible—the more the better.
- *Rule 3: Encourage risk-taking.* The more unique the idea, the better (don't worry yet about whether it's practical).
- *Rule 4: Play.* Build upon, respond to, twist, and invert existing ideas—the more you play, the more creative you'll be.

words: You must not only solicit input, you must also implement it periodically, so people see that you take their ideas and opinions seriously. By asking for help from employees, you model the kind of healthy dependent behavior you want them to exhibit. You also foster connection-based thinking, as people see that *asking for help* isn't the same as *being helpless*. When this idea takes hold, your employees will feel that they can ask for help, too—from colleagues, subordinates, and supervisors alike. They'll know that when they seek support from others, they won't be perceived as having "failed" in some way.

Followership

Because the essence of followership is allowing oneself to be influenced, it is all too easy to take the next step, and give up control completely. Thus, a key challenge of good followership is avoiding overdependence on supervisors and colleagues. To do this, you must replace *mindless* (reflexive) followership with *mindful* (planned) followership.

Mindful followership involves using your healthy dependency skills to connect upward, so you maintain a sense of control even as you work to further another person's agenda. You'll not only be a better follower, but you'll strengthen the skills you need to become an effective leader as well, both now and in the future.

Here are techniques for connecting upward and becoming a more effective follower:

- *Establishing trustworthiness* Just as leaders must establish *trust* to motivate followers, followers need to demonstrate their *trustworthiness* so supervisors feel comfortable delegating responsibility to them. And just as establishing trust requires action (not words), demonstrating trustworthiness is something you do, not something you say. It requires that you follow through on your commitments (so be careful what you promise), meet all your deadlines (no excuses), ask for help when you need it (don't feign omnipotence), and volunteer to pitch in when an extra hand is required (don't wait to be asked). By doing these four things, you'll foster healthy dependency between yourself and your supervisors. You'll know you can rely on them for guidance and direction, and they'll know they can rely on you to help them reach their goals.

- *Avoiding helplessness* To maintain a sense of control when following another person's lead, use connection-based thinking to reframe your role: Don't think of followership as passivity, but as a form of active responsibility. At the same time, use emotional synergy to move beyond childhood stereotypes: Followers are not failures (as many of us were brought up to believe), but integral members of a team. When you use your healthy dependency skills in this way, you'll not only have a greater sense of control, but you'll find it easier to move back and forth smoothly between leadership and followership roles.

- *Accepting responsibility* To err is human. To avoid taking responsibility for our errors is the surest way to torpedo trust among supervisors and colleagues alike. No matter how strong the impulse may be to foist off responsibility on a coworker, fight that impulse. Acknowledge your role in the error (if you had any), but don't call attention to your colleagues' mistakes. If asked directly about shared responsibility for a foul-up, respond with just the facts—no embellishment or interpretation. Mistakes happen—and you *will* make them—but it's easier to accept responsibility gracefully if you use connection-based thinking to separate the *act* from the *person*. Just because you make errors, this does not mean you are error-prone.

- *Communicating openly* Communicating is easy when things are going well. The real challenge comes during difficult times. When dealing with problems, be forthright. Don't hem and haw, or try to "break the news gently." When you disagree with a supervisor's viewpoint or that of a colleague,

BAD FOLLOWERSHIP: GROUPTHINK

* * * * *

What do these three disastrous decisions have in common?

- Kennedy's decision to invade Cuba's Bay of Pigs (which nearly led to a U.S.-Soviet nuclear confrontation)
- Nixon's decision to cover up the Watergate break-in (which destroyed his presidency and harmed the nation)
- NASA's decision to launch the space shuttle Challenger (which exploded seventy-three seconds after liftoff, killing everyone on board)

Answer: In all three decisions, key advisors smelled disaster lurking in the wings, but said nothing because they didn't want to go against the group.

These three disastrous decisions (and countless others) were the result of *groupthink*—a dissent-squelching dynamic wherein peoples' desire to avoid conflict overrides their willingness to say how they feel. Groupthink is a classic example of bad followership because when you allow yourself to go along with an erroneous group judgment, you are abrogating one of your most important followership responsibilities: having the self-confidence to voice your opinion, even when it conflicts with the majority view. Think how different things might have been if just one of NASA's senior scientists had the gumption to stand up to the group and argue forcefully against the Challenger launch.

Psychologist Irvin Janis, who coined the term *groupthink*, suggests several remedies that minimize conformity pressure and encourage healthy dissent:

- Bring into the discussion some devil's advocates who are likely to oppose the majority view.
- Break the group into subgroups who consider the situation separately, then come together to share their perspectives (that way subgroup members can support each other).
- Replace public voting with private ballots (so people feel free to disagree).
- Have the leader save her opinions for later (don't bias the discussion by jumping in too soon).
- Use brainstorming techniques to encourage creative thinking.

state the reasons for your disagreement as diplomatically as possible. Make your case succinctly, argue it forcefully (but respectfully), and let the chips fall where they may. Don't use your platform to impugn others' judgment or effort: You'll just weaken your argument (by delivering two messages at once) and alienate those who perceive your words as an attack. Be sure to choose your battles carefully as well: Ignore trivial details, focus on bigger issues, and remember that the *occasional* differing opinion commands respect, but the *persistent* differing opinion makes you look like a malcontent.

Collegiality

Since the key to collegiality is constructive interdependence, it is easy to see why people in overdependent and detached roles are usually bad colleagues. The overdependent person is too insecure to let down her guard and become a genuine team player. The detached person is too self-involved to put the good of the group ahead of personal gain.

Four strategies will enable you to replace overdependent and detached collegial relationships with healthy dependent collegial relationships:

- *Balancing cooperation and competition* Let's be honest: We all want to get ahead. No one likes being passed over in favor of a colleague—in part because of the financial implications, but also because being passed over is a blow to our self-esteem (it's like sibling rivalry all over again). In many business settings, cooperation is undermined by competition: People believe they must not only perform *well*, but *better* than their colleagues. While there's some truth to this belief (everyone can't get the next promotion), it's also important to recognize that success is not a zero-sum game. It is possible for many people within an organization to succeed, even if some advance more quickly than others. So when you do well, be generous in sharing credit. When a colleague does well, be generous with your praise. You might feel like you're hurting your chances by doing these things, but you're not. You're building good relationships with supervisors (by connecting upward) and with colleagues (by acknowledging their achievements). These relationships will pay off down the line.

- *Delaying gratification* This brings us to the second key strategy for good collegiality: Know that teamwork will bring rewards, even if those rewards don't come as quickly as you'd like. Delaying gratification can be difficult, but it's an important career skill: Studies show that by pushing too hard, you can actually slow career progress. If you feel your contributions are not being recognized, begin by looking inward to determine if your perceptions are accurate. If you decide that they are, schedule an appointment to talk with your supervisor and fill her in on what you've accomplished lately. Don't focus on the promotion you didn't get, but on the contributions you've been making to the organization. Ask if there's anything else you should be doing, and offer to help where it's needed most. And be sure to keep your goals for this meeting in mind as you speak, so you don't veer "off message." You're not asking for special treatment (which would be manipulative and dependent), but setting the stage for future success (by focusing on how to do better).

- *Winning and losing well* No one wins all the time, and if you expect to, you're setting yourself up for frustration and failure. When you don't get that longed-for raise or hoped-for promotion, allow yourself to experience the negative emotions fully and completely (anger, frustration, resentment, hurt). Then, when you've had your fill of self-pity (two days tops), let it go. Use connection-based thinking to separate the act from the person: Even though you lost this time, that does not make you a loser. If you find that the quality of your work is being impaired by lingering anger, consider meeting with your supervisor to clear the air. Use the techniques we just discussed to make this meeting a constructive

NETWORKING

* * * * *

Networking—developing relationships with clients and colleagues to further your career—provides numerous opportunities to use your healthy dependency skills. Here are just a few:

- *One good turn deserves another.* When someone does you a favor, acknowledge it. When the opportunity arises, return it. Networking is a two-way street, and if you don't do your part, the relationships will gradually erode. There's no need to keep a tally of who's done what for whom, but be sure to reciprocate (it's better to do this too often than not often enough).

- *Connect through actions as well as words.* You can't build connections with promises; in the end, it's what you do that counts. So let your behaviors speak for themselves. Follow through on your commitments. Don't disappear for months, then show up on someone's doorstep when you need something. Instead, make a point of reconnecting periodically—especially during those times when you *don't* need a favor.

- *Understand the principles of healthy interdependence.* People who network are *interdependent*—they help each other get ahead. Sometimes that may mean steering a colleague to one of your competitors. If this seems self-defeating, take the long view: Assume that your good deed will pay off down the line.

- *Network with competitors as well as allies.* To the extent they'll allow it, build positive relationships with your competitors as well as your clients and colleagues. Personal relationships keep you in the loop, and make it less likely that a competitor will do something truly nasty and underhanded. Besides, today's competitor may be tomorrow's colleague (or supervisor).

exchange of ideas rather than an angry clash of adversaries. Listen carefully to what your supervisor says, and use this feedback to adjust your behavior so the next promotion will be yours.

- *Building credit* It seems counterintuitive, but sometimes losing well is the best thing that could possibly happen. By accepting an uncomfortable decision, you show your colleagues that you're a genuine team player. You build credit with your supervisor by accepting her decision gracefully, and you can "bank" this credit and cash it in at a later date. If you handle the situation well, others will remember that you've been a good colleague, contributed to the growth of the organization, and made a compelling case for future reward. At some point your patience will pay off, and that reward will come. (And if it doesn't, the problem probably lies in the company, not you. You can then take the next step and disconnect from this dysfunctional organization, as we discuss on page 188.)

Mentorship

To be a good mentor—to nurture another person's career—you must assume a pseudo-parental role and facilitate your mentee's growth. The mentoring relationship provides myriad opportunities to use your healthy dependency skills, but it also entails more risks than other types of professional relationships. Four strategies will help you become a more effective mentor:

- *Setting clear limits* Mentoring brings power, and while there's nothing wrong with enjoying your influence, it is important that you don't exploit it. Begin by setting clear limits on what you will and won't do for your mentee (you *will* provide guidance, but you *won't* give special treatment). Also set limits on what you will and won't ask your mentee to do for you (you *will* ask for that extra bit of effort on key projects, but you *won't* ask for any personal favors). Having

DISCONNECTING FROM A
DYSFUNCTIONAL ORGANIZATION

* * * * *

Sometimes you do all the right things, and the rewards still don't come. This frustrating situation can be caused by any number of factors (badly planned reward system, selfish supervisor, poor person-company fit). Whatever the underlying problem may be, there comes a time when it's best to cut your losses and move on.

Disconnecting from a dysfunctional organization is never pleasant, but by using healthy dependency and a little common sense, you can make the disconnection process go smoothly and keep relationships that will help you down the line.

- *Use your remaining time to build connections.* Resist the urge to trash the company on your way out the door. If you do, your colleagues will shun you (after all, they still want to feel good about where they work). Be as positive as you can about this career transition, and use your colleagues' insights as you plan your next move. You never know: One of your coworkers might know of a company that's looking for someone with exactly your skills and experience.

- *Forget about revenge.* Revenge fantasies trap you into an ongoing dysfunctional relationship with your old company. Have them briefly (everyone does), then let them go. You can't possibly win by getting even, and it's better to put your anger behind you and move on.

- *Think of your exit interview as an opportunity.* Some people make the mistake of unloading during their exit interview—enumerating every wrong they suffered and every employee's flaw. Don't do this. You might feel better in the short run, but you'll hurt yourself in the long run. For one thing, what you say might come back to haunt you later on (word does get around). For another, the exit interview represents your final impression within the organization—and final impressions can last a long time.

clear limits in mind from the outset is critical (though whether you communicate these limits to your mentee is less important than sticking to them in the face of temptation). Whatever you do, resist the urge to make an exception "just this one time": Once a boundary has been crossed it can be difficult—sometimes impossible—to go back.

- *Clarifying your relationship goals* Take time to clarify your mentoring goals. What do you hope to get from this relationship? Why are you invested in helping this person? Selfless mentoring (like selfless parenting) can be among the most rewarding of all relationships, but it's important that you be brutally honest with yourself right from the start. Do you have some sort of hidden agenda? Do you secretly hope to seduce your mentee (or allow her to seduce you)? Are you mentoring this person to acquire power within the organization? Is this a way of showing up your colleagues?

- *Avoiding conflicts of interest* If you answered yes to any of these questions, your mentoring is motivated by personal gain, not mentee growth. It is likely that your mentoring relationship is being compromised by one or more conflicts of interest that will lead you to manipulate your mentee in ways that hurt rather than help. The stage is now set for boundaries to blur, and if this happens, you'll not only undermine your mentee's career, but yours as well.

- *Knowing when boundaries blur* The blurred boundaries that follow from conflicts of interest invariably lead to *destructive enmeshment* between mentor and mentee. Mentors begin to ask for things they shouldn't (like having the mentee do personal errands). Mentees begin to encourage dependency in the mentor (by making themselves "indispensable"). Mentor and mentee may even become involved in a mutually exploitative sexual relationship. Now both people are trapped—destructively dependent on each other in ways they might not even see. At this point each person is likely to engage in a variety of manipulative tactics designed to control the other. It goes without saying (but we'll say it anyway): *A sexual relationship between mentor and mentee is unethical under any and all circumstances.* It not only destroys careers, but lives as well.

Arthur: Model Employee, Nightmare Retiree

Arthur worked for a medical research firm, and he was an ideal employee: Always the first person to arrive in the morning, always the last to leave at night. Arthur worked hard, took on many of the most challenging, unpleasant tasks, and seemed to be one of those rare people who was completely without ambition. Arthur was happy right where he was—in a mid-level laboratory researcher position—and unlike the rest of us (who couldn't wait to get promoted), Arthur showed no signs of wanting to move up into an executive suite.

Everyone who worked with Arthur could tell that he thrived on his routine and genuinely enjoyed having someone else take responsibility for planning the research projects. All he had to do was carry out the protocols that were assigned to him, and this he did flawlessly. We all assumed that Arthur would stay right where he was until he retired, and we were right. He did.

That's when the trouble started. When the structure of day-to-day work was taken away, Arthur lost his center—his reason for being. He seemed lonely and lost, confused and directionless. At first he called the lab frequently, asking how things were going. Then he began stopping by for lunch. Finally one day Arthur showed up at the lab around 10 A.M. "just to say hi."

The problem was he wouldn't leave.

Arthur began showing up every day, hanging around the lab, making conversation, and (to use his word) "puttering." He wasn't doing any harm, really, and perhaps we shouldn't have said anything. But after a couple of weeks of Arthur's daily visits, his replacement complained to the laboratory supervisor, who took it upstairs to the head of personnel. The head of personnel called Arthur in and explained as gently as she could that his presence was preventing his replacement from establishing herself in the lab. It was distracting the researchers, she said, and interfering with their work. He needed to stop showing up at the office. He was hurting the company.

Arthur seemed to take the news well (it wasn't in his nature to complain), and after that day, he never stopped by again. We called him once, on the occasion of a coworker's retirement, and asked him to drop by for the party. But Arthur said no, he didn't feel comfortable, and we didn't press the issue. It's been quite a few years now, and no one has heard from Arthur—not even a card. As far as we know, he's still living at home, but sometimes we wonder how he's doing, and wish he'd come by once in a while.

As we'll see in Chapter 10, retirement can be a difficult transition for anyone, but especially for the overdependent person. The loss of structure and collegial interaction can be particularly hard on someone whose identity revolves around pleasing others. For Arthur, retirement was a negative experience. Perhaps he shouldn't have retired at all. But even for an overdependent person like Arthur, retirement need not be a time of loneliness and loss. Retirement can be an opportunity to deepen one's ties to others rather than severing them, but this takes planning and careful use of a lifetime's worth of healthy dependency skills.

Looking Ahead: Healthy Dependency During Difficult Times

If we allowed ourselves to dwell on every possible catastrophe we might experience, we'd spend all our waking hours pondering life's troubles. Fortunately, nature has equipped the human mind with a set of cognitive avoidance strategies (some psychologists call them *defenses*) that help us fend off our fears, and keep anxiety at bay. Good, strong defenses let us remain *aware* of life's problems without becoming *obsessed* with them.

Not ruminating about potential problems is one thing; coping effectively with problems when they occur is another. It doesn't matter how carefully you plan: Bad things happen to everyone. The trick is to use your healthy dependency skills to reach out to other people and get the help and support you need to make it through difficult times. If you have the self-confidence to lean on others, you'll survive life's inevitable downturns. You might even find that they help you grow stronger.

HEALTHY DEPENDENCY
DURING DIFFICULT TIMES

Michael was not, by nature, a contemplative person, but these were unusual times. He had never lived alone before—stayed at home throughout college, then moved directly from his parents' house to his first apartment with Kathleen. Now that he and Kathleen were separating, Michael would be on his own for the first time.

He was sitting at home, in the den, in the dark, wondering what the next few months would bring. How would it feel to live alone? Would he and Kathleen reconcile, or was this a permanent split? And what about Kimberly—how would she cope? In many ways she was the strongest of the three—the most level-headed, the least perturbable. Would she blame her father for breaking apart the family?

As Michael sat pondering, he looked out the den window. He watched the cars going by, and the shadows in the windows across the street. He was surprised to discover that while he wondered about the future, he wasn't really worried about it. Something had changed within Michael during the past several weeks—something deep inside that he couldn't explain. He'd found a strength—a solid core—he never knew he had. Had it been there all along, untapped, undetected?

Michael was gazing out the window when his attention was captured by silence: The music upstairs had stopped. He heard Kim padding around her room and the sound of a closet door opening and closing. He heard his daughter's footsteps coming down the stairs, then along the hallway that led to the den. There was a soft knock on the door.

"Dad?"

"Kim. Come in." Michael reached for the lamp on the nearby table.

"No, Dad. Leave it. It's nice this way."

Michael eased back into his seat as Kim walked over to the window. She stood for a moment without saying anything. The far-away sound of a barking dog floated into the room.

"I never realized how much of the sky you could see from here," said Kim. She leaned on the windowsill to get a better look. "The view in my room is blocked by trees."

"Really. I never noticed."

"Well, it's kind of nice in the spring and the fall." Kim smiled slightly, still looking up at the stars.

She turned to face her father. Her eyes had adjusted to the darkness of the den.

"Dad, I want you to know things will be okay. Between us, I mean. I've been thinking about it. Even though I'll be living here with Mom, we'll still be able to spend time together."

"I'm looking forward to it," said Michael.

Kim looked at her father, and even in the dark he could see that her eyes were moist. She looked older—much older—than sixteen.

"I'm sorry, Dad."

"It's okay. It's not your fault."

"Oh, I don't mean it that way. I'm just...sorry. I'll miss having things the way they were."

"Me, too," said Michael.

Kim turned back to the window just in time to see a car pull into the driveway. She watched as the car parked and waited, its engine still running, headlights on.

"I'd better go," said Kim. "Melanie's here. We're going over to Andrea's to study. Big chem test tomorrow."

Michael stood up. "Okay. Be careful. Back by eleven, right?"

Kim walked over to her father, paused, looked up.

"Absolutely, Dad," she said. "Back by eleven. You can count on it."

> * * * * *
> **Crises refine life. In them you
> discover what you are.**
> —ALLAN K. CHALMERS

Trouble strips away our veneer and reveals the true person hidden inside. It brings out our strengths, and our weaknesses, too; it exaggerates our differences and predispositions.

Healthy dependency is important when things are going well, but it's even more critical during troubling times. When we experience a significant setback or loss, we're vulnerable—not just emotionally, but physically, too. Studies show that stress—especially chronic stress—puts us at risk for a wide array of health problems, from minor illnesses (like colds and flu) to major ones (like heart disease and cancer).

That's the bad news. Here's the good news: Research also shows that healthy dependency can protect us from the harmful effects of stress. Healthy dependency helps buffer negative emotions, gives us an outlet to express troubling feelings, and lets us feel connected to others, so we don't have to struggle alone.

In this chapter we discuss healthy dependency during difficult times. We begin with an overview of life's transitions and the process of coping with loss and change. We look at how overdependence and detachment undermine our ability to cope and how healthy dependency can help us gain confidence and strength as we face up to a difficult situation.

Life's Transitions

Life is a series of beginnings and endings, gains and losses, victories and defeats. For every joyful surprise, there's an unanticipated setback; for every challenge met, an opportunity missed.

Any life change, whether positive or negative, requires that we *cope*—adjust our thinking, manage our emotions, and alter our behavior to deal with the new situation. Let's take a closer look at this process:

- *The stress response* Stress is the formal term scientists use to describe our physical and psychological reactions to change. Stress isn't something that happens *to* us, it's something that happens *within* us. For the human animal, change signals danger, and when faced with the unexpected we feel threatened. Our heart begins to race, our breathing increases, our palms sweat, and we experience the classic *stress response* first identified by Canadian researcher Hans Selye more than fifty years ago. Once the threat has passed, the body restores its old equilibrium (the heart slows, breathing returns to normal, etc.). But as Selye discovered, bringing the body back to baseline takes energy. It's an active process. That's why stress—especially chronic, unrelenting stress—wears us down, saps our strength, and makes us susceptible to illness and disease.

- *Eustress and distress* Most people think of stress as something that follows a negative event, but stress occurs following *any* significant life change. Divorce is stressful, but so is getting married. Flunking out of school is stressful, but so is graduating with honors. Researchers distinguish negative stress (*distress*) from positive stress (*eustress*), but they've found that at the most basic physical level, our reactions are pretty much the same, no matter what type of event we've experienced.

- *Challenge and opportunity* Though some people (like skydivers and bungee-jumpers) deliberately seek out stress, most of us go out of our way to avoid it. Regardless of whether we chase challenges or shun them, studies show that when we cope effectively, we gain confidence and strength. Nearly twenty years ago, Yale University researcher Jack Tebes found that young adults who coped successfully with the death of a parent reported increased self-confidence and self-awareness months after their loss. Later researchers found the same pattern in cancer survivors and victims of

196

sexual assault. These important *trauma-strength* findings confirm what many of us already suspect: Inside every challenge lies a hidden opportunity—a chance to master a difficult situation and grow from the experience.

STRESS-REDUCTION THROUGH EMOTIONAL UNBURDENING: A BRIEF EXERCISE

* * * * *

As we'll soon see, one of the most important benefits of healthy dependency is that it provides an outlet for expressing negative emotions. By disclosing troubling feelings you release pent-up tension and anxiety, and studies show it doesn't matter whether you open up in private or with a trusted friend: The important thing is that you express your feelings openly and honestly—especially those you haven't talked about before.

If you'd like to experience this yourself, try the following exercise, which is based on the pioneering work of health psychologist James Pennebaker (we've used the procedure successfully as well, in some of our own investigations).

All you need is something to write on. Here's what to do:

On a blank sheet of paper (or a blank computer screen), describe an upsetting or traumatic event that happened to you at some time in the past. The event can be a recent one or one that took place years ago. The important thing is that you describe exactly *how you felt during and after this event* and *how the event affected you*. Be as detailed and descriptive as possible—it's important that you hold nothing back from your description. When you have finished writing, reread the material you've written to be sure it captures the experience fully and completely.

Studies show that this exercise, repeated periodically, can actually reduce stress, boost the immune system, and improve health. To learn more about how unburdening yourself of negative emotions can help you, both physically and psychologically, read on....

CONTRASTING VULNERABILITIES: OVERDEPENDENCE-AND DETACHMENT-RELATED STRESSORS

* * * * *

Some events (like the death of a loved one) are upsetting to everyone. Beyond this, studies show that overdependent and detached people are sensitive to different types of negative life events—they have different *vulnerabilities* (what scientists call contrasting *diatheses*). By knowing your relationship style and the events you're likely to find upsetting, you can prepare yourself ahead of time and minimize the disruptive impact of these experiences.

Among the events most upsetting to overdependent people are:

- interpersonal conflict (for example, an argument with a friend)
- relationship disruption (like a loved one's vacation)
- being thrust into an unwanted leadership position
- changing work environments (even if a promotion is involved)
- having to parent independently, without a partner's support (for example, following a divorce)

Among the events most upsetting to detached people are:

- unstructured social interactions with unfamiliar people
- emotional discussions (heart-to-heart talks)
- being compelled to engage in collaborative work
- medical tests and hospital stays (because of the forced intimacy and loss of control)
- having to intervene on behalf of a troubled family member (like a child who's struggling in school)

Three Phases of Coping

The *body* might not know whether stress is positive or negative, but the *mind* surely does. From a psychological perspective, there's no question: Negative events present the greatest challenge. Any time we lose something we value—be it a loved one, a job, or a dearly-held dream—we go through the same three-stage coping process.

Phase 1: Short-term reaction

Short-term reaction to loss begins immediately, and in most people, this phase lasts anywhere from a few days to a few weeks. Three responses—*recoil, regression,* and *retreat*—are involved.

- *Recoil* When loss is profound, our defenses are temporarily overwhelmed. As a result, we *recoil,* or turn inward. So much mental energy is tied up in dealing with the loss that we have trouble thinking clearly. We experience a kind of "cognitive shutdown"—a mental numbness that is nature's way of protecting us from too-terrible pain.
- *Regression* With recoil comes *regression*—the re-emergence of childlike feelings we thought were gone for good. We may find ourselves crying uncontrollably or falling back into old habits (like hair-twisting or nail-biting). We may even feel like a child again, needing to be held and comforted as if we were four years old.
- *Retreat* As we recoil cognitively and regress emotionally, we withdraw from other people—a process known as *social retreat.* At modest levels, retreat involves distancing ourselves from others, and spending more time on our own. In its extreme form, retreat can turn into complete physical withdrawal: We remain in bed, hopeless and helpless, neither eating nor sleeping, alone in our sorrow.

Phase 2: From chaos to balance

Healing begins as we enter the second stage of coping: We *re-emerge* (both cognitively and emotionally), *reframe* our loss (so we understand what happened), and *review* the situation (to find meaning in our pain).

- *Re-emerging* It can take anywhere from a few days to a few weeks (sometimes longer), but most people eventually *re-emerge* after loss. Tentative at first, re-emergence begins

GRIEVING AND MOURNING

* * * * *

We sometimes use these terms interchangeably, but in fact they mean different things. *Grieving* describes one's immediate, short-term response to loss—the unstable, unsteady feeling that comes quick on the heels of a tragedy. Grieving occurs during Coping Phase 2, and it is characterized by a chaotic, torn-apart, will-I-make-it-through-the-day sensation that usually (but not always) fades within a few weeks of the event.

Mourning comes later, and lasts longer: It refers to a deeper process of coming to terms with loss (Coping Phase 3). As Freud pointed out nearly a century ago, the profound feelings of emptiness that characterize mourning tell us something important: Mourning is not simply sadness about an external loss—it's a process wherein we accept that a part of our *self* has died (the part that was connected to the lost person or dream). That's why mourning hurts so much: When we mourn, we discover that we've not only lost something we cared about, but an important piece of ourselves as well.

when we recapture enough mental energy to think clearly again. The stage is now set for active coping to begin.

- *Reframing* The first task in active coping is *reframing*: We begin to think differently about the troubling event. This involves *shifting our focus* to more positive aspects of the situation ("At least she's no longer suffering") and *revising our interpretation* of our role in the event ("This wasn't really all my fault—he was partly to blame as well").
- *Reviewing* As we reframe, we *review*, and work backward to understand our loss. We put the event into the larger context of our life, and see how it fits with all that came before. Looking backward is a way of regaining control: With the benefit of hindsight we can scrutinize choices made (both ours' and others') and the events that helped create the present situation. Reviewing is the bridge from initial healing to long-term recovery.

Phase 3: Long-term recovery

Long-term recovery can only begin when we're confident we'll survive this crisis. Long-term recovery is measured in years rather than months, but however long it takes, it always involves three stages: *rebirth, reorienting,* and *reconnecting*.

- *Rebirth* When we find meaning in loss, *rebirth* begins, and with it comes a gradual reawakening of hope and optimism. Rebirth can't be rushed (it happens on its own time), and trying to hurry the process only slows it down.
- *Reorienting* Things are never the same after a major loss: Our world has changed, we have changed, and there's no going back. Because of this, a key part of long-term recovery is *reorienting*—finding new ways to relate to ourselves and other people and new ways to create meaning in life.
- *Reconnecting* As we reorient cognitively, we *reconnect* emotionally. First, we look inward and *reconnect with ourselves*, gaining confidence and learning how to feel again. Then we look outward to *reconnect with other people*: To do this we must let down our guard, allow ourselves to be vulnerable, and re-establish trust.

Benjamin and Sarah:
Two Spouses, Two Ways of Coping

Benjamin and Sarah had built a good life together—an ideal life, in many ways. They both had jobs they enjoyed, and took pride in their nine year-old daughter Rachel, who hoped to work with computers some day like her father. Benjamin and Sarah had relationship styles that meshed well—not because they were perfect, but because they complemented each other perfectly. Benjamin's narcissistic detachment caused him to be a bit distant at home, and not as deeply involved in raising Rachel as Sarah would have liked, but it served him well at the office, where he expected (and got) top-quality work from his subordi-

201

nates. Sarah had a more helpless, overdependent style, which sometimes held her back at the office, but worked wonderfully well at home. Sarah's willingness to be led fit nicely with Benjamin's need to lead.

Benjamin and Sarah's comfortable life blew apart on a rainy Wednesday afternoon in May, when Sarah received a phone call from the principal of Rachel's school. Rachel had been in an accident, said Ms. Carskadon. A driver had lost control in front of the school, while the children were waiting for the bus to take them home. The car had skidded on the rain-slicked street, and it swerved up onto the curb, and then....

Sarah should call her husband right away, said the principal, and come to the hospital as soon as she could.

Sometimes a chance event shatters the most well-laid plans, and Rachel's death was one of those events. At first, Benjamin and Sarah tried to put the incident behind them and get on with their lives. Benjamin didn't want to talk about what had happened—didn't want to dwell on it. Sarah tried to go along, but as weeks turned into months, and Sarah's sadness deepened and grew, she finally decided to seek help to cope with her grief.

Therapy went well for Sarah. Her helpless dependent style made her a compliant patient—capable of opening up to the therapist, willing to use the therapist's advice. Therapy focused on helping Sarah strengthen her healthy dependency skills, so she could lean on others to get the support she needed, building new connections and reaffirming old ones.

As Sarah's grief began to resolve, she got in touch with some very angry feelings she'd harbored toward her husband—long-buried emotions just starting to surface. As therapy progressed, Sarah asked Benjamin to join in, but he refused. She pleaded, then begged, but Benjamin held his ground. To Benjamin, the prospect of dwelling on feelings—especially uncomfortable, vulnerable feelings—was too threatening. He was unwilling (or perhaps unable) to enter into a process that he knew would compel him to give up control.

Though their marriage held together for more than a year after Rachel's death, Benjamin and Sarah eventually divorced, and went their separate ways. Since then Sarah has returned to therapy periodically to wrestle with difficult issues in her life and overcome challenges at work and at home. Sarah remarried about three years after her divorce, to a man with two teenage children. Not surprisingly, she became a devoted mother to both of them. Bit by bit Sarah created a new life for herself—a life that was better than her old one in many ways.

Benjamin quickly put both events—death and divorce—behind him. He threw himself into his work, continued to rise through the ranks of his company, and committed suicide four years after his daughter's accident. Since we'd lost contact with him, it was impossible to know what drove Benjamin to end his own life. We can only guess, but it seems likely that Benjamin's narcissistic detachment—his unwillingness to connect, grieve, and mourn Rachel's tragic death—ultimately destroyed him.

The Risks of Overdependence

Overdependence—like detachment—makes it difficult to move beyond the initial stages of coping. However, overdependence traps us in a different way: We become so caught up in leaning on others we find it difficult (sometimes impossible) to forge ahead on our own. Without realizing it, we slip quietly into overdependent "victim mode," setting the stage for an extended period of helpless self-pity. Four things follow:

- *Emotional staging* If a person copes by looking to others for protection, her reflexive response to stress will be to escalate her support-seeking. One common outcome is *emotional staging*—exaggerating internal pain to obtain the desired response from other people. Emotional staging sometimes works in the short term, but in the long term it has two important costs. First, *it alienates potential caregivers* (after a while, they see through the charade). Second, *it makes the person doing the emotional staging feel worse, not better.* Studies show that when we *act* upset, we *feel* upset—even if we weren't upset to begin with. In this case our

203

emotions actually follow from our behaviors, rather than the other way around.

- *Downward spiraling* Repeated emotional staging leads to *downward spiraling*—increased anxiety, more emotional staging, more anxiety, and so on. The process goes something like this: When "rewards" for our emotional displays stop coming, we increase our care-eliciting efforts; when our increased dramatics are ultimately reinforced, we escalate even further next time. The situation is complicated by the fact that as we alienate potential caregivers through repetitive emotional staging, we create a new problem on top of our old one: Now we've disrupted some important relationships, and made it less likely we'll obtain support when we need it.

- *Hypochondriasis* While detached people tend to develop psychosomatic (stress-based) disorders, overdependent people develop *hypochondriacal* syndromes—imagined illnesses that reflect emotional upset and inner turmoil. Hypochondriacal disorders are not faked or made up: The stressed-out person genuinely feels sick. But closer examination reveals that there's no biological basis for the illness—it truly is "all in the person's head." Aches and pains, dizziness and nausea, stiff joints and chronic tiredness—these are just a few symptom patterns that sometimes (but not always) reflect a hypochondriacal process at work. (Note: It's always better to err on the side of caution, so if you develop a bothersome physical symptom, don't assume it's just stress—have it checked out by a physician to be sure.)

- *Exploitation* The final risk of an overdependent coping style is exploitation: Consciously or unconsciously, those you look to for comfort may begin to exploit the power you've given them. The process is slow and subtle, but it usually takes place in two stages. First, caregivers begin to look down upon those who depend on them, and perceive the care receiver as weak, childlike, and manipulative. Second, caregivers begin to take advantage of the care-receiver's vulnerability, making demands they wouldn't otherwise make, and exploiting the power differential that has emerged in the relationship. In its extreme, exploitation can turn into emotional (even physical) abuse, as the frustrated caregiver lashes out at the "powerless" care-receiver.

The Risks of Detachment

As Benjamin's sad situation illustrates, detachment deprives us of external support, and makes it less likely that we will cope effectively during difficult periods. Stress lingers, tension builds, and long-term recovery is impaired. Detachment interferes with coping in four major ways:

- *Ruminating/obsessing* When we don't talk to others about an upsetting event, we *ruminate*—we obsessively rehash the event in our mind. Ruminating is a way of trying to regain control, but in this situation it doesn't work. In fact, the more a detached person ruminates, the more upset she becomes. She remains mired in the past, feeling less—not more—in control. And when that happens the typical response of the detached person is...more rumination! This pattern can persist for weeks (sometimes months) but since the person is essentially "thinking in circles," she never gains ground. Ruminating rarely deepens the detached person's understanding of the event, nor does it help her feel better about her role in it. Instead, it traps her in Coping Phase 1: cognitive recoil.
- *Autistic withdrawal* As we ruminate, anxiety and guilt build up, and we retreat even further from those around us. When withdrawal becomes extreme, it takes on a kind of autistic quality: Not only are we cut off from other people, but we begin to screen out aspects of the environment, literally not perceiving things that are happening around us. We no longer see the world as others do, and we feel oddly "split-off" from external events. If withdrawal persists, we may begin behaving strangely as well (misinterpreting

OVERDEPENDENCE AND OVERUSE
OF MEDICAL SERVICES

* * * * *

As you might expect, hypochondriasis sometimes leads people to seek medical help for illnesses that don't exist. In fact, the overdependent person's tendency to look to others for nurturance and reassurance may lead him to overuse clinic and hospital services even when hypochondriasis is not present. During the past fifteen years we conducted several studies of this issue. We found that the link between overdependence and overuse of medical services occurs in several domains.

Consider:

- Overdependent students use the college's health center three times as often as do nondependent students, and they make six times as many appointments with private physicians.
- Overdependent hospital patients receive twice as many medical consultations and nearly 50 percent more medication prescriptions than do nondependent patients with similar diagnoses.
- Overdependent patients have significantly longer hospital stays than do healthy dependent or detached patients with similar illnesses.
- Overdependent medical patients initiate a greater number of after-hours contacts with their physicians, and report a greater number of "pseudo-emergencies" (false alarms) that require a physician's response.

communications, forgetting appointments and promises made). In the end, work and family relationships are compromised, as pent-up stress spills over into multiple areas of life.

- *Bottled-up emotions* In 1972 Harvard University researcher Peter Sifneos coined the term *alexithymia* (literally, "no words for feelings") to describe the detached person's reflexive reaction to stress and loss. Sifneos observed that even as dysfunctionally detached people spend more and more time ruminating, they become less and less able to describe their internal states. They cannot articulate how they feel, even if they want to. They become *alexithymic*, and lose access to their inner world (emotions, wishes, fantasies, desires). A vicious cycle ensues: The detached person's withdrawal interferes with his ability to talk about feelings, and the anxiety that results from his bottled-up emotions increases his urge to retreat and withdraw.

- *Psychosomatic illness* Alexithymia sets the stage for *psychosomatic illness*—stress-based illness—to occur. Psychosomatic illnesses are not imaginary, as many people believe, but genuine physical ailments that are caused in part by stress and anxiety. Ulcers, headaches, hypertension, heart disease—all are related in part to bottled-up stress and unexpressed negative emotion. Once a psychosomatic illness has developed, it takes on a life of its own: Disclosing troubling feelings can help manage the illness and reduce its negative impact, but now the illness requires a medical intervention as well, to alter its biological components.

The Benefits of Healthy Dependency

Healthy dependency helps us deal effectively with loss in several different ways. It lets us share troubling feelings without feeling weak (emotional synergy), and look to others for help without seeing ourselves as helpless (connection-based thinking). Healthy dependency enables us to use a difficult situation to strengthen ties to other people (relationship flexibility), and build connections that will help us thrive, both now and in the future (growth motivation).

Let's take a closer look at the benefits of healthy dependency during life's most difficult times:

- *Unleashing negative emotions* It's a powerful effect that has now been confirmed in dozens of independent studies: Expressing negative feelings combats depression, strengthens

> ### INTERPERSONAL STRESS AND SOCIAL SUPPORT: THE YIN AND YANG OF OVERDEPENDENT ILLNESS
>
> * * * * *
>
> Scientists had long suspected that social support could buffer the negative effects of stress in overdependent people, but it wasn't until 1995 that we obtained hard data supporting this idea. For three months we had healthy young adults make daily diary entries describing their most important life events (both positive and negative) and ongoing social support (helpful contacts with friends, family members, romantic partners, etc). We also tracked participants' health status throughout the study. Here's what we found:
>
> - Overdependent people with high levels of interpersonal stress (that is, interpersonal conflict and relationship disruption) showed higher illness rates than overdependent people with more modest stress levels.
> - Social support protected overdependent people against stress's negative effects: Even if they experienced a great amount of relationship conflict, overdependent people with strong social support systems still showed below-average illness rates.

the immune system, helps prevent both minor and major illnesses, and even speeds recovery from existing illnesses. It doesn't matter whether your confidant is a family member, friend, or stranger, nor it is important *how* you disclose what you feel (a written message is as effective as a spoken one). All you need do to bolster your immune system is unburden yourself fully and completely: You must describe as honestly as you can exactly how you're feeling, without holding anything back.

- *Sharing the burden* Healthy dependency not only provides an emotional outlet, but also an opportunity to gain *respite*—a break from dealing with the troubling event. Studies show that people trapped in stressful situations (like caring for an aging loved one) benefit tremendously from brief "stress breaks": Their mood improves significantly and they report fewer illness episodes. Even if the respite lasts only an hour or two, it's enough to let the body recharge, renew its resources, and prepare to confront the stressful task again. Psychologically, respite helps us gain perspective, reaffirm our commitment, and approach the challenge with a more optimistic, focused outlook.

- *Obtaining information* A hidden benefit of healthy dependent help-seeking: Other people provide information that lets us cope more effectively with loss and change. Two types of information are particularly useful in this context: *fact-based information* and *experience-based information*. Fact-based information is exactly that—objective data about an event (like an illness) that help you prepare for what lies ahead. Experience-based information is more subjective and more personal: It's the sharing of someone's previous struggles with similar problems. In contrast to fact-based information (which is mostly cognitive), experience-based information prepares you to confront the more private, emotional aspects of the challenge.

REACHING OUT FOR INFORMATION

* * * * *

Friends and family members can be tremendous resources, but these are not the only sources of information to consider. Many associations and advocacy groups (like the *American Cancer Society* and *Children of Aging Parents*) have web pages chock-full of useful data. Adult education classes and seminars are also good sources of fact-based information.

If experience-based information is what you seek, consider joining a support group (hospitals and social service agencies can usually hook you up). Certain forms of individual, marital, and group psychotherapy may also be useful in providing fact- or experience-based information (or both).

9-11

* * * * *

The terrorist attacks in Washington, New York, and Pennsylvania were just a few hours old when the calls began to come in. Like mental health professionals throughout the country, we were contacted by members of the news media—health reporters mostly—and they all wanted to know the same thing: How can we help people get through this crisis?

We answered their questions as best we could, and we described the various things people could do to cope. But our bottom-line advice was simple and direct: In the midst of terrible tragedy, people need to reconnect.

The events of 9-11 were so upsetting—so terrifying—that many of us recoiled emotionally, reflexively protecting ourselves from overwhelming anxiety and fear. And as we recoiled, we began to experience *cognitive shutdown*—mental numbness—which is why so many people described feeling "unreal" that day, as if it was all a "bad dream."

But we knew that turning inward was the worst thing people could do. Tragedy demands that we reach out to others, first to survive, then to mourn and heal. So we advised people to lean on those close to them—to actively seek support. And we asked people to reach out to others as well—to offer support to those who were having difficulty coping. We encouraged people to unburden themselves—to talk about how they were feeling until the emotional weight begin to lift. And we encouraged people to lend an ear, so others could unburden themselves, too.

In the days following 9-11, we found inner strength we never knew we had. We discovered heroes all around us: firefighters in New York, EMS workers in Washington, D.C., and courageous, selfless passengers on Flight 93. And as we found our strength, we rediscovered connections we'd taken for granted. We saw how people around the world were touched by the tragedy, and seeing this, we began to feel better because we knew we weren't alone.

- *Forging connections* A final benefit of healthy dependency during difficult times is that it allows you to forge new connections. Not only do you get the help you need right now, but you create bonds that will let you get the help you need down the line, when unexpected challenges arise. These new connections also provide you with an opportunity to give help to others—an equally important aspect of healthy dependency. Forging connections is a good example of how a difficult situation can be turned into a positive event— how trauma can be turned into strength. Not only are you surviving and thriving despite your loss, but you've gained confidence that you can cope with other challenges in the future.

Looking Ahead: Healthy Dependency and Successful Aging

If we got all our information from popular media, it would be easy to conclude that growing old is like a long, slow death. Aging, so we're told, is a time of inexorable decline and decay: Vision clouds, reaction time slows, memory fades, and the body becomes brittle and frail. Society pushes us aside, telling us in no uncertain terms that we've outlived our usefulness—we've nothing left to contribute. Is it any wonder that older adults in many Western societies report increased isolation, and decreased self-esteem?

There's no question about it: Aging is a challenge, especially in a culture that worships youth. But aging can be an opportunity as well—a chance to develop long-neglected interests and renew relationships that were put on hold to meet family and career demands. With old age come the dual benefits of *wisdom* and *experience*. The trick is to use these gifts wisely, and find ways to adapt a lifetime's worth of skills and talents to an environment that is not always receptive to the older adult.

Aging researcher Margaret Baltes of Berlin's Free University has found that many late-life difficulties are more a product of

211

HEALTHY DEPENDENCY DURING DIFFICULT TIMES: BUILDING CONNECTIONS FOR NOW AND LATER

* * * * *

Whatever your relationship style may be, developing healthy dependent relationships during difficult times takes effort. You must use your healthy dependency skills to strengthen connections, get the help you need right now, and set the stage for future support. Here are six useful strategies:

- *Strategy #1: Time your requests.* Don't interrupt someone during their busiest time, but wait (if you can), until the person is less stressed. They'll be more receptive to your request and better able to put their own concerns aside to listen to what you have to say.
- *Strategy #2: Be flexible.* Not everyone is capable of responding exactly as you'd hope. Let people offer support as they see fit, and be grateful for it. If your friend's helping style doesn't work well for you, don't get annoyed. Instead, seek out someone whose style fits better with yours.
- *Strategy #3: Acknowledge help (but not too much).* It is important that you acknowledge help when you receive it, but it's also important that you know when to stop. Repeated thank-you's can be off-putting, and may alienate potential caregivers.
- *Strategy #4: Give help as well as getting it.* If you always ask but never offer, people close to you will drift away. It is important that you return the favor when the time is right. When a supportive person needs a hand or a shoulder to cry on, make yourself available—don't wait to be asked.
- *Strategy #5: Communicate clearly.* Even those who know you best can't read your mind. You have to communicate your needs clearly. It might feel awkward to specify what kind of support you want, but it's the best way to get the help you're hoping for.
- *Strategy #6: Be selective.* Not everyone is comfortable offering help and support, so be selective in choosing who to ask. If you have a friend who is somewhat detached, this might not be the best person to seek out when you need to unburden yourself of heavy emotional baggage.

society's expectations than any real decline in physical or psychological functioning. Cultural messages are critical here: Older adults feel and act helpless when they're told they're *expected* to be this way. What if instead of entering late life with the expectation of helpless overdependence, we approached later adulthood with the expectation of healthy dependency? Might we be able to create a different outcome—a happier, healthier old age?

The research says yes, and that's what we'll look at in Chapter 10: healthy dependency and successful aging.

10

HEALTHY DEPENDENCY
AND SUCCESSFUL AGING

Ellen had been at the trade show for four days now, and she was having the time of her life. Phoenix was fun—new restaurants to try, nice neighborhoods to explore—and for the first time in years Ellen was enjoying spending time with her colleagues. She felt more relaxed now than at any time she could remember.

When the Friday afternoon workshop broke at four, Ellen headed up to her room to call Theresa. That was their arrangement: Ellen would check in once each day, get caught up on the office goings-on, and make some long-distance decisions about pressing issues. Ellen took the elevator upstairs, went to her room, kicked off her shoes, and dialed.

Theresa picked up on the second ring. She had been expecting Ellen's call. And Ellen knew right away what was coming—she could tell from Theresa's tone when she answered the phone.

"Nothing to report here," said Theresa. "Everything's under control."

This was, by now, a familiar refrain. Ellen had heard it every day this week. But today Ellen surprised herself. When Theresa told her everything was under control, Ellen laughed.

She actually laughed.

It was such an odd reaction from Ellen, who was usually so stiff and starched when talking about the office, that Theresa was taken aback.

"Excuse me?" she said.

Ellen took a moment to catch her breath. "Sorry, Theresa. It's just funny."

"What's that?"

"Hearing you say everything's under control. 'Nothing to report here!' I mean, it used to bother me, but now...."

"Now what?"

"Well, I'm glad. I'm actually glad to hear you say it."

"Good for you."

Ellen's voice changed then—became secretive, almost playful.

"What do you think, Theresa? Should I go for a swim?"

"Are you kidding? Did you bring a suit?"

"No."

"I didn't think so."

"Tell you what, though."

"What's that?"

"Next time I think I will."

When Ellen got off the phone with Theresa, she was still full of energy. She wasn't due downstairs until six—she was meeting some colleagues for a drink—so she had plenty of time to kill. What should she do?

Ellen debated going for a walk, but it looked like it was starting to drizzle. The going-for-a-swim idea bubbled up again, and Ellen seriously considered calling down to the lobby shop to see if they had a suit in her size. She decided against it though. Ellen felt relaxed, but not that *relaxed*, and these were, after all, her business associates.

Then it hit her. She knew what to do. She dug through her bag until she found the slip of paper she was looking for. Then she hurriedly dialed the phone—quick, before she had time to change her mind.

The voice on the other end sounded tired and sad.

"Mom?"

"Ellen? Is that you?"

"Yes. How are you? I've been thinking about you."

"About me? Aren't you in Phoenix?"

"Yeah, but the meeting got done early, and I felt like talking."

"Well, this is a first."

"I guess it is, Mom. I don't call to chat very often, do I?"

"Well, no."

"I'm sorry about that. I think I owe you an apology."

"Ellen, dear, no apologies necessary. I'm just glad you called."

Ellen had been pacing back and forth by her bed, but now she sat down. She filled her mother in on the meeting, and her mother brought her up to date on how rehab was going. Half an hour later Ellen wasn't sitting anymore; she was sprawled on the bed, lost in talk.

Ellen was midway through a story about this morning's breakfast meeting when out of the corner of her eye she saw the clock on the nightstand.

"Oh Mom, I'm late. I didn't realize how long we'd been on. I've got to meet some friends downstairs."

"Go, Ellen. Have fun. It was so nice to hear from you." The sad voice that had answered the phone was long gone now, replaced by a voice that sounded energetic, optimistic—and twenty years younger.

"I'll call you when I get back to town, okay? I'm flying in tomorrow."

"Okay. Oh, Ellen?"

"Yes?"

"We should do this more often."

"We will, Mom. I promise."

As we age, we rely more on other people. In many Eastern cultures, this is seen as a natural—even enviable—part of growing old. But in most Western societies, late-life dependency is seen as a sign of frailty and failure—something to be ashamed of, hidden, and denied.

There's no question about it: In later adulthood most of us need the occasional helping hand with things we once did on our own. It's not a question of *whether* we need to rely on others as we age; it's really a question of *how*. We can deal with late-life dependency in an unhealthy way (by becoming increasingly overdependent or rigidly detached), or we can deal with it in a way that allows us to feel confident regarding challenges that await us and connected to those who want to help.

TEST YOUR KNOWLEDGE:
AGING AND ITS EFFECTS

* * * * *

Two primary obstacles to healthy dependent aging are *myth* and *stereotype*. So many people are convinced that late adulthood is a time of decline and decay they allow a self-fulfilling prophecy to take over: They become overdependent or detached because they think it's inevitable—that they have no choice in the matter.

Let's approach late life mindfully instead of mindlessly. Which of the following statements are true?

- By age seventy-five, people begin to show impairment in most areas of memory.
- About 20 percent of the eighty-year-old population currently resides in nursing homes.
- Life satisfaction declines with age, especially after age seventy.
- The rate at which neurons (brain cells) die increases rapidly after age sixty-five.
- Intelligence test scores decline in older adults.

Believe it or not, *every one of these statements is false*. Here are the facts:

- Certain types of memory (like memory for well-learned skills) are completely unaffected by age.
- Less than 10 percent of the eighty-year-old population resides in nursing homes.
- Life satisfaction ratings are stable throughout adulthood; seventy-year-olds are as satisfied with life as forty-year-olds are.
- The rate of neural death is unrelated to age (though older people form fewer new neural connections than younger people do).
- Some forms of intelligence actually increase in late life (it just takes us a bit longer to retrieve information).

This chapter focuses on healthy dependency and successful aging—for you and those you love. We begin by contrasting successful and unsuccessful aging patterns, then look at ways you can use your healthy dependency skills to make older adulthood a time of strength and adaptation, growth and positive change.

Unsuccessful Aging: Old Problems Re-Emerge

The roles and scripts we create early in life persist through the years. The cast of characters may change, but our core relationship style remains pretty much the same. Those who were once dependent on parents, then spouses, now shift their dependency to children and other caregivers. Those who learned to cope by detaching find that with increasing age, their detachment persists.

As we move through late adulthood, we undergo a process called *disinhibition*: Our predispositions and behavioral tendencies become even more pronounced. Disinhibition results from subtle changes in brain structure and function that occur in later life—changes that interfere with our ability to moderate urges and impulses. As a result, our lifelong relationship style not only persists, but actually accentuates as we age. The mildly dependent person becomes increasingly clingy, while the moderately detached individual withdraws even more sharply. Relationship patterns that worked fairly well in our forties and fifties can create significant problems in our seventies and beyond.

Late-life overdependence

For the overdependent person with a fragile core of self-doubt, the challenges of aging can seem overwhelming. The urge to lean on others grows stronger, and three things follow:

- *Helplessness* For most of us, the awareness that we no longer function as we once did is very frightening. Some people

> ## PSEUDODEMENTIA
>
> ✳ ✳ ✳ ✳ ✳
>
> Researchers have long known that people express needs and fears in age-appropriate ways. For example, anxious children who don't have the vocabulary to describe their feelings will instead report physical aches and pains ("my tummy hurts") that mirror the anxiety they're experiencing. One of the most striking late-life examples of this phenomenon is a syndrome called *pseudodementia* ("false dementia"). Pseudodementia occurs when an overdependent older adult becomes anxious or depressed. Instead of asking for help directly, the person develops "age-appropriate" symptoms that elicit help from others without their having to ask. Memory deficits, confused thinking, rambling conversation—these are just a few common symptoms of pseudodementia.
>
> Because the symptoms of pseudodementia mimic those of genuine dementia (like Alzheimer's disease), careful testing by a psychologist experienced in assessing older adults is necessary to get to the root of the problem. If an older adult under your care (a parent for example, or an aging spouse) develops dementia-like symptoms, it is critical that formal testing be done to determine whether these symptoms reflect neurological impairment, or are simply an indirect manifestation of late-life dependency.

cope by developing a philosophical approach to late-life limitations, accommodating their losses as best they can. But for the overdependent person, "I can't" becomes a mantra—a reflexive response to every challenge. The idea of developing new ways of coping seems too difficult, and the overdependent person falls back on old habits, trapping others into doing things they're afraid to do themselves.

- *Regression* In at least one respect, the limitations of old age parallel those of childhood: During both stages of life, we rely on others for help with some basic life tasks. In people with a lifelong pattern of destructive overdependence, old age sometimes triggers *regression*—a return to old childhood behaviors (though the original targets of those behaviors are long gone). Even if the overdependent older adult is capable of functioning independently, he may insist on relating to others in a helpless, childlike way. At first this regression elicits nurturance and support, but after a while it backfires, frustrating and angering all but the most devoted caregivers.

- *Ambivalence* As the overdependent person copes with late-life losses, identity issues re-emerge, albeit in a slightly different form than they did the first time around. Conflicts between dependency and self-sufficiency return to center stage, which can lead to unpredictable behavior. In contrast to the adolescent (who expresses his ambivalence through attitude shifts and mood swings), the overdependent older adult may display a pattern of uneven coping skills (for example, asking for help with medical matters while steadfastly refusing financial advice). This ambivalent, conflicted pattern is confusing to caregivers, who feel caught between a rock and a hard place—simultaneously pulled in and pushed away by the person they're trying to help.

Late-life detachment

As detached people begin to confront troubling end-of-life issues, their reflexive response is to withdraw even further into their protective shell. Three processes ensue:

- *Disengagement* Many detached people respond to the challenges of aging by *disengaging*—cutting ties with those close to them and distancing themselves from friends and family members. Oftentimes this process begins with retirement: Deprived of the daily social contact that comes with work, the detached person slides slowly into isolation. Some detached people rationalize their withdrawal, asserting that it's "too much trouble" to stay connected and involved. For other detached people the process is less deliberate: Depressed by illness, loss, or perceived lack of purpose, they simply fade away and disappear.

> * * * * *
> **As one grows older, one becomes**
> **wiser and more foolish.**
> —FRANCOIS DE LA ROCHEFOUCALD

- *Rebellion* While some detached people seem to disappear in late adulthood, others show the opposite pattern. These individuals really do (to borrow Dylan Thomas's famous phrase) "rage, rage against the dying of the light." Angered by their limitations, envious of those who enjoy the health and vitality they no longer possess, these rebellious people respond to even minor challenges with bitterness and resentment. They shove others away with a rancor that serves in part to mask their loneliness and fear (not just from those around them, but from themselves as well).
- *Regret* The psychoanalyst Erik Erikson believed that quiet introspective reflection is a key late-life task. For many detached people, this reflection reveals more missed opportunities than victories, more disappointments than successes. The person may feel as though he's wasted his life and made poor choices along the way. Worse, there's no time left to correct past errors. Such people experience what Erikson called *late-life despair*. When this despair becomes profound, the detached person is likely to dismiss any sort of encouragement or support as pointless and useless—too little, too late.

Wilma and Al: Destructive Grandmother-Grandson Enmeshment—From Compliance to Anger to the Edge of Abuse

Wilma was a hostile overdependent person—controlling, manipulative, always on the verge of a theatrical breakdown. For most of her adult years, Wilma directed this behavior at her husband Al, who assumed the role of long-suffering spouse,

HELPING A "STUCK" CARE RECEIVER
GET "UNSTUCK"

✳ ✳ ✳ ✳ ✳

If someone under your care is "stuck" in overdependent or detached mode, don't get frustrated. Instead, help the person get "unstuck" and find new ways to cope with challenges. Here are some useful strategies:

- *Reframe the situation.* The way we label tasks affects how we feel about them (which is why an "intelligence test" is a whole lot more intimidating than a "problem-solving test"). If a detached care receiver is reluctant to join a group to meet new people, present it instead as a way of "developing new interests." If an overdependent person is afraid to go grocery shopping without your help, don't describe the task as "going shopping on your own," but as "doing me a favor" or "helping me out." By reframing a frightening situation in this way, you detoxify it, and make it easier for the person to attempt it.

- *Offer examples from the past.* Sometimes reminding a person of past successes can boost their confidence and help them approach a new challenge with greater resolve. Remind the person of times in the past where she confronted a feared situation and overcame it. Or flip it around, and remind the care receiver of times when *she* encouraged *you* to take a risk. Hearing one's own advice in a new situation can have a powerful positive effect (plus, it reassures the person you were listening the first time—her words had an impact).

- *Be a role model.* If words aren't effective, try actions instead. Be a role model and let the stuck person see you moving forward—confronting a feared situation despite your misgivings. You might have to do this more than once, and it sometimes helps if you describe aloud your feelings about the challenge: The fear you felt when you decided to take the plunge, and the satisfaction you experienced by conquering your fear. For many people, seeing someone confront a difficult situation helps them confront it more easily themselves.

- *Reinforce adaptive behavior.* As we discussed in Chapter 9, there are times when our behaviors shape our feelings, not the other way around. So use rewards (reinforcements) to encourage the person to engage in a feared activity. Once they begin, and disaster doesn't follow, their fear will likely subside. Rewards need not be obvious to be effective: Subtle reinforcers like a smile, a nod, or a pat on the back are surprisingly powerful in shaping people's behavior.

- *Use a paradoxical intervention.* If all else fails, you might want to try a *paradoxical intervention*—an intervention wherein you encourage the person to do the opposite of what you really want them to do. Paradoxical interventions are not without risk (the person might say "okay" and leave it at that), but they can be quite effective in altering the behavior of oppositional people who are ambivalent about a challenge. For these individuals, saying "you can't do this" might be vexing enough that they go ahead and do it…just to prove you wrong.

and kowtowed to Wilma's many demands. Over time, Wilma and Al co-authored a marital script wherein she held all the power, and in return for giving up control, Al was allowed certain freedoms he might not otherwise have had (like drinking excessively most every night).

Two events conspired to destroy the fragile balance that Wilma and Al had created together. First, Al developed diabetes, and as his health declined he could no longer meet Wilma's many demands. Second, Wilma developed a progressive arthritic condition that limited her mobility significantly. So at the same time Wilma's dependency needs increased, Al became less able to meet them.

Fortunately (or unfortunately, depending upon how you see it), Wilma and Al had a grandson with an overdependent style as well. Eddie was devoted to his grandparents, and since he lived nearby, he volunteered to take over many of the daily household tasks (like laundry and shopping) that Wilma and Al could no longer manage on their own. After work each day Eddie drove to his grandparents' home and did whatever chores and errands were needed to get them through the evening. As time went on,

Eddie became more and more invested in his caregiver role, and ultimately he put many parts of his life on hold so he could spend all his free time (including weekends) with his grandparents.

Sadly (but predictably), the harder Eddie tried to be a good caregiver, the more strained his relationship with his grandmother became. His work was always "sloppy" and "careless"— never good enough to please perfectionistic Wilma. Eddie began to harbor considerable anger toward both his grandparents, though he was unable to express this anger directly, even in therapy. Instead, Eddie denied any negative feelings toward Wilma and Al, and he rationalized each hostile or controlling behavior they directed toward him, asserting that "they really can't help it" and "that's just the way they are." Any effort to help Eddie get in touch with his hidden resentment merely strengthened his resolve and hardened his defenses.

After a while, Eddie's anger built to the point that it began to leak out in various ways. He occasionally ignored his grandmother's requests for assistance, deliberately making her wait as a way of regaining control (he pretended he couldn't hear her calls from a distant part of the house). Eddie became uncommunicative as well, responding to his grandparents' questions with one-word answers that precluded further interaction. Eddie finally reached his breaking point one Saturday in May, when Wilma spilled a pot of spaghetti sauce in the kitchen. He lost his temper and handled his grandmother roughly, grabbing her wrist and pulling her sharply away from the stove. Eddie was crossing the line into elder abuse, and he knew it.

His grandmother knew it, too, and she tried to exploit Eddie's lapse by making him feel guilty. Eddie was in fact wracked with guilt (he needed no help from Wilma in that regard). But rather than allowing himself to be manipulated further, Eddie used the incident to change a longstanding dysfunctional pattern that— he finally realized—was hurting everyone. Eddie decided he could no longer handle caregiving responsibilities by himself, and he insisted that his grandparents hire a home health aide to be with them several hours each day. Eddie still helped out one or two evenings a week, but he began to set limits on Wilma's demands and rebuild the life he had interrupted.

Ironically, Eddie's relationship with his grandparents improved when he set limits on his caregiving, and over time, they found a new, healthier way of relating. Wilma continued to be manipulative at times, and Al never did free himself from his long-suffering husband role. However, with the benefit of limit-setting—and the perspective that came from having more time to himself—Eddie was better able to tolerate his grandparents' demands with understanding rather than rancor. He became a better caregiver, and Wilma learned how to moderate her dependency needs more effectively than she had in the past.

Successful Aging: Strength and Adaptation

Successful aging doesn't mean doing everything on your own or denying life's losses as long as possible. On the contrary, successful aging means maximizing your strengths—whatever they may be—while you adapt to the challenges of late adulthood. In this respect, Wilma and Al did not age successfully. Instead, they clung ever more tightly to old, familiar ways—behavior patterns that no longer served them well in the context of changing circumstances.

Rather than trying to maintain the status quo, Wilma and Al should have set in motion two transitions that are critical to the successful aging process. First, they needed to *accept their changing roles* so they could flourish in these new roles instead of fighting them. Second, they should have made a deliberate effort to *deepen ties to others* so they could get the help they needed to succeed, meeting late-life challenges head-on instead of shrinking from them.

If you (like Eddie) are the caregiver of an aging loved one, your job is to facilitate these two tasks in the care receiver. By doing this you'll set the stage for successful aging in the person you love—and for yourself as well, when you make the transition to later adulthood.

Accepting a changing role

Accepting a changing role is not something that happens quickly or easily. It's a process that evolves throughout late adulthood. Three things are involved:

- *Stepping down: The challenge of retirement* In most Western societies, people are what they do. (No one says, "I work as a teacher" or "My job is being a lawyer"; instead they say, "I *am* a teacher" and "I *am* a lawyer.") Because we identify so strongly with what we do, retirement can be a rocky time. We not only lose income, status, and the structure of the workday, but we actually lose a part of our *self*—a part of our identity—as well. To set the stage for successful aging, we must find a way to step down gracefully and give up our professional identity without losing ourself in the process. For some people this means finding new ways to stay connected to their profession post-retirement (for example, through consulting or mentoring). For others it means shifting energy to new challenges and using their new-found freedom to focus on tasks they'd put off to meet the demands of family and work (like long-neglected hobbies and interests).
- *Stepping up: Matriarchy and patriarchy* At the same time as we step down professionally, we step up within the family. In many cultures, it's simply expected that the older adult will assume a family leadership role. In other cultures (particularly those that emphasize youth), matriarchy and patriarchy don't come easy. They must be cultivated through words and deeds that earn the respect of other family members and make them want to care for you as they follow your lead. To step up into matriarchy or patriarchy, you'll find that gentle persuasion and leading by example work

COMPENSATORY DEPENDENCIES

* * * * *

Sometimes people show increased dependency in one area in order to maintain (or even increase) their autonomous functioning in some other area. Psychologists refer to these as *compensatory dependencies* because the person's enhanced functioning in one domain *compensates* for their increased dependency in the other. Compensatory dependencies are healthy (they facilitate adaptation and growth), so be careful: If an older adult begins to show increased dependency in some aspect of their behavior, don't overreact. First analyze the situation to see if the increased dependency may be facilitating the person's functioning in another area. If so, you should support the compensatory (healthy) dependency.

A few examples:

- A person requires increased help with transportation...but she needs it to join an interest group (like a bridge club) that allows her to connect with others.
- A person asks for assistance with bill-paying...because it helps him maintain control over his personal finances (and the self-esteem that comes with financial independence).
- A person requires in-home health care...but uses it to manage her diabetes carefully and live independently for as long as she can.

better than coercion and intimidation. Some older adults use their accumulated wealth to gain leverage over loved ones, threatening (either subtly or directly) to disinherit those who question their authority. Resist this temptation. It might allow you to control those closest to you in the short term, but in the long term you'll lose their love and respect.

- *Life at a different pace* The third challenge of accepting a changing role is recognizing that life moves at a different pace during life's final phase. To some extent the slower pace of late adulthood stems from decreased work demands, but it also reflects normal physical decline that occurs as

> * * * * *
> **In the middle of difficulty lies opportunity.**
> —ALBERT EINSTEIN

we move through our sixties and seventies. Muscle mass shrinks, reflexes slow, vision and hearing become less acute. These losses can be accommodated, but they can't be reversed (at least not yet). Some people enjoy the less hectic, more contemplative lifestyle that comes with late adulthood; other people find the slower pace and lack of structure disconcerting. The trick is to find the rhythm that works best for you: busy enough to keep you energized and motivated, but not so crammed with activities that you have no time to relax, step back, and enjoy life's little gifts.

Deepening ties to others

Like accepting a changing role, deepening ties to others is a process that unfolds over time and evolves throughout the years. But it doesn't happen all by itself. It takes effort to strengthen connections—especially in later life. Again, three things are involved:

- *A fresh perspective* With age comes increased empathy—a deeper appreciation for other peoples' struggles (after all, you've been through many of these struggles yourself by now). Age also helps us understand the importance of small victories and the pointlessness of dwelling on trivial defeats. Treatable health problems, minor financial setbacks, the inevitable conflicts that occur in every relationship—all these things lose the power to bedevil us as we gain perspective and experience. Though for most people increased empathy is a natural part of aging, that doesn't mean we should take it for granted. On the contrary, it's all too easy to become preoccupied with late-life losses and lose sight of what we've gained. When this happens the only solution is to replace mindless pessimism with mindful realism: Step back, take a deep breath, and try to put everything into perspective.

- *Sharing wisdom and experience* Successful aging doesn't just mean gaining a fresh perspective—we must also share our wisdom and experience with others. Sharing wisdom doesn't mean forcing it on those close to you or lording it over them. In this situation, *how* you share is as important as *what* you share. Education experts long ago recognized that effective teaching involves tailoring information to meet others' needs—framing what you say so it resonates with peoples' personal experiences. The same is true here, even if you're passing on wisdom to adults rather than children. To share wisdom effectively, you must communicate it in ways that people can grasp (not just cognitively, but emotionally too). You must find those elusive "teachable moments" that life provides every once in a while—those golden moments when someone is not merely ready to be taught, but literally hungers for guidance and inspiration.

- *Accepting others' gifts* Late life is a time for receiving gifts as well as sharing them. It's ironic that most of us find it easier to give help than receive it, but successful aging means accepting help gracefully—with genuine gratitude that makes the helper feel good, not trapped. It doesn't matter whether the help you receive is physical (a ride to the doctor), social (companionship), financial (help with paying bills), or emotional (a shoulder to cry on, a hand to hold). The important thing is that you use the help to adapt, not regress. Effective help-receiving in later adulthood requires that you use connection-based thinking to remind yourself that accepting help doesn't mean you are helpless. When you do this, growth motivation will follow, and you'll use the help you receive to confront life's challenges, and strengthen connections to those around you.

CAREGIVER STRESS

* * * * *

If you are a caregiver for an ill or aging loved one, be forewarned: Caregiver stress can be a significant problem, with the potential to spill over into multiple areas of life. Studies show that nearly 60 percent of at-home caregivers report significant problems with depression. More than 20 percent of caregivers report health problems stemming from caregiver stress.

To minimize the effects of caregiver stress, you must use your healthy dependency skills to get help and support at the same time as you're giving it. Here are some steps you can take:

- *Don't try to go it alone.* Formal support (an established support group) and informal support (a caring friend or colleague) are both useful here. Use your healthy dependency skills to unburden yourself of pent-up emotions without feeling weak (scream or cry if you need to). And use a variety of sources to get the fact-based information and experience-based information you need to make it through a difficult period.
- *Get respite from caregiving.* As we discussed in Chapter 9, even a brief break from caregiving can have tremendous psychological and physical benefits. This "respite effect" is particularly powerful for caregivers of aging loved ones who are seriously ill or cognitively impaired. Not only does respite help us recharge our batteries and renew our commitment to caregiving, it makes it less likely that we'll become overwhelmed, lose our temper, lash out, and say or do something we'd regret later on.
- *Use all the available services.* Sometimes people are reluctant to use the support services available through charitable organizations and government agencies. We find all sorts of excuses to avoid using these resources, from "Dad would never accept a handout" to "there are so many other people worse off than we are." These excuses are just that—excuses. Healthy dependency means giving and getting good help—in this case, using every resource at your disposal to be a more effective caregiver.
- *Take care of yourself.* In the midst of caregiving, we sometimes forget to take care of ourselves. So set aside some private time when you refuse to dwell on the care-receiver and his needs (you might

feel guilty about this, but do it anyway). Take a walk, see a movie, or go out to dinner with friends. You'll not only reduce your own stress level, you'll be a better caregiver as well—more patient, more understanding, more tolerant, more upbeat.

- *Don't get down on yourself.* No one is perfect, and even the most devoted caregiver makes the occasional mistake. When these occur (and believe us, they will), don't beat yourself up about them. Instead, try to understand what caused the error. Was it misinformation? Stress? Plain old clumsiness? Once you know what caused the error, take steps to correct it, so it doesn't happen again.

Late-Life Healthy Dependency: Turning Possibility to Reality

By *accepting a changing role* and *deepening ties to others* you create a context for successful aging. But to turn late-life healthy dependency from possibility into reality, you need to take some additional steps as well—some concrete actions that enhance autonomy and connectedness throughout later adulthood. Here's what you should do:

- *Become informed.* There are a tremendous number of resources and support services available for older adults. Pretending you don't need them because you're "not really old" is both dishonest and self-defeating. Healthy dependency means accepting help from others to learn and grow, so use library and Internet resources to get the information you need (government websites, and those of reputable national organizations like the AARP are particularly useful). Once you've gotten the information you need, use it.
- *Take charge of your health.* There's no denying it: Health problems increase with age. But by taking charge of your health, you can minimize future illness risk and manage more effectively those illnesses you already have. Consult with experts (physicians, dieticians, physical therapists),

then develop a written plan for maximizing wellness. Stick to your plan as best you can, and don't fall off the wagon when setbacks occur. If you eat something you shouldn't or miss a scheduled exercise, just put it behind you, and stay with your plan.

- *Shape your environment.* The findings are clear: Older adults who take an active role in shaping their environment are healthier and happier than those who do not. So don't be shy about reshaping your surroundings to fit your needs. For some older adults, independent living is best (even if they relocate to a smaller, more accessible house). For others, a continuing care community or other form of assisted living is needed. You mustn't let pride (or worse, misinformation) prevent you from finding the best living environment for you. Asking for help with the tasks of daily living is a natural part of successful aging—not a sign of helplessness or decline.

- *Stay in touch.* Staying connected to others becomes more difficult post-retirement, so you'll have to make a special effort to remain in touch. More free time means more time to travel, and this is one way to revitalize longstanding relationships. If you haven't ventured onto the information highway yet, now is the time to do it. E-mail is not that complicated; with today's sophisticated software you can master it in an afternoon (even if you're a computer novice). If you don't use all the communication resources available to you, you'll be left behind, and out of touch. (Besides, studies show that older Internet users actually spend more time online than younger users do.)

- *Pass the torch.* Teaching and mentoring are gratifying at any age, but especially during late adulthood. By passing along the wisdom and knowledge you've acquired over the years, you'll not only help others, but you'll feel more competent and confident yourself—fully connected and deeply engaged. The confidence you gain by passing the torch will make it easier for you to accept help in other areas without feeling weak or helpless.

- *Share the wealth.* By now the advice has reached almost all of us: Don't wait until you die to begin distributing your assets. By sharing the wealth while you're still alive you'll not only minimize tax burdens on your heirs, but you'll get the joy of experiencing first-hand the effects of your generosity. If you haven't done it yet, make time to consult with a financial advisor (preferably a Certified Financial Planner), so you can develop a plan for sharing the wealth.

- *Find meaning.* Erik Erikson was right: The final phase of life is an ideal time to reflect and review. Set aside a few minutes each day to think about how far you've come, and how far you still want to go. Don't dwell on mistakes (but don't ignore them either). Instead, use this period of reflection to find meaning in life's journey. When you take time to create your life's narrative—to literally tell your tale—you'll be amazed at how much you've done. So write your story down (even if you never intend for anyone else to see it). Sometimes the mere act of writing helps us discover meanings and connections we might otherwise miss.

- *Live your dreams.* Late life really is your last chance—your final opportunity to live your dreams. Most of us put off doing the things we'd love to do (taking a cruise, writing poetry, visiting a part of the world we've always wanted to see). When we're young we think we'll have time to do these things later, when life slows down. We're here to tell you: Now is later. If you don't start living your dreams today, you might never live them at all.

ANNA MARY ROBERTSON MOSES

* * * * *

Think post-retirement is too late to cultivate a new interest? Try telling that to Anna Mary Robertson Moses (better known as Grandma Moses), who first began painting seriously in her late seventies. By the time she finally put down the brush more than twenty years later she had produced more than 1,600 paintings—an impressive output by any measure. If she could do it, why can't you?

HEALTHY DEPENDENCY, NOW AND TOMORROW

When the meal was done and the dishes were cleared, Michael and Ellen finally got a chance to sneak off by themselves. From the quiet of the den they could hear the clatter of pots and pans, bursts of laughter, and snatches of conversation about who would get which leftovers. They sank into the cushions of the deep, soft chairs, door closed, blinds drawn, and they rested there quietly, savoring the mood of the day.

After a few minutes the noise in the kitchen faded. Ellen turned toward her brother, and she saw that his eyes were closed.

"Michael?"

"Hm?" His response was slow, relaxed.

"I've made a decision."

"Mm...What's that?"

"Well, I've decided I'd like to have Mother stay at my place for a while."

Michael rubbed his eyes. He looked over at his sister.

"Ellen, are you serious? Why would you want to do that? You know how fragile she is right now. She needs a lot of looking after."

Ellen stirred in her seat, sat up straighter. "I know," she said, "but that's okay. It's something I want to do."

"How come?"

"Well, I guess I feel like it's our last chance to spend some time together." Ellen gazed at the portraits lined up over the couch. "I missed a lot of Thanksgivings over the years."

Michael smiled.

"I know what you're thinking, Michael, but I've decided something else, too."

"What's that?"

"I'm going to cut back on my work schedule."

"Whoa." Michael's eyes opened wide. "Is that really you over there?" He pulled himself up into a sitting position. "Ellen, are you sure you haven't been taken over by aliens?"

Ellen laughed softly. "No, it's really me. I'm just…I don't know… sort of reorganizing my priorities."

Michael nodded. "Good for you."

"I mean look, I have terrific people working with me. I trust them. I think it might be time to delegate a bit more. Let them carry some of the burden for a change."

Michael said nothing.

"Anyway," Ellen said, "that's how I feel. I hope it's okay with you. About Mother, I mean."

"Sure," said Michael. He paused to collect his thoughts. "I've got to tell you, though. I think she'll be pretty surprised."

Michael looked at his sister. She was nodding slowly, smiling slightly, and he saw on her face an expression he recognized instantly. It was that same look of contentment she used to get when they were playing together, the two of them alone in the woods behind the house. He hadn't seen that expression in ages. How long had it been? Thirty years? Forty?

Michael sank back into his chair, pondering what he'd heard, and as he thought he began to drift into a dreamy half-sleep. Ellen watched him for a while, feeling warm and flushed and a bit sleepy herself. But she had one last thing she wanted to say.

"Michael?"

"Hm?"

"I'm sorry about Kathleen."

His eyelids fluttered. "Oh, yes. Well, thanks."

"Are you okay?"

"Sure. I mean, I will be. We'd gotten to a point where we both sort of needed a fresh start."

"Oh."

"So it was something we felt we had to do. It was a mutual thing."

"Oh." Ellen hesitated. "Aren't you scared?"

"Um...sure. Of course. We've been together a long time, Kathleen and me."

"You sound all right about it, though."

"I am. I mean, I know there'll be rough spots, but what can I do? I'll survive."

Ellen looked at the fading sunlight through the venetian blinds. It was nearly dark.

"Michael?"

"Hm?"

"If you ever need to...talk or anything, call me, okay?"

"Okay," he said softly. "I will."

They drifted off to sleep for real then, first Michael, then Ellen. By the time Aunt Eileen found them twenty minutes later, Michael was snoring deeply, and Ellen's chest was rising and falling in a slow, steady rhythm. Eileen smiled, shook her head, and before she woke them she fetched the camera and snapped a half-dozen pictures of brother and sister, curled up in chairs, side by side, fast asleep. And those pictures got dragged out of the closet every year after that—every Thanksgiving that the family got together.

Now that we've reached the end, let's remind ourselves of something we noted at the beginning: Healthy dependency is a lifelong journey—an ongoing process that unfolds over the years. As you change and grow, the strategies you use to build your healthy dependency skills will change and grow with you. In this sense, healthy dependency is like life itself—never static, ever-changing.

Don't hesitate to reread parts of this book as the need arises, and as you do, remember five principles that will guide you now and tomorrow:

- *Enjoy the journey.* Sometimes we become so fixated on where we're going that we forget to enjoy the time we spend getting there. There's no harm in having clear goals, but re-member: The journey is as important as the destination.

Even if you don't meet every goal you've set (and who does?), you'll be better for having tried.

- *Adapt our strategies to fit your style.* The guidelines we've discussed in this book are just that—guidelines. Use the ones that work best for you, and adapt them to fit your needs. These guidelines are not set in stone, but are intended to create a context within which you can strengthen your healthy dependency skills, now and in the future.

- *Don't try to be perfect.* Everyone makes mistakes, and we all backslide on occasion. Mistakes aren't something to be avoided. On the contrary, they're a sign that you're moving forward—taking on new challenges rather than resting on your laurels. Expect mistakes to happen, and learn from them when they occur.

- *Be tolerant of others' imperfections.* It's a natural human instinct: When we find something we believe in—be it a religion, a political cause, or a personal philosophy—we want to shout it from the rooftops and bring everyone else on board. Don't be reluctant to share your insights with others, but resist the urge to proselytize. Other people might not be ready to change in the same way you are. Maybe they will be at some point...or maybe not. That's for them—not you—to decide.

- *Be a lifelong learner.* Once you've internalized the principles of healthy dependency—really made them a part of you— you'll discover that every day brings new opportunities for growth and positive change. As new challenges arise, think of each one as a chance to use your healthy dependency skills. If you make it a point to be a lifelong learner, you'll discover surprising new truths every day—new ways to connect with other people, and to connect more deeply with yourself as well.

LET US KNOW....

$$* \; * \; * \; * \; *$$

If you found some parts of this book especially useful, please let us know. If some parts of the book could be improved, let us know that too. We wrote this book to help, and we want to learn how we can do better. So if you have a moment, please e-mail us at *HealthyDependency@hotmail.com*. We can't respond to every message we receive, but we will read every one carefully and take it seriously. You have our word on it.

BIBLIOGRAPHY

Aamodt, M. G. (1991). *Applied Industrial/Organizational Psychology*. Belmont, CA: Wadsworth.

Abelson, R. (1981). "Psychological status of the script concept." *American Psychologist*, 36, 715-729.

Abrams, R. C., & Horowitz, S. V. (1996). "Personality disorders after age 50." *Journal of Personality Disorders*, 10, 271-281.

Adler, A. (1969). The *Science of Living*. NY: Doubleday.

Ainsworth, M. D. S. (1978). *Patterns of Attachment: A Psychological Study of the Strange Situation*. Hillsdale, NJ: Erlbaum.

Ainsworth, M. D. S. (1989). "Attachments beyond infancy." *American Psychologist*, 44, 709-716.

Alarcorn, R. D. (1996). "Personality disorders and culture in DSM-IV." *Journal of Personality Disorders*, 10, 260-270.

Alperin, R. M. (2001). "Barriers to intimacy: An object relations perspective." *Psychoanalytic Psychology*, 18, 137-156.

American Psychiatric Association. (2000). *Diagnostic and Statistical Manual of Mental Disorders* (4th edition, text revision). Washington, DC: American Psychiatric Press.

Ansbacher, H. L., & Ansbacher, R. R. (Eds.) (1956). *The Individual Psychology of Alfred Adler*. NY: Basic Books.

Archer, J. (1996). "Sex differences in social behavior." *American Psychologist*, 51, 909-917.

Archer, S. (1994). *Interventions for Identity*. Thousand Oaks, CA: Sage.

Argyle, M., & Henderson, M. (1984). "The rules of friendship." *Journal of Social and Personal Relationships*, 1, 211-237.

Babcock, M., & McKay, C. (Eds.) (1995). *Challenging Codependency: Feminist Critiques*. Minneapolis, MN: University of Minnesota Press.

Baltes, M. M. (1996). *The Many Faces of Dependency in Old Age*. Cambridge, UK: Cambridge University Press.

Baumeister, R. (1986). *Identity: Cultural Change and the Struggle for Self*. NY: Oxford University Press.

Birtchnell, J. (1975). "The personality characteristics of early-bereaved psychiatric patients." *Social Psychiatry*, 10, 97-103.

Blake, R. R., Shepard, H., & Mouton, J. S. (1964). *Managing Intergroup Conflict in Industry*. Houston: Gulf Publishing.

Blieszner, R., & Adams, R. G. (1992). *Adult Friendship*. Beverly Hills, CA: Sage.

Bornstein, R. F. (1992). "The dependent personality: Developmental, social, and clinical perspectives." *Psychological Bulletin*, 112, 3-23.

Bornstein, R. F. (1993). *The Dependent Personality*. NY: Guilford Press.

Bornstein, R. F. (1994). "Adaptive and maladaptive aspects of dependency: An integrative review." *American Journal of Orthopsychiatry*, 64, 622-635.

Bornstein, R. F. (1995). "Interpersonal dependency and physical illness: The mediating roles of stress and social support." *Journal of Social and Clinical Psychology*, 14, 225-243.

Bornstein, R. F. (1995). "Sex differences in objective and projective dependency tests: A meta-analytic review." *Assessment*, 2, 319-331.

Bornstein, R. F. (1998). "Depathologizing dependency." *Journal of Nervous and Mental Disease*, 186, 67-73.

Bornstein, R. F. (1998). "Implicit and self-attributed dependency needs: Differential relationships to laboratory and field measures of help-seeking." *Journal of Personality and Social Psychology*, 75, 778-787.

Bornstein, R. F., Bowers, K. S., & Bonner, S. (1996). "Effects of induced mood states on objective and projective dependency scores." *Journal of Personality Assessment*, 324-340.

Bornstein, R. F., Geiselman, K. J., Eisenhart, E. A., & Languirand, M. A. (2002). "Construct validity of the Relationship Profile Test: Links with identity, relatedness, and attachment style." Paper presented at the 73rd meeting of the Eastern Psychological Association, Boston, MA; March 2002.

Bornstein, R. F., & Kennedy, T. D. (1994). "Interpersonal dependency and academic performance." *Journal of Personality Disorders*, 8, 240-248.

Bornstein, R. F., Krukonis, A. B., Manning, K. A., Mastrosimone, C. C., & Rossner, S. C. (1993). "Interpersonal dependency and health service utilization in a college student sample." *Journal of Social and Clinical Psychology*, 12, 262-279.

Bornstein, R. F., & Languirand, M. A. (2001). *When Someone You Love Needs Nursing Home Care: The Complete Guide*. NY: Newmarket Press.

Bornstein, R. F., Languirand, M. A., Creighton, J. A., West, M. A., & Geiselman, K. J. (2001). "Construct validity of the Relationship Profile Test: A self-report measure of dependency-detachment." Paper presented at the 72nd meeting of the Eastern Psychological Association, Washington, DC; April 2001.

Bornstein, R. F., Riggs, J. M., Hill, E. L., & Calabrese, C. (1996). "Activity, passivity, self-denigration, and self-promotion: Toward an interactionist model of interpersonal dependency." *Journal of Personality*, 64, 637-673.

Bowen, M. (1978). *Family Therapy in Clinical Practice*. NY: Jason Aronson.

Brazelton, T. B. (1994). *Touchpoints: Your Child's Emotional and Behavioral Development*. Boulder, CO: Perseus Press.

Brink, T. L. (Ed.) (1986). *Clinical Gerontology*. NY: Haworth Press.

Brock, G. W., & Barnard, C. P. (1988). *Procedures in Family Therapy*. Boston, MA: Allyn & Bacon.

Brown, J. D., & McGill, K. L. (1989). "The cost of good fortune: When positive life events produce negative health consequences." *Journal of Personality and Social Psychology*, 57. 1103-1110.

Burke, R. J., & McKeen, C. A. (1996). "Gender effects in mentoring relationships." *Journal of Social Behavior and Personality*, 11, 91-104.

Buunk, B. (1982). "Anticipated sexual jealousy: Its relationship to self-esteem, dependency, and reciprocity." *Personality and Social Psychology Bulletin*, 8, 310-316.

Carlson, G. A., & Kashani, J. H. (1988). "Phenomenology of major depression from childhood through adulthood." *American Journal of Psychiatry*, 145, 1222-1225.

Cherlin, A. (1993). *Marriage, Divorce, Remarriage*. Cambridge, MA: Harvard University Press.

Christensen, A., & Shenk, J. L. (1991). "Communication, conflict, and psychological distance in nondistressed, clinic, and divorcing couples." *Journal of Consulting and Clinical Psychology*, 59, 458-463.

Clark, K. E., & Ladd, G. W. (2000). "Connectedness and autonomy support in parent-child relationships." *Developmental Psychology*, 36, 485-498.

Clark, L. A., Kochanska, G., & Ready, R. (2000). "Mothers' personality and its interaction with child temperament as predictors of parenting behavior." *Journal of Personality and Social Psychology*, 79, 274-285.

Cohen, S. (1988). "Psychosocial models of the role of social support in the etiology of physical disease." *Health Psychology*, 7, 269-297.

Cohen, S., & Herbert, T. B. (1996). "Health psychology." *Annual Review of Psychology*, 47, 113-123.

Compas, B. E. (1987). "Coping with stress during childhood and adolescence." *Psychological Bulletin*, 101, 393-403.

Costello, C. G. (Ed.) (1995). *Personality Characteristics of the Personality Disordered*. NY: Wiley.

Coyne, J. C. (1991). "Social factors and psychopathology: Stress, social support, and coping processes." *Annual Review of Psychology*, 42, 401-425.

Deci, E. L. (1971). "Effects of externally mediated rewards on intrinsic motivation." *Journal of Personality and Social Psychology*, 18, 105-115.

Deci, E. L. (1975). *Intrinsic Motivation*. NY: Plenum Press.

Dollard, J., & Miller, N. E. (1950). *Personality and Psychotherapy*. NY: McGraw-Hill.

Eisenberg, A. (1996). *What to Expect the Toddler Years*. NY: Workman Publishing.

Ellis, A. (1960). *The Art and Science of Love*. NY: Lyle Stuart.

Ellis, A. (1989). *Rational-Emotive Couples Therapy*. Boston, MA: Allyn & Bacon.

Ellis, A. (1999). *How to Make Yourself Happy and Remarkably Less Perturbable*. Atascadero, CA: Impact Publishers.

Erikson, E. H. (1968). *Identity, Youth, and Crisis*. NY: W. W. Norton.

Erikson, E. H. (1982). *The Life Cycle Completed*. NY: W. W. Norton.

Fichman, L., Koestner, R., & Zuroff, D. C. (1996). "Dependency, self-criticism, and perceptions of inferiority at summer camp." *Journal of Youth and Adolescence*, 25, 113-126.

Fichman, L., Koestner, R., & Zuroff, D. C. (1997). "Dependency and distress at summer camp." *Journal of Youth and Adolescence*, 26, 217-232.

Field, T. (1996). "Attachment and separation in young children." *Annual Review of Psychology*, 47, 541-561.

Freud, A., & Burlingam, D. (1944). "Infants without families." In *The Writings of Anna Freud*. NY: International Universities Press, 1974.

Freud, S. (1909). "Notes upon a case of obsessional neurosis." In *The Standard Edition of the Complete Psychological Works of Sigmund Freud* (Volume 10). London: Hogarth Press, 1955.

Freud, S. (1917). "Mourning and melancholia." In *The Standard Edition of the Complete Psychological Works of Sigmund Freud* (Volume 14). London: Hogarth Press, 1957.

Freud, S. (1926). "Inhibitions, symptoms, and anxiety." In *The Standard Edition of the Complete Psychological Works of Sigmund Freud* (Volume 20). London: Hogarth Press, 1964.

Fu, V. R., Hinkle, D. E., & Hanna, M. A. (1986). "A three-generational study of the development of individual dependency and family interdependence." *Genetic, Social, and General Psychology Monographs*, 112, 153-171.

Gelles, R. J. (1994). *Contemporary Families*. Beverly Hills, CA: Sage.

Gibran, K. (1923). *The Prophet*. NY: Alfred A. Knopf.

Goldenberg, H., & Goldenberg, I. (2000). *Family Therapy*. Pacific Grove, CA: Brooks/Cole.

Goodstein, R. K. (1985). "Common clinical problems in the elderly: Camouflaged by ageism and atypical presentation." *Psychiatric Annals*, 15, 299-312.

Greenberg, J., & Baron, R. A. (1997). *Behavior in Organizations*. Upper Saddle River, NJ: Prentice Hall.

Greenberg, J. R., & Mitchell, S. J. (1983). *Object Relations in Psychoanalytic Theory*. Cambridge, MA: Harvard University Press.

Greenberg, R. P., & Bornstein, R. F. (1989). "Length of psychiatric hospitalization and oral dependency." *Journal of Personality Disorders*, 3, 199-204.

Greve, A. (1995). "Networks and entrepeneurship." *Scandinavian Journal of Management*, 11, 1-24.

Haley, J. (1976). *Problem Solving Therapy*. San Francisco, CA: Jossey-Bass.

Harris, J. R. (2000). "Context-specific learning, personality, and birth order." *Current Directions in Psychological Science*, 9, 174-177.

Hetherington, E. M., & Blechman, E. A. (1996). *Stress, Coping, and Resiliency in Children and Families*. Hillsdale, NJ: Erlbaum.

Hill, R., & Davis, P. (2000). "Platonic jealousy: A reconceptualization and review of the literature on non-romantic pathological jealousy." *British Journal of Medical Psychology*, 73, 505-517.

Horowitz, M. J. (Ed.) (1991). *Person Schemas and Maladaptive Interper-*

sonal Patterns. Chicago: University of Chicago Press.

Hartup, W. (1989). "Social relationships and their developmental significance." *American Psychologist*, 44, 120-126.

Hartup, W. (1999). "Friendships and adaptation across the life span." *Current Directions in Psychological Science*, 8, 76-79.

Ihilevich, D., & Gleser, G. C. (1991). *Defenses in Psychotherapy*. Owosso, MI: DMI Associates.

Jacobson, K. C., & Rowe, D. C. (1999). "Genetic and environmental influences on the relationship between family connectedness, school connectedness, and adolescent depressed mood." *Developmental Psychology*, 35, 926-939.

Janis, I. (1982). *Victims of Groupthink*. Boston, MA: Houghton Mifflin.

Johnson, J. G., & Bornstein, R. F. (1992). "Utility of the Personality Disorder Questionnaire-Revised in a nonclinical population." *Journal of Personality Disorders*, 6, 450-457.

Kagan, J. (1984). *The Nature of the Child*. NY: Basic Books.

Kantor, M. (1993). *Distancing*. Westport, CT: Praeger.

Kazdin, A. E. (1995). *Conduct Disorders in Childhood and Adolescence*. Beverly Hills, CA: Sage.

Kernberg, O. F. (1984). *Severe Personality Disorders*. New Haven, CT: Yale University Press.

Kernberg, O. F. (1992). *Aggression in Personality Disorders and Perversions*. New Haven, CT: Yale University Press.

Khan, S. A., & Sinha, J. B. P. (1971). "Social anxiety in dependence-prone persons." *Psychological Studies*, 16, 42-44.

Kiecolt-Glaser, J., & Glaser, R. (1992). "Psychoneuroimmunology." *Journal of Consulting and Clinical Psychology*, 60, 569-575.

Kobayashi, J. (1989). "Depathologizing dependency: Two perspectives." *Psychiatric Annals*, 19, 653-658.

Kramer, R. M., Tyler, T. R. (1995). *Trust in Organizations*. Beverly Hills, CA: Sage.

Kurdek, L. A., & Schmitt, J. P. (1986). "Relationship quality of partners in heterosexual married, heterosexual cohabiting, gay, and lesbian relationships." *Journal of Personality and Social Psychology*, 51, 711-720.

Lamb, M. J. (1999). *Parenting and Child Development in Nontraditional Families*. Mahwah, NJ: Erlbaum.

Langer, E. J. (1989). *Mindfulness*. Reading, MA: Addison-Wesley.

Langer, E. J., & Rodin, J. (1976). "The effects of choice and enhanced personal responsibility for the aged." *Journal of Personality and Social Psychology,* 34, 191-198.

Larson, C. E., & LaFasto, M. J. (1989). *TeamWork.* Beverly Hills, CA: Sage.

Lawton, M. P., & Salthouse, T. A. (Eds.) (1998). *Essential Papers on the Psychology of Aging.* NY: New York University Press.

Lazarus, A. (1990). *Emotion and Adaptation.* NY: Oxford University Press.

Levinson, H. (1994). "Why the behemoths fell: Psychological roots of corporate failure." *American Psychologist,* 49, 428-436.

Locke, E. A., & Latham, G. P. (1990). *A Theory of Goal-Setting and Task Performance.* Upper Saddle River, NJ: Prentice Hall.

Lovallo, W. R. (1997). *Stress and Health: Biological and Psychological Interactions.* Thousand Oaks, CA: Sage.

Mahler, M. S. (1982). *The Selected Papers of Margaret S. Mahler.* NY: Jason Aronson.

Main, M., Kaplan, M., & Cassidy, J. (1985). "Security in infancy, childhood, and adulthood." *Monographs of the Society for Research in Child Development,* 50, 66-104.

Manuck, S. B. (Ed.) (2000). *Behavior, Health, and Aging.* Mahwah, NJ: Erlbaum.

Marcia, J. (1993). *Ego Identity: A Handbook for Social Research.* NY: Springer-Verlag.

Masling, J. M., & Bornstein, R. F. (Eds.) (1994). *Empirical Perspectives on Object Relations Theory.* Washington, DC: American Psychological Association.

Meehl, P. M. (1989). "Schizotaxia revisited." *Archives of General Psychiatry,* 46, 935-944.

Miller, L. C. (1990). "Intimacy and liking." *Journal of Personality and Social Psychology,* 59, 50-60.

Millon, T. (1996). *Disorders of Personality.* NY: Wiley.

Millon, T., Blaney, P. H., & Davis, R. D. (Eds.) (1999). *Oxford Textbook of Psychopathology.* NY: Oxford University Press.

Millon, T. & Davis, R. D. (2000). *Personality Disorders and Modern Life.* NY: Wiley.

Minuchin, S. (1974). *Families and Family Therapy.* Cambridge, MA: Harvard University Press.

Morgan, J. P. (1991). "What is codependency?" *Journal of Clinical Psychology,* 47, 720-729.

Mullen, E. J. (1998). "Vocational and psychosocial mentoring functions." *Human Resource Development Quarterly*, 9, 319-331.

Neimeier, R. A. (Ed.) (2001). *Meaning Reconstruction and the Experience of Loss*. Washington, DC: American Psychological Association.

Nemiah, J. C. (1978). "Alexithymia and psychosomatic illness." *Journal of Continuing Education in Psychiatry*, 35, 25-37.

Olshevski, J. L., Katz, A. D., & Knight, B. G. (1999). *Stress Reduction for Caregivers*. NY: Brunner/Mazel.

O'Neill, R. M., & Bornstein, R. F. (2001). "The dependent patient in a psychiatric inpatient setting: Relationship of interpersonal dependency to consultation and medication frequencies." *Journal of Clinical Psychology*, 57, 289-298.

Osborne, A. F. (1953). *Applied Imagination*. NY: Scribner.

Parks, C. D., & Komorita, S. S. (1997). "Reciprocal strategies for large groups." *Personality and Social Psychology Review*, 1, 314-322.

Parlee, M. (1979). "The friendship bond." *Psychology Today*, 43-45.

Pashler, H. (1992). "Attentional limitations on doing two things at the same time." *Current Directions in Psychological Science*, 1, 44-48.

Pennebaker, J. (1990). "Accelerating the coping process." *Journal of Personality and Social Psychology*, 58, 528-537.

Pennebaker, J. (1990). *Opening Up: The Healing Power of Confiding in Others*. NY: William Morrow.

Pennebaker, J. (Ed.) (1995). *Emotion, Disclosure, and Health*. Washington, DC: American Psychological Association.

Pennebaker, J. (1997). "Writing about emotional experiences as a therapeutic process." *Psychological Science*, 8, 162-166.

Pincus, A. L., & Gurtman, M. B. (1995). "The three faces of interpersonal dependency." *Journal of Personality and Social Psychology*, 69, 744-758.

Pincus, A. L., & Wilson, K. R. (2001). "Interpersonal variability in dependent personality." *Journal of Personality*, 69, 223-251.

Reardon, R. C. (2000). *Career Development and Planning*. Belmont, CA: Brooks/Cole.

Rubin, K. H., Nelson, L. J., Hastings, P., & Asendorpf, J. (1999). "The transaction between parents' perceptions of their children's shyness and their parenting styles." *International Journal of Behavioral Development*, 23, 937-958.

Rubin, Z. (1993). *Liking and Loving*. NY: Holt, Rinehart & Winston.

Rutter, M. (1980). *Patterns of Adolescent Development*. Cambridge, MA: Harvard University Press.

Sagi, A. (1990). "Attachment theory and research from a cross-cultural perspective." *Human Development*, 33, 10-22.

Schafer, W. (1992). *Stress Management for Wellness*. NY: Holt.

Schlenker, B. R., & Weigold, M. F. (1990). "Self-consciousness and self-presentation: Being autonomous versus appearing autonomous." *Journal of Personality and Social Psychology*, 59, 820-828.

Selye, H. (1950). *The Physiology and Pathology of Exposure to Stress*. NY: Acta Publications.

Seymour, N. (1977). "The dependency cycle." *Transactional Analysis Journal*, 7, 37-43.

Shonkoff, J. P., & Meisels, S. J. (Eds.) (2000). *Handbook of early childhood intervention*. Mahwah, NJ: Erlbaum.

Sifneos, P. (1972). *Short-Term Therapy and Emotional Crisis*. Cambridge, MA: Harvard University Press.

Sifneos, P. (1983). "Psychotherapies for psychosomatic and alexithymic patients." *Psychotherapy and Psychosomatics*, 40, 66-73.

Simpson, J. A., & Gangestad, S. W. (1991). "Individual differences in sociosexuality." *Journal of Personality and Social Psychology*, 60, 870-883.

Sinnot, J. D. (1994). *Interdisciplinary Handbook of Adult Lifespan Learning*. Westport, CT: Greenwood Press.

Skinner, B. F. (1971). *Beyond Freedom and Dignity*. NY: Knopf.

Skinner, B. F. (1974). *About Behaviorism*. NY: Knopf.

Stern, B. L., Kim, Y., Trull, T. J., Scarpa, A., & Pilkonis, P. (2000). "Inventory of Interpersonal Problems personality disorder scales." *Journal of Personality Assessment*, 74, 459-471.

Sternberg, R. J. (1986). "The triangular theory of love." *Psychological Review*, 93, 119-135.

Stocker, C. M., Lanthier, R. P., & Furman, W. (1997). "Sibling relationships in early adulthood." *Journal of Family Psychology*, 11, 210-221.

Stocker, C. M., & Youngblade, L. (1999). "Marital conflict and parental hostility: Links with children's sibling and peer relationships." *Journal of Family Psychology*, 13, 598-609.

Sulloway, F. (1996). *Born to Rebel: Birth Order, Family Dynamics, and Creative Lives*. NY: Vintage Books.

Taylor, S., Repetti, R. L., & Seeman, T. (1997). "Health psychology." *Annual Review of Psychology*, 48, 411-447.

Tebes, J. (1985). *Construct validation of the trauma-stren conversion*. Dissertation Abstracts International, 45, 2704.

Thomas, A., & Chess, S. (1984). "Genesis and evolution of behavioral disorders: From infancy to early adult life." *American Journal of Orthopsychiatry*, 141, 1-9.

Thompson, R., & Zuroff, D. C. (1998). "Dependent and self-critical mothers' responses to adolescent autonomy and competence." *Personality and Individual Differences*, 24, 311-324.

Thompson, R., & Zuroff, D. C. (1998). "Dependent and self-critical mothers' responses to adolescent sons' autonomy and competence." *Journal of Youth and Adolescence*, 28, 365-384.

Tjosvold, D. (1997). "Networking by professionals to manage change." *Journal of Organizational Behavior*, 18, 745-752.

van Ijzendoorn, M. H. (1988). "Cross-cultural patterns of attachment." *Child Development*, 59, 147-156.

Wallerstein, J. (1985). "Children of divorce." *Journal of the American Academy of Child Psychiatry*, 24, 545-553.

Whiffen, J., & Aube, J. A. (1999). "Personality, interpersonal context, and depression in couples." *Journal of Social and Personal Relationships*, 16, 369-383.

Winnicott, D. W. (1958). *Through Pediatrics to Psychoanalysis*. London: Hogarth Press.

Winnicott, D. W. (1965). *The Maturational Process and the Facilitating Environment*. NY: International Universities Press.

Complete citations for all the books and articles mentioned here may be found in the Bibliography.

CHAPTER 1

Healthy Dependency and Life Success
The many positive effects of healthy dependency are described in two articles by Robert F. Bornstein: "Adaptive and maladaptive aspects of dependency" and "Depathologizing dependency." An excellent recent study of this issue is Aaron L. Pincus & Kelly R. Wilson's "Interpersonal variability in dependent personality."

Taking a somewhat more narrow focus, the links between healthy dependency and academic success (along with the results of our 1994 study) are discussed in "Interpersonal dependency and academic performance" by Robert F. Bornstein & Timothy D. Kennedy.

The Relationship Profile Test
The Relationship Profile Test was developed over several years, and involved literally hundreds of research subjects from different walks of life. This process is described in two papers by Robert F. Bornstein, Mary A. Languirand, and others: "Construct validity of the Relationship Profile Test: A self-report measure of dependency-detachment" and "Construct validity of the Relationship Profile Test: Links with identity, relatedness, and attachment style."

Destructive Overdependence and Dysfunctional Detachment

The dynamics of destructive overdependence are described in Robert F. Bornstein's *The Dependent Personality* (Guilford Press, 1993); Chapters 3, 4, 6, and 8 are particularly relevant. The negative impact of dysfunctional detachment is discussed in Martin Kantor's *Distancing* (Praeger, 1993), a readable overview of the childhood roots and present-day consequences of this relationship style.

Information regarding the frequency of overdependence and detachment can be found in our 1992 study, "Utility of the Personality Diagnostic Questionnaire-Revised in a nonclinical population" by Jeffrey G. Johnson & Robert F. Bornstein. It's the first broad-based survey of destructive overdependence and dysfunctional detachment in high-achieving young women and men.

CHAPTER 2

Attachment Styles

Jerome Kagan's *The Nature of the Child* (Basic Books, 1984), and Tiffany Field's "Attachment and separation in young children" discuss the psychological consequences of our prolonged period of parental dependence. Other important works on this topic include A. Sagi's "Attachment theory and research from a cross-cultural perspective" and M. H. van Ijzendoorn's "Cross-cultural patterns of attachment."

Relationship Scripts

Mardi Horowitz's edited volume, *Person Schemas and Maladaptive Interpersonal Patterns* (University of Chicago Press, 1991), contains several excellent reviews of research on relationship scripts. Robert Abelson's article "Psychological status of the script concept" discusses his important work on this topic in straightforward, non-technical language.

Overdependence Patterns

Research on destructive overdependence patterns is summarized in Chapters 3 and 4 of Robert F. Bornstein's *The Dependent Personality* (Guilford Press, 1993). These patterns are also discussed in Aaron L. Pincus & Michael B. Gurtman's "The three faces of interpersonal dependency." Two other good sources of information are by the psychoanalyst Otto Kernberg: *Severe Personality Disorders* (Yale University Press, 1984), and *Aggression in Personality Disorders and Perversions* (Yale University Press, 1992).

Detachment Patterns
The range of dysfunctional detachment patterns identified by mental health professionals is discussed in John Birtchnell's chapter entitled *Detachment,* which appears in Charles G. Costello's edited volume *Personality Characteristics of the Personality Disordered* (Wiley, 1995). Chapter 12 of Theodore Millon & Roger Davis's *Personality Disorders and Modern Life* (Wiley, 2000) analyzes angry detachment in detail.

CHAPTER 3

Relationship Games and Relationship Traps
Relationship games almost always reflect well-learned relationship scripts played out in a new context. Nola Seymour's "The dependency cycle" discusses the dynamics of relationship games, with special emphasis on overdependent people and their partners. Richard M. Alperin's *Barriers to intimacy* discusses many of these same issues from a Freudian perspective.

Codependency
There has been a tremendous amount of writing on codependency during the past 20 years, much of it bad. James P. Morgan's article "What is codependency?," and Marguerite Babcock & Christine McKay's edited volume entitled *Challenging Codependency: Feminist Critiques* (University of Minnesota Press, 1995) are exceptions. Both present accurate, critical, research-based information on this controversial topic.

Overdependence and Abuse
Studies of the link between overdependence and abuse are summarized in Chapter 5 of Robert F. Bornstein's *The Dependent Personality* (Guilford Press, 1993). Key warning signs of abuse are outlined in Robert F. Bornstein & Mary A. Languirand's *When Someone You Love Needs Nursing Home Care: The Complete Guide* (Newmarket Press, 2001), which also provides practical advice for dealing with abuse situations.

Coping with Negative Emotions
James Pennebaker's *Opening Up: The Healing Power of Confiding in Others* (William Morrow, 1990) describes a wealth of studies which show that releasing negative emotions has positive effects on health and well-being. On the other side of the coin, David Ihilevich and

Goldine Gleser's *Defenses in Psychotherapy* (DMI Associates, 1991) reviews research on how difficult it can be to alter a longstanding anger-turned-inward coping style.

CHAPTER 4

Perspectives on Love
Albert Ellis's classic work on the practical challenges of romance is his book *The Art and Science of Love* (Lyle Stuart, 1960). More recent books by Ellis include *Rational-Emotive Couples Therapy* (Allyn & Bacon, 1989) and *How to Make Yourself Happy and Remarkably Less Disturbable* (Impact Publishers, 1999).

A very different perspective on this issue can be found in Robert Sternberg's article "The triangular theory of love," which is considered the definitive statement of his intimacy-passion-commitment model.

Marital Conflict and Communication
A useful overview of the literature on communication and marital satisfaction can be found in A. Christensen & J. L. Shenk's article "Communication, conflict, and psychological distance in nondistressed, clinic, and divorcing couples." L. A. Kurdek's paper entitled "Relationship quality of partners in heterosexual married, heterosexual cohabiting, gay, and lesbian relationships" discusses these same issues from the perspective of lesbian and gay relationships.

Overdependence, Detachment, and Intimacy
James Marcia's edited volume *Ego Identity: A Handbook for Psychosocial Research* (Springer-Verlag, 1993) contains chapters on the various "intimacy styles" (including superficial intimacy) that psychologists have identified. Taking a more narrow, focused approach, Valerie E. Whiffen and Jennifer A. Aube's "Personality, interpersonal context, and depression in couples" deals specifically with the negative impact of overdependence on romantic intimacy.

CHAPTER 5

The Friendship Bond
Two good articles on the evolution of friendship, both by Willard Hartup, are "Social relationships and their developmental signifi-

cance" and "Friendships and adaptation across the life span." The emotional bonds between lifelong friends are discussed in R. Blieszner & R. G. Adams' very readable book, *Adult Friendship* (Sage, 1992).

Friendship Styles

Key friendship subtypes were originally described in Zick Rubin's *Liking and Loving* (Holt, Rinehart & Winston, 1993). Mary Ainsworth's "Attachments beyond infancy," and John Archer's "Sex differences in social behavior" are other good sources of information on different styles of friendship.

Overdependent and Detached Friendship

Howard Berenbaum's chapter entitled "Peculiarity," in Charles G. Costello's *Personality Characteristics of the Personality Disordered* (Wiley, 1995) summarizes much of what we know about the friendship over-identification process. Information on friendship detachment (and on overdependent friendship as well) can be found in Theodore Millon's *Disorders of Personality* (Wiley, 1996).

CHAPTER 6

Family Dynamics

Jay Haley's *Problem Solving Therapy* (Jossey-Bass, 1976) is his most influential book—the classic introduction to family systems theory. Other important works on this topic are Murray Bowen's *Family Therapy in Clinical Practice* (Jason Aronson, 1978) and Salvador Minuchin's *Families and Family Therapy* (Harvard University Press, 1974).

Sibling Bonds

Anna Freud & Dorothy Burlingham's groundbreaking 1944 study of sibling bonding ("Infants without families") is reprinted in *The Writings of Anna Freud* (International Universities Press, 1974). Much of the sibling research conducted during the past several decades has been influenced by this pioneering investigation.

Approaching the sibling bonding issue from a very different perspective, "Sibling relationships in early adulthood" by Clare M. Stocker and others discusses power differentials between siblings. Robert Hill & Paul Davis describe the dynamics of sibling jealousy in their article "Platonic jealousy."

Overdependence, Divorce, and Loss

The links between overdependence and early parental loss are described in "The personality characteristics of early-bereaved psychiatric patients" by John Birtchnell. Two good sources of information on the divorce-overdependence link are A. Cherlin's *Marriage, Divorce, Remarriage* (Harvard University Press, 1993) and R. J. Gelles's *Contemporary Families* (Sage, 1994), both of which discuss the long-term effects of divorce on family dynamics and children's adjustment.

Healthy Dependency Within the Family

The link between healthy dependency and children's school adjustment is discussed in Kristen C. Jacobson & David C. Rowe's article, "Genetic and environmental influences on the relationship between family connectedness, school connectedness, and adolescent depressed mood." Two books—one recent, one a bit older—are also useful here. *Stress, Coping, and Resiliency in Children and Families* by E. M. Hetherington & E. A. Blechman (Erlbaum, 1996) provides a tremendous amount of information on the psychological dynamics of blended families. Michael Rutter's *Patterns of Adolescent Development and Disorder* (Harvard University Press, 1980) reviews research on family communication patterns and children's well-being.

CHAPTER 7

Developmental Milestones

Two good sources of information on developmental norms are Arlene Eisenberg's *What to Expect the Toddler Years* (Workman Publishing, 1996) and T. Berry Brazelton's *Touchpoints: Your Child's Emotional and Behavioral Development* (Perseus Press, 1994). Both are very readable books written in straightforward, nontechnical language.

Overdependence- and Detachment-Fostering Behaviors

Detachment-fostering parenting practices are discussed in Theodore Millon's *Disorders of Personality* (Wiley, 1996) and George C. Costello's *Personality Characteristics of the Personality Disordered* (Wiley, 1996). Sally Archer's *Interventions for Identity* (Sage, 1994) and Roy Baumeister's *Identity: Cultural Change and the Struggle for Self* (Oxford University Press, 1986) describe the causes and consequences of a "negative identity."

Richard Thompson & David C. Zuroff look at the other end of the dependency-detachment spectrum, and focus on overdependent mothers' autonomy-squelching behaviors. Two companion articles are useful: "Dependent and self-critical mothers' responses to adolescent autonomy and competence" and the follow-up paper entitled "Dependency, self-criticism, and mothers' responses to adolescent sons' autonomy and competence."

Parent-Child Dynamics and Healthy Dependent Parenting
Two excellent sources of information on the complex interaction of temperament, parenting, and attachment style are "Mothers' personality and its interaction with child temperament as predictors of parenting behavior" by Lee Anna Clark and others, and "The transaction between parents' perceptions of their children's shyness and their parenting styles" by Kenneth H. Rubin and others. Jack P. Shonkoff & Samuel J. Meisels' *Handbook of Early Childhood Intervention* (Erlbaum, 2000) contains additional advice for healthy dependent parenting.

CHAPTER 8

Organizational Dynamics
J. Greenberg & R. A. Baron's *Behavior in Organizations* (Prentice-Hall, 1997) discusses the forces that shape organizational roles and alliances. Though it's been around for quite a while, R. R. Blake, H. Shephard, & J. S. Mouton's *Managing Intergroup Conflict in Industry* (Gulf Publishing, 1964) remains one of the definitive discussions of organizational overdependence and detachment.

Constructive Interdependence in Organizations
Carl E. Larson & Frank M. J. LaFasto's *TeamWork* (Sage, 1989) provides an extensive analysis of the positive effects of constructive interdependence on collegial relationships. A related discussion of organizational commitment is found in R. M. Kramer & T. R. Tyler's *Trust in Organizations* (Sage, 1995).

In a related vein, E. A. Locke & G. P. Latham's *A Theory of Goal Setting and Task Performance* (Prentice-Hall, 1990) and Edward L. Deci's *Intrinsic Motivation* (Plenum Press, 1975) analyze various aspects of reward structure within organizations. These books can be useful if you are in a supervisory role or if you just want to understand more fully the dynamics of supervision and leadership.

Career Development and Networking
Career Development and Planning by Robert C. Reardon (Brooks/ Cole, 2000) reviews research on factors that foster and impede career progress. The career networking process is analyzed in Arent Greve's "Networks and entrepreneurship" and in Dean Tjosvold's "Networking by professionals to manage change." Information on the rewards and risks of mentoring can be found in Ellen J. Mullen's "Vocational and psychosocial mentoring functions" and Ronald J. Burke & Carol A. McKeen's "Gender effects in mentoring relationships."

CHAPTER 9

Stress and Coping
Shelley Taylor's article "Health psychology" reviews evidence on the health-compromising effects of stress—a very active area of medical and psychological research today. The stress-coping process is also discussed in William R. Lovallo's *Stress and Health: Biological and Psychological Interactions* (Sage, 1997).

Practical advice on strategies for managing your own stress level is summarized in Chapter 2 of *When Someone You Love Needs Nursing Home Care* by Robert F. Bornstein & Mary A. Languirand (Newmarket Press, 2001).

Grieving and Mourning
Freud's classic work on grieving and mourning is "Mourning and Melancholia," which is available in *The Complete Psychological Works of Sigmund Freud* (Volume 14), published by Hogarth Press. Recent research on this topic is summarized in Robert A. Neimeier's edited volume *Meaning Reconstruction and the Experience of Loss* (American Psychological Association, 2001).

Detachment, Health, and Illness
Peter Sifneos's classic work on alexithymia is *Short-Term Therapy and Emotional Crisis* (Harvard University Press, 1972). Two more recent articles—John C. Nemiah's "Alexithymia and psychosomatic illness" and Peter Sifneos's "Psychotherapies for psychosomatic and alexithymic patients"—contain a wealth of information on the links between alexithymia and psychosomatic disorders.

Overdependence, Health, and Illness

Robert F. Bornstein's chapter "Dependent and histrionic personality disorders," in Theodore Millon's *Oxford Textbook of Psychopathology* (Oxford University Press, 1999) discusses the health-related dynamics of emotional staging. Other findings regarding the negative effects of overdependence on health are described in "Interpersonal dependency and health service utilization in a college student sample" by Robert F. Bornstein and others and "The dependent patient in a psychiatric inpatient setting: Relationship of interpersonal dependency to consultation and medication frequencies" by Richard M. O'Neill & Robert F. Bornstein.

CHAPTER 10

Late-Life Overdependence and Detachment

Richard K. Goodstein's article "Common clinical problems in the elderly" discusses the psychological dynamics of late-life dependency. M. Powell Lawton & Timothy A. Salthouse's edited volume *Essential Papers on The Psychology of Aging* (New York University Press, 1998) reviews the various causes of late-life disengagement.

Promoting Healthy Aging

The breakthrough study of enhanced control and health in nursing home residents was Ellen J. Langer & Judith Rodin's 1976 article, "The effects of choice and enhanced personal responsibility for the aged." Stephen B. Manuck's edited volume *Behavior, Health, and Aging* (Erlbaum, 2000) summarizes recent research in this area. Another useful reference is Margaret M. Baltes's *The Many Faces of Dependency in Old Age* (Cambridge University Press, 1996), which describes late-life compensatory (adaptive) dependencies.

Resources for Caregivers

Numerous resources on aging and caregiving (including telephone and Internet contact information) are summarized in Robert F. Bornstein & Mary A. Languirand's *When Someone You Love Needs Nursing Home Care* (Newmarket Press, 2001). This book also discusses effective strategies for late-life financial planning, and provides tips for coping with caregiver stress.

INDEX

Robert F. Bornstein received his Ph.D. in Clinical Psychology from the State University of New York at Buffalo in 1986, completed a year-long internship at the Upstate Medical Center in Syracuse, N.Y., and is Professor of Psychology at Gettysburg College. Dr. Bornstein has published more than 100 articles and 30 book chapters on personality dynamics, diagnosis, and treatment. Dr. Bornstein wrote *The Dependent Personality* (Guilford Press, 1993), co-authored (with Mary Languirand) *When Someone You Love Needs Nursing Home Care* (Newmarket Press, 2001), and edited seven other volumes of psychological and psychiatric research. He is a Fellow of the American Psychological Association, American Psychological Society, Pennsylvania Psychological Association, and Society for Personality Assessment. Dr. Bornstein's research has been funded by grants from the National Institute of Mental Health and the National Science Foundation. He sits on the editorial boards of several professional journals and received the Society for Personality Assessment's 1995 and 1999 Walter Klopfer Awards for Distinguished Contributions to the Personality Assessment Literature.

Mary A. Languirand received her Ph.D. in Clinical Psychology from the State University of New York at Buffalo in 1987, and completed a year-long internship in clinical geropsychology at the R. H. Hutchings Psychiatric Center in Syracuse, N.Y. Dr. Languirand co-authored *The Thinking Skills Workbook* (Charles C. Thomas, 1980, 1984, 2000) and co-authored (with Robert Bornstein) *When Someone You Love Needs Nursing Home Care* (Newmarket Press, 2001). Dr. Languirand is a Fellow of the Maryland and Pennsylvania Psychological Associations and a Member of the American Psychological Association and Society for Personality Assessment. Dr. Languirand has worked as a geriatric counselor, coordinator of a mental health crisis unit in York, PA, and Director of the Psychology Department at Brook Lane Psychiatric Center in Hagerstown, MD, where she developed a multidisciplinary treatment program for older adults. Now in full-time private practice in Gettysburg, PA, Dr. Languirand continues to provide direct service to individuals, couples, and families, as well as offering consultation and training to educators, administrators, physicians, mental health professionals, and allied health professionals in a variety of educational and treatment settings.